THE FIRST BOLSHEVIK

THE FIRST BOLSHEVIK

A Political Biography of Peter Tkachev

by Albert L. Weeks

NEW YORK—New York University Press
LONDON—University of London Press Limited
1968

Foreword

In my opinion, Professor Weeks has made a valuable contribution to the study of Russian and Soviet political thought. His study of a neglected but significant revolutionary should be of interest both to historians and to political scientists. Peter Nikitich Tkachev is important both as a product of the backward, but rapidly developing and disequilibrated, Russian society of the second third of the nineteenth century and as a precursor of, and in some ways an inspiration to, Lenin. However, there is more to Tkachev than this. His life and thought shed fascinating light on the interplay between ideas, personality, political cultures, and rapidly changing social conditions. Perhaps most interesting is the light shed by Tkachev's intellectual development upon the highly significant and in some ways distinctively Russian phenomenon of the rootless, radical intellectual, who compensates for his social isolation and powerlessness by fashioning intellectual weapons designed to confer upon him mastery over mankind.

Professor Weeks has sought to relate Tkachev's ideas to his life, times, and experience. The contextual and biographical elements of his book, in which Tkachev's revolutionary outlook is related to the contributions of such men as Dobrolyubov, Chernyshevsky, Pisarev, and others, shed considerable light on the still by no means fully explored social, intellectual, and journalistic history of Russia in the 1860's and 1870's. However, the greatest value of this study consists in its systematic exposition of what might be described as the Jacobin socialism of Tkachev. Although many of Tkachev's ideas were borrowed from Western European as well as Russian radical and revolutionary thinkers, Tkachev achieved a rather original synthesis, or at least aggregation of theories, demands, and programs.

In several significant aspects, Tkachev's findings and prescriptions resembled those later developed by Lenin. The parallels between Tkachev and Lenin with respect to the peculiarities in the situation and revolutionary potential of Russia, the necessity, in Tkachev's and Lenin's opinion, for the welfare of the Russian people, of an elite and dictatorial revolutionary organization, their common belief in the need for a long period of postrevolutionary reeducation of the hitherto passive and inert masses by their self-appointed guardians—these and other similarities are explored, but with due regard to the considerable differences between the thought, temperament, and actions of unsuccessful Jacobins and the victorious founder of bolshevism. Skillfully using both original sources and a wide range of Soviet monographic literature, Professor Weeks succeeds very well in relating Tkachev's pessimistic elitism to the harsh realities which helped to shape it. In so doing, he contributes to understanding of the development of Leninism. It is clear that Lenin was not only influenced by factors similar to those which shaped Tkachev but that he was directly influenced by the latter, to whom he acknowledged his indebtedness and respect in a number of striking statements. Weeks documents Lenin's appreciation of Tkachev's contribution, in respect, for example, to the important concept of "preemptive revolution."

Thus the reader of this book cannot help feeling that he has at least to some degree enhanced his understanding of the Leninist and even of the contemporary Soviet political mentality. The reader will also gain enhanced understanding of Stalinism from Dr. Weeks's careful tracing of the shifting and selective treatment of Tkachev in Soviet scholarly literature. Finally, it should be said that in a severely objective but compassionate manner Professor Weeks has not only placed his subject in the context of Russian and world history but has presented him as a significant contributor to the shaping of the contemporary Soviet world outlook—and as a somewhat frightening but understandable specimen of *homo politicus*.

FREDERICK C. BARGHOORN

November, 1967

Preface

The description of Peter Tkachev (1844–1886) as the "forerunner of Lenin"—or, as I have put it somewhat unoriginally, "the first Bolshevik"—may surprise that reader who has either not examined the works of Tkachev or has not familiarized himself with the considerable literature in the Russian language on Tkachevism and Russian Jacobinism.

Perhaps the first essay in English describing the enormous debt owed to Tkachev by Vladimir Ilyich Ulyanov (Lenin [1870–1924]) was a modest article written by the late Professor Mikhail Karpovich of Harvard University in *The Review of Politics* in 1944 entitled "A Forerunner of Lenin: P. N. Tkachev." Indeed, it was after reading and pondering this article that the author, then a graduate student at the University of Chicago, decided to embark on the study of Tkachev.

By no means was Karpovich the first to discover important similarities between Tkachevism and Leninism. A few of Lenin's confreres and, in fact, Lenin himself had alluded to proto-Bolshevist elements in Tkachev's writings, published articles which, as we will see, Lenin recommended as "required reading" for his followers. But the most extended discussion of this resemblance may be found in the writings of Bolsheviks, ex-Bolsheviks, Russian Socialists, and exiles of various persuasions who have published books or essays on Russian revolutionism. Many of these authors and their writings are listed in the Bibliography and include works by B. I. Nicolaevsky, V. D. Bonch-Bruyevich, F. I. Dan, B. I. Gorev, S. P. Melgunov, Avrahm Yarmolinsky, N. V. Valentinov (Volskii), S. I. Mitskevich,* and others. Any number of contemporary Western writers on Russia or revolutionary thought have referred, although briefly, to various proto-Bolshevist concepts in the writings of Tkachev. Such references may be found in works by Bertram Wolfe, Leonard Shapiro, Franco Venturi, Max Nomad, Werner Scharndorff, Merle Fainsod, Alfred Meyer, to name only a few who have cited the kinship between the ideas of Tkachev and his Jacobin successor, Lenin.

This kinship is impressive. Tkachev had laid down a number of key, Bolshevist-like principles of revolution and post-revolutionary rule over thirty years before the exiled Lenin was to spend those many evenings in the library of "legal" and "illegal" revolutionary literature in Geneva, Switzerland, reading and digesting the "magnificent" Tkachev, as he called him. Some of these concepts were:

1. Formation of a band or party of *déclassé* intellectual-conspirators who would teach socialism to the masses;
2. Seizure of power by this small group (in the midst of mass unrest) in military fashion in the urban "power centers" of Russia;
3. Extreme centralism within the elitist political party;
4. Establishment of a powerful, postrevolutionary "socialist dictatorship" headed by the same *déclassé* intellectuals who had "made" the revolution;
5. Carrying out of "permanent revolution," remaking society into a new socialist order;
6. Postponement or lack of definition of the withering away of the state;
7. Intolerance of political opposition after the revolution; scorn for "liberal bourgeois democracy"; establishment

---

* Mitskevich wrote in the Soviet magazine, *Proletarskaya revolyutsiya* (*Proletarian Revolution*), in 1923: "It is an irrefutable fact that the Russian Revolution proceeded to a significant degree according to the ideas of Tkachev, with the seizure of power made at a time determined in advance by a revolutionary party which was organized on the principle of strict centralization and discipline. And this party, having seized power, is working in many respects as Tkachev advised." In the same article, Mitskevich actually uses the words "first Bolshevik" to describe Tkachev (see discussion in last chapter, pp. 178–187).

of a punitive Commission for Public Security (the K. O. B.) to protect the dictatorship;

8. Distinction between agitation and propaganda and the use-any-means-to-reach-the-ends tactic in designing agitation;
9. Quasi-Marxist economic theory;
10. Russia as a special case, an especially suitable "weak link" in the bourgeois chain where revolution could be made and socialism undertaken.

This book is about the kinship between the ideas of Tkachev and Lenin, but it is just as much about the total outlook of "the first Bolshevik" against the background of revolutionary thought in Russia which had influenced Tkachev—and which Lenin was to draw upon too. A short biography of Tkachev as told by his contemporaries, memoirists, historians, and editors of his writings is contained in one of the chapters.

The author is much indebted to a number of persons and institutions who assisted in the research, editing, or physical preparation of this book. Surely the late Boris Ivanovich Nicolaevsky belongs near the top of such a list along with Professor George V. Bobrinskoy of the University of Chicago, and Professors John N. Hazard, Herbert A. Deane, and H. L. Dyck of Columbia University. Mrs. Lynn Taheri, Mary Williamson, Dwight Miles, and Frederick Duda all provided invaluable aid in the typing and proofing of the manuscript. The author is grateful to the Tamiment Institute in New York, the libraries of New York University, Columbia University, Yale University, and the University of Chicago for speedy and valuable assistance in obtaining books, pamphlets, and microfilms and for the generous gift of a valuable Tkachev pamphlet to the author by the library of the University of Chicago. The able and cooperative librarians working in the Slavonic Division of the New York Public Library deserve special mention.

Note on Transliteration

I have tried to compromise between the phonetic spellings of Russian words in English, complete with diacritical marks, as they are used by the Library of Congress, and the less precise but more familiar and, perhaps, more intelligible usage of current English-language books and newspapers. Names familiar in the West, such as Turgenev, Berdaev, Herzen, Dostoyevsky, and the city of Velikie-Luki, are given in their common form. Other names follow the Library of Congress system of transliteration except that ligatures and diacritical marks have been omitted. Soft signs (indicated by apostrophes) have been retained in ordinary words but dropped in family names. Thus Boris P. Kozmin's name, for example, would be spelled Koz'min by the Library of Congress.

The *dve tochki* or umlaut, indicating an *o* sound in words like Tkachëv, has also been dropped, as it usually is in Russian publications. Tkachev's name, which means tailor, is pronounced t-kah-CHOFF.

The name of Tkachev's revolutionary journal, *Nabat,* has been variously translated into English as *Tocsin, Alarm Bell,* and *Alarm* by other writers. I have preferred the latter of these alternatives as the most plausible name for such a journal in English. The exact meaning of *nabat* is discussed fully in n. 39 on p. 69. The names of other revolutionary organs of Tkachev's time are given in Russian, followed by an English translation the first time they appear.

The Julian calendar was in use in Russia until 1918, when the Gregorian calendar already in use in the West was adopted. I have used Gregorian dating throughout so that, for instance, Tkachev's birth year is given as 1844 instead of the date he knew, 1843.

ALBERT L. WEEKS

New York, December 1967

The average representative of the people is a dispassionate person; this is particularly true of the Russian people. Slave-like impulses have been encouraged in the Russians by centuries' old slavery. Secretiveness, untrustworthiness, servility . . . have all served to atrophy the energy of the Russian people. They are phlegmatic by nature. It is impossible to place any hope in their enthusiasm. Their stoical passivity is like the encrusted shell of a snail.

> —P. N. Tkachev, "Our Illusions," *Nabat*, 1876.

Once, in a dispute with a Tkachevist, I asked him: "Do you, as a member of a minority, consider it right that you force the people to be happy?"

This question greatly animated my co-debater.

"Why, of course!" he answered. "Since the people themselves do not understand their own good, what is truly good for them must be forced upon them."

> —P. B. Axelrod, *Perezhitoye i peredumannoye.*

To be forever carrying about in one's head ideas which are not permitted to be put into practice is in itself tormenting, a dreadfully excruciating torture.

> —P. N. Tkachev, "Sick People," *Delo*, No. 4, 1873.

You are wrong; what you oppose is so logical that you yourself do not believe it.

> —P. N. Tkachev, quoted by B. P. Kozmin, *Literaturnoye
> Nasledstvo*, Nos. 7, 8, 1933.

The success of revolution depends on the formation and organized unity of scattered revolutionary elements into a living organism which is able to act according to a single, common plan and be subordinated to a single, common leadership—an organization based on centralization of power and decentralization of function.

> —P. N. Tkachev, *Sochineniya*, III.

If you leave the people to themselves, they will build nothing new. They will only spread the old way of life to which they are already accustomed.

> —P. N. Tkachev, *Sochineniya*, I.

Contents

Determinism • Utilitarianism • Tkachev's Views
on Psychology and Aesthetics

THE FIRST BOLSHEVIK

CHAPTER I

Introduction

TKACHEV'S REVOLUTIONISM FINDS A DISCIPLE

In the summer of 1900, the younger brother of a famous Russian revolutionary martyr arrived in Geneva, Switzerland, European headquarters of Russian revolutionary *émigrés*. He had sworn to avenge the heroic death of his beloved older brother, Alexander. Alexander had died on the Tsarist gallows in 1887 for having participated in an ill-conceived and basically ineffective attempt to assassinate Tsar Alexander III, son of the assassinated "Tsar Liberator," Alexander II.

This newcomer to Geneva, known as N. Tulin or sometimes as *Starik* (or the "Old Man," although he was a young man of thirty), had just completed a prestigious three-year exile in Siberia. His sentence was the consequence of having taken the road of vengeance to which he had dedicated himself partly in memory of his brother and which he swore would end in the complete overthrow of the Tsarist old order and the establishment of a Socialist new order. This young "Old Man" was, of course, Vladimir Ilyich Ulyanov (Lenin).[1]

Lenin was now in the *émigré* haven of Geneva to enlist the aid of the authoritative Russian Marxist *troika* consisting of Plekhanov, Axelrod, and Zasulich, in the realization of his most cherished immediate goal, which he set for himself while serving his term in the "white desert" of eastern Siberia—the founding of a truly radical Russian Marxist newspaper. This organ, Lenin thought, must equip potential Russian revolutionaries of the younger generation (meaning for the most part university students or ex-students) with truly militant tactics and strategy informed by a frankly Russian-oriented Marxism.

Protracted meetings took place in Geneva between the *troika* and the enthusiastic young newcomer, Lenin. But despite pressing organizational matters, he used a large part of his spare time, according to one of his intimate friends, to examine closely the impressive collection of revolutionary literature—books, pamphlets, manuscripts, and periodicals—bound in large, thick, wine-colored buckram volumes labeled Miscellany (*Razn'*). These finds had been sedulously accumulated in Geneva largely through the efforts of the veteran publisher of clandestine literature in Russia, Vladimir Dmitriyevich Bonch-Bruyevich. Bonch, or "B. B." as he was addressed affectionately by co-workers, had been serving as unofficial librarian of revolutionary literature of all types ever since his arrival in Switzerland in 1894. He had met the young Ulyanov in 1895, when the latter had made his first visit to Geneva, and was keenly aware of the young man's preference for revolutionary literature "of a very special type," as Bonch-Bruyevich wrote in his memoirs. In them he recalls:

> Vladimir Ilyich knew how to connect the present with the past, borrowing from the past whatever was militant and expedient for the contemporary proletarian class struggle. . . . From the very beginning, Vladimir Ilyich gave serious attention to our library and began to work in it evenings. . . . We gave him a special key with which he could enter the library and work there whenever he pleased. In the area where the Archive was located, we set up a large work-table and placed on this table for him to use all the books which he had himself requested from our stacks. . . . He was especially interested in the whole of the old revolutionary literature [of Russia]. . . . Whenever we received a given outstanding writer such as, for example, Tkachev and his *Nabat* publication, we wanted to share any of these finds with him so much that we often dropped by the library in the evening to point out these rarities to him.[2]

Bonch-Bruyevich continues the description of Lenin's activities in the library revealing (as has never before been recorded in

4

English) Lenin's great interest in the writings of Peter Nikitich Tkachev:

> Vladimir Ilyich read through and examined most
> carefully all of this old revolutionary literature paying
> particular attention [*osoboye vnimaniye*] to Tkachev,
> *remarking that this writer was closer to our viewpoint
> than any of the others.* We wanted very much to collect
> everything that Tkachev had ever written in the legal
> press. So we instructed [G. A.] Kuklin to examine all
> the various journals of the 1870's in order to find
> everything that Tkachev had written. And Kuklin did.
> *We collected these articles and handed them over to
> Vladimir Ilyich. Not only did V. I. himself read these
> works of Tkachev, he also recommended that all of us
> familiarize ourselves with the valuable writings of this
> original thinker. More than once, he asked newly-
> arrived comrades if they wished to study the illegal
> literature. "Begin," V. I. would advise, "by reading and
> familiarizing yourself with Tkachev's* Nabat. . . .
> *This is basic and will give you tremendous knowledge."*
> (italics are mine—A. L. W.)

The memoirist then offers an interesting opinion on the effect
of this reading on Lenin which he says was noticeable in the
immediate post-1917 period:

> I think that Vladimir Ilyich's research [into the
> old Russian revolutionary tradition] helped him when
> the proletariat seized power and our Party took over
> the administration of the country.

It was Lenin's reading of this type of revolutionary literature—not only in Geneva, it should be added, but also in his
earlier years in Kazan and Samara[3]—that appeared to exert a
lasting influence on his thinking.

Another rather impressive link between the Russian
Jacobin-Blanquist tradition and Lenin's own family has been
established by N. V. Volskii (Valentinov) who, like Bonch-
Bruyevich, was acquainted with Lenin in Geneva and who was
able to examine a detailed and unpublished biography of Lenin
written by V. V. Vorovskii, chief of the Soviet State Publishing House in the early 1920's.[4]

Valentinov recounts how a follower of an early Russian

Jacobin contemporary of Tkachev's later became a close friend of the Ulyanov family. Her name was M. P. Yaseneva; she was a dedicated follower of P. G. Zaichnevsky, a Russian Jacobin who in turn strongly influenced Tkachev.[5] Yaseneva, who was nine years Lenin's senior, became acquainted with Lenin in Samara around 1891. Vorovskii asserts that the impressive woman-revolutionary Yaseneva exerted a strong influence on the twenty-one-year-old Lenin, an influence, he writes, which lay in a "Jacobin-Blanquist" direction.[6]

From these and several other sources it is quite obvious that the young Lenin was strongly attracted to the writings and concepts of the Russian Jacobins and to those of Tkachev in particular. It appears that this attraction began quite early in his life and became more intense as the years went on.

This early commitment to Russian Jacobinism and Tkachevism cropped up later in several forms—in Lenin's position in the Menshevik-Bolshevik split within the Russian Social-Democratic Labor Party; in his comprehensive set of revolutionary tactics and strategy essentially designed to suit Russian conditions; in fact, in his overall world view and political theory. Much of Lenin's thinking bore a strong resemblance to Tkachevism, a fact which is often pointed out in scholarly writings on Bolshevism published in the West.[7] This Tkachevist-Leninist kinship provoked an eruption of lively polemics in the USSR during the 1920's around the issue of Lenin's indebtedness to Tkachev. The debate was silenced with the rise of Stalin and the Lenin cult to which Lenin's "absolute originality" was essential; the debate has never been resumed on the scale or with the objectivity of the 1920's, even in the post-Stalin period (1953–1967).

The Tkachevian logic of the 1870's was to become Lenin's reasoning in several respects thirty years later. The pressure of events within the RSDLP and Tsarist Russia impelled Lenin, supported by his elitist cast of mind, toward an expression of Bolshevism which bore a strong resemblance to the conclusions that Tkachev had reached previously and in which Lenin was well versed. What had been impossible to achieve in Tkachev's era became temptingly feasible by the time of World War I. The chaotic conditions prevailing in Russia in 1917 made the country, as Lenin said, "the weakest link" in the chain of bourgeois imperialism and a most suitable battleground on which the spark of proletarian revolution could first be ignited in the world.[8]

NOTES

1. Lenin employed some fifty pseudonyms in his prerevolutionary legal and illegal writings and appears to have taken a certain amount of pleasure in being as revolutionary and secretive as possible, even when the necessity to be so was not present. Robert Payne in his *Life and Death of Lenin* (New York: Simon and Schuster, 1964), p. 147, asserts that Lenin used seventy-five pseudonyms; this is true only if one counts each use of a name as a different pseudonym. A complete list of Lenin's pseudonyms may be found neatly collected in the volume of Vladimir Ilyich Lenin's *Sochineniya* (4th ed.) entitled *A Supplemental Index and Chronological Listing of the Works of V. I. Lenin (Vospomogatel'niye ukazateli i khronologicheskii ukazatel' proizvedenii V. I. Lenina* [Moscow: Gosudarstvennoye Izdatel'stvo Politicheskoi Literatury, 1963]), pp. 389–92.

2. Vladimir Dmitriyevich Bonch-Bruyevich, *Selected Works in Three Volumes (Izbranniye sochineniya v trekh tomakh* [Moscow: Izdatel'stvo Akademii Nauk SSSR, 1961]), II, 314–16. Italics in the quotations are mine. The *Little Soviet Encyclopedia* (1958) describes Bonch-Bruyevich as "one of the elder officials of the Communist Party and Soviet Government . . . who functioned as an active collaborator on Lenin's *Iskra (Spark)*." *(Malaya sovetskaya entsiklopediya* [Moscow: Gosudarstvennoye Nauchnoye Izdatel'stvo, 1958], I, 1141. Bonch-Bruyevich died on July 14, 1955, at the age of eighty-two.)

3. Lenin attended Kazan University off and on from 1887 to 1889 where he further acquainted himself with secret or illegal revolutionary literature, exceptionally large stores of which were (and still are) located both in Kazan and Samara. After 1889, Lenin lived in Samara for a total of four years and there began to fall under the influence of radical Populism and Russian Jacobinism. For a description of the libraries of revolutionary literature to be found in Kazan and Samara in that period, see Y. Z. Polevoy, *The Birth of Marxism in Russia (Zarozhdeniye marksizma v Rossii* [Moscow: Izdatel'stvo Akademii Nauk SSSR, 1959]), pp. 360–66. David Shub asserts in his biography, *Lenin* (New York: Mentor, 1948), p. 19, that Lenin's acquaintance with the works of Tkachev, Nechayev, and Bakunin started about the time of his brother's death in 1887.

4. N. V. Volskii (Valentinov), *Encounters with Lenin (Vstrechi s Leninym* [New York: Izdatel'stvo imeni Chekhova, 1953]), pp. 113–19, including a preface by Mikhail N. Karpovich. This work is cited in the Soviet book by Polevoy (n. 3) but Polevoy is silent about Yaseneva and the Blanquist influence.

5. See this study below, pp. 29–32. Yaseneva's maiden name is sometimes rendered "Yasneva." Yaseneva later married V. S. Golubev, an ex-Populist and collector of revolutionary literature. Yaseneva-Golubeva became a terrorist "judge" in the Bolshevik Cheka (see Stefan T. Possony, *Lenin: the Compulsive Revolutionary* [Chicago: Henry Regnery Company, 1964], p. 26).

6. Valentinov wrote of Lenin's ripened point of view by 1904: "Lenin came to the firmly-held conclusion that any orthodox Marxist Social-Democrat inevitably must follow Jacobinism, that Jacobinism demanded a dictatorship of the proletariat and that 'without a Jacobin purge it would be impossible to carry out the revolution' and 'without Jacobin force the dictatorship of the proletariat would become only a word whose meaning had been castrated.' " Valentinov notes that Yaseneva later became an ardent Bolshevik seeing in Bolshevism a continuation of the Russian Jacobin tradition (Valentinov, *op. cit.,* p. 118). Valentinov offers the intriguing opinion that Lenin's Bolshevist theory and practice would have looked essentially the same *even without the admixture of Marxism into it.*

7. See below for some recently published observations by Russian specialists in the West attributing a large degree of Tkachevist influence to Lenin, pp. 72–73. Soviet discussion of Tkachev may be found below, pp. 176–87.

8. Examined below is the whole Tkachevist (implicitly Leninist) conception of the advantageous weakness and lack of power and force in the Tsarist state; in the weak and scarcely-developed roots of a Russian middle class; in the Russian urban workers who were increasingly falling under "petty-bourgeois" influences and whose links with the petty-bourgeois village were strong—this latter weakness making a *preemptive* revolution all the more urgent. Tkachev and Lenin kept their eyes fixed squarely on the levers of political *power,* sometimes with utter disregard for socio-economic factors.

CHAPTER II

Development of the Russian
Revolutionary Spirit Before Tkachev

Although the term *intelligentsiya* was introduced into Russian parlance only by the 1860's,[1] a stratum of Russian society which could be described as an intelligentsia had existed in Russia at least since the end of the seventeenth century in the form of a "small minority of liberally educated and secular-minded people."[2] This minority grew rapidly in that century as the result of two major enactments by the Russian monarchy: the introduction of compulsory education for the gentry (by the imperial manifesto of December 31, 1736) and the freeing of the nobility from compulsory service to the state (by the imperial manifesto of February 18, 1762).[3] This in turn led to the emergence of a leisure class.

In the nineteenth century this "internal proletariat"[4] continued to expand and distinguish itself from the mass of Russian society and above all underwent a process of variegated Westernization. By mid-nineteenth century an intelligentsia in the "narrower, more subjective sense" began to appear.[5] An important element of this group followed the tradition of radicalism already established among such writers on social and political themes (*publitsisty*) as Alexander Radishchev and Nikolai Novikov, critical thinkers in the reign of Catherine II; Novikov, a Freemason, founded the largest and most influential publishing house that had ever existed in Russia up to that time.[6] The mid-nineteenth-century "Westernizing" group of *intelligenty* accepted in more extreme form contemporary French and German positivist thought and deliberately detached itself from the rest of the population to form something resembling a dedicated sect. This was an intensely curious, intellectually inclined group borrowing ideas from the French Utopian Socialists, Left Hegelians, Schelling, Fichte, Feuerbach, *et al.* Extensive discussions of these ideas could be found in the writings of Herzen, Belinsky, the members of the Stankevich and *Petrashevtsi* circles.

Beginning early in the nineteenth century, another wing within the Russian intelligentsia, besides the Westernizers, became discernible. This was the Slavophils, who strove to work out a Christian world-conception like that found in the teaching of the Eastern Fathers and Russian Orthodoxy. They idealized the Russian past and Russian national characteristics. They insisted that Russia follow its own peculiar historical path which was strikingly different from that of the Western nations. The Slavophils began to develop a messianic attitude toward the West, seeking to carry to it the allegedly superior spirituality of Russian Orthodoxy and of Russian social ideals.[7]

Although the Slavophils may be said to have been basically conservative and hostile toward the secularized, revolutionary, and predominantly socialistic ideas of the radical Westernists, they were among the very founders of independent philosophical thought in Russia.[8] Moreover, their extreme nationalistic and messianic bias undoubtedly exerted an influence—although indirect and unintentional—on certain of their antagonists in the Westernist camp.[9] Certain Westernizers had passed through Slavophil phases in their own intellectual development, while certain Slavophils had at some time or other inclined toward Westernism.[10]

At the same time, however, a good deal of cross-fertilization was evident in both Slavophils and Westernizers. Professor Venturi has written on this point:

> Moscow was the natural center of the Slavophils. . . . Herzen lived and worked in their capital, and there established that complex relationship made up of love and hatred, opposition and agreement, which was to continue in various forms throughout his life, and which finally led him to Populism. [The Slavo-

phils] helped to transform socialism from an intellectual reflection of the problems of the West to a question which was closely related to the peasants of their own country. This is certainly not what they had intended, but thanks to Herzen, their opponent, this is what they achieved. By keeping alive the discussion on the earliest forms of agrarian communities in Russia, which had begun in the eighteenth century and had already assumed such importance for the Decembrists, these supporters of a backward and patriarchal country life prepared the ground for Herzen's Populism.[11]

S. V. Utechin points out in *Russian Political Thought:*

Herzen's romantic Westernism received a great shock when, traveling through Western Europe after his emigration, and particularly during the 1848 revolution, which he experienced in Paris, he saw egoism, vulgarity, and corruption not only of the bourgeoisie but also of the proletariat. After this, he no longer expected the light to come to Russia from the West, though he appreciated the far greater freedom enjoyed by people in Western Europe. He still believed that the establishment of socialism was a necessary condition for a free and full development of the human personality, but he now thought that the prospects for socialism were far better in Russia than in Western Europe. . . . By blending Westernist socialism with Slavophil admiration for the peasant commune, Herzen originated the notion of a specifically Russian socialism.[12]

Herzen's most important writings for showing his faith in the embryonic and indigenous socialist institutions in Russia were his *Letters from France and Italy* and *From the Other Shore,* both written in 1848–1849, and *The Russian People and Socialism,* 1851. In those works one may see the blend of Westernist socialism with Slavophil admiration of the peasant commune, as noted above by Utechin. At the same time, it is important to note that in the philosophy of Herzen, the "founder of Russian Populism," there is a strong undercurrent of criticism of both revolutionary and Tsarist authoritarianism, a form of criticism which is passed on to the populist movements of the 1870's and 1880's. Herzen deliberately and emphatically dissociated himself from the Jacobin tradition in Russia, which is discussed below.

In the early period before the 1860's, noblemen of a special stamp began to appear, the so-called "repentant noblemen." Often they were Utopian Socialists, or else intensely self-critical and socially conscious intellectuals. Some of these noblemen represented the embryonic form of Russian Populism. Taken together, these intellectuals are usually referred to in Russian history as the "Old Generation" of Russian radicals.

To certain members of this older generation for whom the central problem was the land and peasant question, the solution of all of Russia's problems lay in a vast, large-scale metamorphosis of Russian life. Some of these early Russian radicals insisted that the Russian peasant was basically, even "instinctively," communist and collectivist in his outlook and way of life in the peasant commune (or *obshchina* as Baron August F. L. N. von Haxthausen has described it in his *Russian Studies*).[13] Had not the peasant preserved the *obshchina* down through several centuries—this ancient seedbed of a communist regeneration, with its collective ownership and collective distribution of the land and harvest? And had not those of the old generation who had traveled to the West seen ample evidence of the bitter fruit of capitalist development, the kind of nascent capitalism described in the all-too-realistic fiction of Dickens and Hugo? These proto-Populists and agrarian socialists of the older generation began to frame the question: Must the Russian people, who tend toward natural communism, suffer the consequences of a bourgeois-capitalist development in Russia? Must they endure the proliferation of large cities and slums, child labor, and the sweat and toil of incredibly long hours of labor in cold, dark, impersonal factories? To these questions most of the radicals, whether of a a Westernist or outright Slavophil point of view, answered with an unequivocal No. Cottage industry (*Artel'*) and agrarian socialism via the commune were to spare Russia—Russia, the special case—from the plight of the new Western proletariat of whose poor condition the Russian intelligentsia, even those who had never traveled abroad, were thoroughly cognizant.

How was the metamorphosis of agrarian socialism to take place in the midst of the semifeudal conditions of early nineteenth-century Russia?

As we shall see in the case of the Decembrists, most of the older generation before the sixties feared and opposed a bloody social revolution—that is, a general nationwide insurrection.[14] Some of these educated noblemen thought that to unleash suddenly the pent-up energy of a sprawling mass of ignorant and restive peasants might well end in mass destruction of lives and property. The Decembrist answer in 1825 had been an attempt at a court *coup d'état*.[15] After the failure of the Decembrist soldiers in Senate Square in St. Petersburg,[16] the slogan for Herzen and others was essentially "reform from above," official reform by Tsarist institutions of government.

But frustration of the Decembrist revolt and the Decembrists' projects for reform "precipitated the full development of the intelligentsia they had adumbrated"[17] and began to lead it in a more radical direction. The post-Decembrist development generally bore an extremely idealistic cast. Also, in this period, alienation of the educated nobility and gentry from the Tsarist state increased, as did Tsarist repressions against the more outspoken *intelligenty*. "Red" disorders erupting in the Polish provinces of the Empire in 1830 and all over Europe in 1848 served to increase this alienation and radicalization of the intelligentsia. In addition to this, the coming of the men of mixed classes (*raznochinstvo*) became manifest. By the mid-nineteenth century, this alienation and radicalization were aggravated by other issues revolving about the peasants' emancipation. The slogan, "reform from above," a notion sometimes employed by less radical members of the "old generation" of the 1840's and 1850's, began to be scorned and discarded by the new "young generation" of intellectuals, who were so clearly distinguishable from their forebears.[18] We will examine this group in the next section of this chapter.

Hegel's logic had been read as—in Herzen's phrase—"the algebra of revolution"; the seeds of a future Russian Populist movement had been sown by Herzen and Bakunin; the Decembrist challenge to autocracy had been made in 1825 by the Jacobins, Pestel and Rileyev; but it was not until the sixties and seventies that the crystallization of Russian revolutionism, as well as the mounting frustration of its practical accomplishment, took place. This revolutionism was to serve, until the advent of Marxism in Russia and the grafting of the Western Marxist addition to the Russian revolutionary tradition, as the solid base for the development of secret terrorist societies inside Russia. It was the basis for establishing the Russian Section of the International Workingmen's Association and was the foundation for the publication of numerous legal and illegal articles, pamphlets, proclamations, and journals,[19] all discussing either openly or covertly in the "language of Aesop" the true philosophy which should underlie the future grandiose transformation of Russian society.

This was the beginning of the whole intellectual milieu and the development of the Russian revolutionary spirit of which Tkachev was to partake and to which he was to contribute. The first stage was the sixties.

RUSSIAN REVOLUTIONISM AND THE HERITAGE OF THE SIXTIES

In nineteenth-century Russia, revolution was as common a topic of debate and discussion as, say transcendentalism, perfectionism, free silver, or tariffs in the United States. The Russian topic of revolution had the quality of dynamite, an explosive, which, until 1905 and 1917 lacked a political fuse to ignite it. American intellectual ferment tended to be lofty and philosophical, and when it concerned political issues, it was easily ingested by the reigning political factions or parties of the day and concretized in the form of, for example, a free silver plank or the American Populist Party. In Russia, no such political expression of contending ideas was possible. Ideas, no matter how realistic and practicable, became sealed up in men's minds or exchanged in clandestine fashion between members of secret debating societies called "circles" (*kruzhki*), or couched in the censor-dodging language of Aesop. Many suffered the misery of pent-up ideas, condemned to residence in the mind without the opportunity of testing them in practice. Ideas became fugitives from the stolid, suspicious, and reactionary forces of Tsarism with its political police and a censorship which regarded Hobbes's *Leviathan,* for example, as subversive.[20]

This isolated and sealed-off quality of the circles, especially those in the stream of *radical* political and social thought, had the effect of deepening and complicating the debates on revolution with hair-splitting argumentation and of narrowing the participants into a miniscule, radical intelligentsia constituting a fraction of one per cent of the total Russian population. Around the topic of revolution developed a veritable tradition or *Geist,* a self-subsisting body of argumentation, a spiritual environment which nourished the minds of Russian radicals throughout the whole nineteenth century and which they in turn nourished. Included under the main topic of revolution were such philosophical (and ultimately practical) problems as the Individual vs. Society, Anarchy vs. the State, Capitalism vs. Agrarian Socialism, Postrevolutionary Dictatorship vs. Liberal Democracy, and, of course, that portentous topic of debate on the eve of the cataclysmic twentieth century, *Marxism vs. Marxism,* that is, *Liberal* Marxism vs. *Radical* Marxism.

The spectre of radical socialism, which Marx and Engels said in *The Communist Manifesto* was haunting Europe, was also haunting Russia. But the spectre was almost a total stranger to the Russian toiling masses in their own land. Not even the suspicious Tsarist police took accurate measure of it or appreciated its importance—and ominousness. And, needless to say, the sprawling masses of ignorant, illiterate peasants of Russia were oblivious to the debates about revolution and the concepts which were later to shape their lives so drastically.

The manner in which the debates about revolution were carried on in Russia tended to foster a particular strain of revolutionary (and postrevolutionary) theory above all others: the outwardly rational and logical presentation tended to dominate, especially toward the end of the century, over the romantic and irrational. Seemingly, logical argument tended to appeal more to the well-read radical intelligentsia than did catchalls like "intuition," "revolutionary instinct," "collective widsom," and the like. Furthermore, alienation of the intelligentsia from the "black masses" of Russia encouraged this abstract rationalism.

As a result, the involved arguments of the intellectuals

and revolutionaries were free of the *adulteration of compromise.*
A social or political argument did not have to be diluted in
order to win support "in the party" or "in the country." Under conditions of Tsarist Russia, there was no party, and, in
fact, there was no country, in the sense of a free and informed
public and electorate. If there had been a party or a country
to worry them, to temper their pure radicalism and the un-
yielding pure logic and alleged reason of their arguments, these
radical intellectuals would have had to admit that no matter
how rational their point of view might be in itself, there were,
after all, *other* forces and factors, *other* opinions to contend
with in the society. Their unadulterated and sometimes ponder-
ous theoretical apparatus would have had as a result a strong
and much-needed democratic strain introduced into it. But because of their almost eremitic isolation, at times scorn for the
popular masses, they never had to make this adulteration and
compromise of their theories, although, of course, some did in
halfhearted imitation of what they had seen or read of the
democratic West. F. I. Dan once wrote that the intellectualist
debates on revolution in Russia essentially amounted to conflicting and baffling definitions of just "who or what were
the people."[21]

Of the three strains running through the Russian intelligentsia as a whole in the last century—conservative, liberal
and radical—the radical grew steadily dominant. Finally, in
1917, in a stormy environment of the kind in which radicalism is likely to find a home, the radical strain overcame the
other two and at last engulfed the past, present, and future of
Russia.

By the Tsar's *ukaz* of February 19, 1861, and by a later
decree of 1863, the Russian serfs had been given the *de jure*
opportunity of being released from their bondage to the land-
lords by means of redemption payments made in the course of
forty-nine years. But by 1880 some 15 per cent of the peasantry still remained outside the redemption scheme, and
those ex-serfs who did avail themselves of the optional deal
with their squires were compelled by law to hand over their
allotment to the peasant commune, whose economic authority,
granted to it by the state, was great.[22]

Problems in the early sixties tended to group themselves

around the following aspects of the Tsarist peasant reform: peasants' dissatisfaction with receiving only about half the total arable land as the result of the decrees; the strong interference of the commune and later government officials (*zemskiye nachal'niki*) in both land and private affairs of the peasants; the practical administration of the land-parceling accomplished in the villages by Tsar-appointed "arbitrators of the peace"; the chronic poverty of both peasants and landowners, which made the latter dependent upon the government for advances on redemption payments in the form of bonds (that began to lose their face value) and which made the peasants impatient with redemption payments so high they were seldom able to pay the one-fifth earnest money. Serfdom had been replaced by a kind of economic enslavement.

Out of this legacy of dissatisfaction came the first revolutionary movements of the 1860's. Planks on the peasant questions made up the programs of all these movements and formed their backbone. But it is important to note in this connection that a position taken on the peasant question, although basic, was only a part of the total revolutionary program of many circles or groups. The peasant question often acted as the agitative portion of a particular revolutionary doctrine. The larger, more fundamental or "pure" part of a revolutionism contained the basis and determinant philosophy.

The measures advanced by the leaflets, *The Great Russian* (*Velikoruss*) and *The Young Russia* (*Molodaya Rossiya*), the *Nechayevtsi* and *Chaikovtsi* groups, and the various illegal proclamations throughout the sixties were directed primarily toward a solution of the immediate peasant land question. Behind these panaceas, however, lay the whole revolutionary philosophy containing the principles for a total reorganization of society. This metaphysical portion of the revolutionary program contained first principles relating to political economy, the state, ethics, science, and aesthetics. Because of the insularity of the Russian intelligentsia with respect to the general population and the development of a self-contained revolutionary spirit, this principle-minded revolutionism began to develop in depth and sophistication. It tended to become increasingly complex and radical, and at the same time more divorced from reality.[23]

The Russian sources from which Tkachev was to draw

some of his important first principles were the writings and traditions represented by three men of the sixties, N. G. Chernyshevsky (1828–1889), N. A. Dobrolyubov (1836–1861), and D. I. Pisarev (1840–1868). Each contributed a unique element to the later Tkachevian system, although they by no means contributed all the elements making up Tkachevism. The coming of such figures as Chernyshevsky, Dobrolyubov, and Pisarev also marked the opening of a new era, the appearance of a new type of intellectual, the *raznochinets*.[24]

Perhaps the first *raznochinets* occupying an authoritative position in the Russian intelligentsia was V. G. Belinsky (1811–1848), son of a provincial doctor. Differences between him and Herzen—Belinsky taking in typical *raznochinets* fashion a more radical position on most social and political questions—were well known to both the noble and *raznochinets* youth of the time. Belinsky is most important for having freed the *raznochinets* intellectuals from the spiritual domination of the older noblemen-intellectuals. Chernyshevsky and Dobrolyubov became the offshoots of the more radical tendencies represented by Belinsky, whose influence consisted mainly of his utterances, letters and articles rather than personal contact (he died in 1848 at the early age of thirty-seven).

Besides the advent of the *raznochinstvo* were the events in Europe which occurred toward the middle of the century and which exerted a strong influence on the *raznochintsi*. Radical Russian intellectuals viewed the frustrated revolutions of Europe of the thirties and forties (particularly those of 1848) as evidence of what Herzen had once asserted: "Political revolution without social revolution is impossible."[25] And in his letter to the French sociologist Edgar Quinet, in which he criticized the course of the revolution of 1848, Herzen stated that the roads to be followed by Russia and Western Europe would necessarily differ: "You will attain socialism by means of the proletariat while we will attain freedom by means of socialism."[26] This conception of the primacy of social welfare and equalitarianism over political freedom was a dominant idea in radical revolutionary thought and runs through Tkachev into the Bolshevik period. It grew mainly out of the inferences drawn by Russian radicals from the failure of the revolution in Europe. In the manner of Marx and Engels, they viewed this

18

failure as the consequence of a superstructure of "sham political democracy" rationalizing, ignoring, and erected over an economic base which, they said, was shot through with inequality and which stood in need of total reformation. Reference to European events also served to distinguish Russian experience—the Russian future also—from European experience in the sense that Russia for various special reasons would be able to avoid the West and Central European frustration. This in turn led to the notion of Russia *"skipping"* the capitalist stage of development altogether and passing directly to socialism, abetted in this process by the "instinctively communist" institutions of the *obshchina.*

CHERNYSHEVSKY'S CONTRIBUTION

Like most social theorists in the sixties both in Russia and abroad, Nikolai G. Chernyshevsky embraced the ethic of utilitarianism. He believed that the good and the useful were identical, that the truth of utilitarianism was rational and a priori.[27] In a manner unlike that of some Western utilitarians, however, the starting point in Chernyshevsky's ethics was the individual, whose "natural rights" as a free personality he considered "the true, holy rights of the individual person"; the enlightened egoism of each person in a properly established society could minister to the welfare of every other individual participating in the society. Chernyshevsky illustrated this point by the character, Rakhmetov, in his novel, so popular among the educated youth of the time, *What Is To Be Done?,*[28] written in the Peter and Paul Fortress. Rakhmetov's rationally selfish calculation merges with the best interests of society. If it is assumed that everyone were as rational as Rakhmetov in his calculation of the useful, society would flourish in harmony and bounty. Accordingly, it was Chernyshevsky's strong belief that enlightenment—specifically, education—was the *sine qua non* if such an ethic were to be put into practice. The passionate articles written by Chernyshevsky in *Sovremennik (Contemporary;* the legal journal of the time expressing a liberal and sometimes socialist line) on the ethic of utilitarianism exerted a great influence on Tkachev, as did Tkachev's own reading of Mill.[29]

The idea of primitive socialism within the peasant commune was not of course unique with Chernyshevsky, as we have seen. But it was Chernyshevsky who broadened the idea of *Mir* socialism, elaborating upon it in such a way as to influence succeeding revolutionists up to and including fully-developed Russian Populism.

Chernyshevsky was no Slavophil; he did not view the commune as something indigenously Russian. But he did consider it to be the means for avoiding the Western road of social development, and this idea became imbedded in embryonic Russian Populism. Russia could bypass Western economic misery by merely extending the system of social ownership of land and socialistic distribution of the product already latent in the ancient Russian peasant commune. In the field of manufacture, the *artel'* system of cooperative workshops was to be extended and modeled after Kirsanova's dressmaking establishment in *What Is To Be Done?*

In presenting this "avoidance principle" for Russian society and the direct passage into socialism—the skipping concept which omitted for Russia various stages of social and economic development—Chernyshevsky anticipated Tkachev's own skipping theory as well as his idea of the *"historical jump."* The radical revolutionism of the *jump* and *skip* theories and the denial of a rigorous Hegelian dialectical historical process provided a great stimulus to the youth of the sixties and seventies who read Chernyshevsky's articles in *Sovremennik*. This revolutionary spirit was evident when Chernyshevsky applied it practically in his proclamation *To the Russian Peasants*[30] and helped win for him the title of founder of the *Land and Liberty Society (Zemlya i Volya)*.

To political economy Chernyshevsky contributed the strong ethical and equalitarian point of view toward economics, and in this his natural fellow travelers were the French Utopians and Marx. Not "national wealth," wrote Chernyshevsky, "but national well-being is the true criterion of the good of a nation's economy."[31] National wealth distributed unequally meant nothing; "for a democrat," he wrote, "our Siberia enjoying the simplest of human welfare stands much above England in which a majority of the people suffer terrible need."[32] (Incidentally, note in the above quotation the conception of a simple and primitive justice existing in Russia.) This moral criterion for tooting any economy was transferred to Tkachev's thought. The latent Populism of Chernyshevsky was carried over into Lavrovism of the seventies. Also, it should be added, Chernyshevsky emphasized that "capital is the product of labor" and in this he could be associated with the school of Ricardo and Marx, both of whom developed a labor theory of value.[33]

The advance of science in the nineteenth century stimulated impatient thinkers of all kinds to extend scientific procedure and its resultant truth into heretofore strictly unscientific realms, like literature and politics. Chernyshevsky was a realist and devotee of science. Like the character Bazarov in Turgenev's *Fathers and Children*, he sought to subsume human psychological data under scientific postulates taken from fields related to psychology, physiology, and medicine. If the mind could be studied on the basis of medical and physiological science, could not the production of the mind—philosophy, for example—be studied with the same cool scientific objectivity? Chernyshevsky answered:

Philosophy may see in man only what medicine, physiology, and chemistry see in him. These sciences prove that in man no dualism is discoverable; but philosophy adds that if man did have a second nature in addition to his real bio-chemical nature, that second nature would have to manifest itself in some way.[34]

But no second nature reveals itself, said Chernyshevsky. Psychology was for him, therefore, merely an arm of physiology; "the laws of nature apply equally in the domain of the psyche." These beliefs were posited with the confidence of scientific truth, although he admitted that "they lack precision and universal truth." It is this side of Chernyshevsky's thought which might be termed "materialistic monism."[35]

In psychological matters Chernyshevsky's eagerness to invade the realm of disorderly passions, imagination, and even the intellect, to order mental phenomena according to scientific law, contributed to the extremist and hyper-rationalist atmosphere pervading the era of the sixties. It was left for later thinkers to attempt an extension of scientific procedures into those other "anarchical realms" of literary creation and criticism, politics, and finally ethics.

As for politics, Chernyshevsky was one of the first—and certainly the best known figures of the sixties—to express disillusionment with the Tsar's Emancipation Decree and inadequate land reform. But in positing a tacitly revolutionary solution to the problem, Chernyshevsky seemed hesitant about unleashing the destructive force of the ignorant peasant masses. In his *Letters Without an Address*, written in early 1862, Chernyshevsky predicted resignedly that the peasants would eventually take matters into their own hands in any case. While he viewed this prospect of mass action more or less favorably, at the same time he warned:

> The people are ignorant, dominated by primitive prejudices and by blind hatred for anything different from their own barbaric customs, make no distinction between one and the other in the class that wears different dress from themselves. They will go against them all indiscriminantly sparing neither our science, our poetry, nor our arts, destroying our civilization.[36]

At this time, Chernyshevsky evidently foresaw a gradually widening democratic mass base—that is, the people—abetted by education, a broad mass participation in democratic government and democratic solution of the peasant problem. Despite his later imprisonment and the implicit revolutionism at least of his *What Is To Be Done?* and his personal correspondence, and even in the midst of disillusionment with reform from above, Chernyshevsky appeared to have retained a certain faith in democratic and gradualistic solutions to social problems. At the same time he seemed to expect the Russian masses to make a revolution which he neither altogether feared nor altogether welcomed.[37]

The important elements in Chernyshevsky passed on to the seventies and to Tkachev were: 1) suggestions of economic determinism; 2) the Utopian-Socialist outlook of *What Is To Be Done?*, the political *Eugene Onegin* of radical Russian social and political writers;[38] 3) the fear expressed in Chernyshevsky's younger days of the destructive force (if left uncontrolled) of the peasant masses unleashed in a spontaneous revolution;

4) Russia as a special case; 5) the typically Russian dedication to the cause, the renunciation of "Oblomovism."

DOBROLYUBOV'S CONTRIBUTION

As though the application of strict scientific procedures to psychology were not enough, the "illusioned realm," as Tkachev was to call it, of literary creation and criticism became the next target for irrevocable truth, in the hands of Nikolai A. Dobrolyubov.

Dobrolyubov, a fellow writer with Chernyshevsky on *Sovremennik* and like his co-worker the offspring of a family of priests, contributed the idea that all art "must directly and naturally flow from life, or else art would be deformed and unthinkable"; he maintained that the accurate portrayal of a leaf of a tree is actually more useful than the accurate portrayal of the character of some person.[39] Utility, not beauty, was to be the principal criterion for art. A suggestion that utilitarianism should be applied to the aesthetic realm had already come earlier in the writings of Chernyshevsky, who had rated art as follows:

A work of art is always petty in comparison with nature and life itself of which art is a mere depiction.[40]

The real tree, he seemed to be saying, is always superior to the described one; the described tree will *always* be bathed in the "petty" individuality of the artist; it is the concrete seen as a useful object which supersedes any other *depicted* tree.[41] Dobrolyubov went to the extreme of dropping the words "art" and "beauty" out of his vocabulary altogether.[42] In his article "Characteristics of the Simple Russian Folk,"[43] he stated emphatically that for him the importance of an artistic work—and of all activity—was its aim, not its artistic execution or form. The aim of the content, its utility in the social sense, was the criterion. In a manner anticipating Tkachev and reminiscent of Plato, Dobrolyubov at times questioned the need in society for any poets at all.[44] His devotion to the "real" and the "concrete" had political overtones.

In his political views Dobrolyubov displayed a greater faith in tangible mass action than some of his predecessors, even though such action was not backed up with formal education. While by no means inattentive to the intelligentsia's duty to educate the masses, Dobrolyubov began to introduce into the Russian revolutionary spirit the notion that the "half-mad society which claims to be educated" had something to learn from the masses as well.[45] However, Dobrolyubov stressed strongly the responsibility of the intelligentsia—particularly its young, university-educated members—as the only body capable of bringing education to the people while at the same time representing it.[46] In this Dobrolyubov established the ideal for a Populist intelligentsia, an ideal which was to exert a profound influence on the coming generation.

Dobrolyubov frequently stressed the need, indeed the urgency, for placing thoughts and ideas on the same level with action; to do otherwise, he said, was to fall into Oblomovism.[47] For this reason it has been said that Dobrolyubov gave shape to the psychology of Populism.[48]

In general, Dobrolyubov displayed more impatience than some of his predecessors with delayed solution of Russia's many social problems and, like Tkachev, began to demand immediate action.

> When will the real day come? What has our society done in the last twenty to thirty years? Until now—nothing. It has educated itself, it has seen development, it has sat around listening to Rudins [Rudin was the hero of Turgenev's novel, a talkative idealist] and has grieved over their lack of success in the noble fight for ideals. It has prepared itself for action but has done nothing. After the stage in which given ideas are recognized, there must come the moment when they are *put into action*. Action must follow meditation and talk.[49]

This was, in fact, not only a condemnation of the older generation represented by Herzen, but a condemnation of all those who would sit and wait for problems to solve themselves or for Tsarist institutions to solve them ("Popular Tsarism"). In many respects, Dobrolyubov was one of the first true revolutionaries of the new era marked by the frustrating years of 1848, 1855, 1863 and intervening years—i.e., successively the abortive revolutions in Europe, failure of a peasant revolt to materialize in Russia, Russia's defeat in the Crimean War, and the Polish revolt. He was one of the first social and political writers (before he died in Chernyshevsky's arms in 1861) to inspire the next, post-Emancipation generation to all manner of revolutionary and going-to-the-people activity. The note of extremism characteristic of Dobrolyubov's writings inspired the men of the next decade, including Tkachev, but the latter was to make important modifications and elaborations which set him apart in several aspects from his predecessors.

As to Dobrolyubov's basic philosophy and his ideals for the future, he seems to have attempted only rarely to delineate them, and then in a somewhat unclear way.[50] Except for occasional favorable treatment of Robert Owen and French Utopian Socialists, Dobrolyubov ignored social doctrines. His influence lay not so much in what he said (in the sense of the content of his teaching qua teaching) as in the vehement manner in which he criticized existing social conditions, the impatience which he showed toward what he called Oblomov-like inaction. He called for members of the intelligentsia to roll up their sleeves, go to the masses, become part of them, and arm-in-arm with them change the old order into a new one.

PISAREV'S CONTRIBUTION

Dimitri I. Pisarev, who wrote in the late sixties for the radical journal *Russkoye slovo* (*Russian Word*) for which Tkachev also wrote, taught that all critics should be well versed in the latest discoveries of scientific research since they provided suitable material for the arts.[51] He remained true to this belief amidst other great changes of viewpoint which took place during his short life.

In his early nihilistic period Pisarev exclaimed, "Down with theory and ethics!" He wrote at that time:

> It would be a very good idea if the faith in the necessity of theory were demolished amongst the reading public. A strict carrying out of theory means only the suffering of the individual personality, and to be-

lieve in such suffering means to look at the world
through the eyes of an ascetic, to torment oneself with
the love of art. . . . Idealists are prepared to wreck
anything for the sake of their conclusions—any person's or anyone's interests. They are certainly unable
to sense that a person is always dearer than any
thought-up conclusions whatsoever.[52]

All truth is relative, he said; "there is only A's truth, B's
truth, etc. . . . Truth is what each says is true." Intellectual
and moral propaganda is to some extent an encroachment upon
the freedom of each person.[53] This rejection of ideals and theory
and the ultra-individualism permeating it were only temporary
phenomena in Pisarev's thoughts. But this nihilism, as it came
to be called, was joined to the tradition of Turgenev's Bazarov
and his strictly scientific approach to all life. The doctrine of
Pisarev was a denial of all past and contemporary values (aesthetic and moralistic) and a positive glorification of strictly
verifiable scientific postulates. This scientism of the youthful
pisarevshchina probably exerted a direct influence upon the
young Tkachev who was, of course, personally acquainted
with him. And Pisarev's purely negative response to artificial
"thought-up" values undoubtedly provided Tkachev with a positive stimulus to treat thought-up tradition lightly, too, and to
foresee an eventual total revolutionary change in all values,
the laying down of new basic principles of society as a real
possibility and desirable goal.

In his later phase Pisarev developed the idea of the "thinking proletariat" or "consistent realists,"[54] which probably also
exerted an influence on Tkachev. The thinking proletariat was
an intellectual minority economizing its strength, as it were,
in order to devote all its time to natural-scientific research,
social-scientific research, literary (didactic) criticism, and so
forth. As the result of its research, Pisarev's thinking proletariat would formulate great ideas and standards for social life
which all should follow. This later phase witnessed a partial
renunciation of Pisarev's former nihilism and his search for
the union of the individual and society in a common utilitarian
bond. The thinking proletariat was transformed in Tkachev's
thought into "the radical minority—the cultured group . . .
the civilized group."[55]

LATENT JACOBINISM

Chernyshevsky was a revolutionary democrat who believed that some day the people would throw off the yoke of autocracy and usher in a new era of popular, representative government.[56] The same may be said of Herzen, as well as of many of his contemporaries in the sixties, who, writing in *Sovremennik* or *Russkoye slovo,* gave vent to similar ideas. Later revolutionists such as Lavrov, members of *Land and Liberty* (*Zemlya i Volya*), most of the People's Will society (*Narodovol'tsi*)[57] and the Populists of the seventies and eighties, and liberal university professors and *zemstva* administrators who believed in popularly based revolution. On the other hand, in the midst of a disenfranchised, illiterate peasantry, other thinkers posited the necessity of the introduction of enlightenment *from the outside,* either by means of a thinking proletariat (said the *Pisarevshchina*) or by means of a movement to the people by enlightened individuals who would participate realistically in peasant village life (*Mikhailovtsi* and *Chaikovtsi*) ; others thought that the peasants should be passionately urged to social revolt after which a constituent assembly, with popular and universal representation, would be called to settle economic and social questions on the basis of majority rule (*Narodovol'tsi*). But there were a few *who differed strikingly from all these viewpoints.*

These few believed in a minority, instead of the "vulgar and ignorant masses," leading or even making the revolution; after the revolution, this minority should carry out certain prescribed revolutionary principles for the reorganization of society. These revolutionists made up the tradition of Jacobinism and (later) Blanquism in Russia—descending-mode power theory and a tradition which rested dormant in the midst of more popular revolutionary principles throughout most of late nineteenth-century Russian history.[58]

Colonel Pavel I. Pestel, the Decembrist, represents one of the earliest and greatest of Russian Jacobins. It was Pestel who called for the radical-nobleman minority to make a palace revolution in 1825, a "preventive" revolution against an anarchical peasant insurrection which was sure to come, he said, and which would only weaken the nation economically and militarily. A provisional "dictatorship," he said, should prevail after the *coup* to complete the parceling out of former landlord land to the peasants and the instituting of a national assembly.[59] Until the sixties no other significant Jacobin appears on the Russian revolutionary scene with the exception of Speshnev.[60]

Nikolai A. Speshnev (1821–1882) and some of his concepts represent still another early appearance of Jacobinism in Russian revolutionary thought. One of the wealthiest of revolutionaries, he was educated in a Paris *lycée* and was strongly influenced by the French political thought and action of the 1840's. He was also sympathetic with Polish revolutionary exiles whom he had met in France. Speshnev was one of the active participants in the *Petrashevtsi* socialist revolutionary circle in St. Petersburg, which functioned during a part of the reign of Nicholas I. Dostoyevsky, who had also been a member of the circle, once asserted that it was the *Petrashevtsi* who had "sown many seeds" among Russian revolutionaries and had influenced later Russian socialists. While the *Petrashevtsi* agreed with each other on the metaphysics of revolution and revolutionary transformation of Russian society, by no means all of them agreed with Speshnev that:

—a central committee should be formed in which centralized leadership of all revolutionary groups and revolutionary activity could be organized and led;

—the revolutionary program should be avowedly conspiratorial and Babeuvian-communist;

—revolutionary tactics should be Machiavellian;

—a postrevolutionary dictatorship should be established;

—collectivization of Russian agriculture should be encouraged.

Speshnev, like many of the Jacobins of later times, found himself almost alone in his views among his comrades. Petrashevsky himself called Speshnev a victim of self-glorification; he said that he, Petrashevsky, "would be the first to raise my hand against a dictator."[61]

The debates among the *Petrashevtsi*—between the moderates and the radical socialists—foreshadow the later controversies revolving about the issue of moderation, gradualism, and democracy vs. radicalism, the *coup* tactic, and dictatorship, controversies which were to beset Russian Populism and Russian Social Democracy in both the nineteenth and twentieth centuries.

The proclamation *Young Russia*,[62] written in 1862 by Peter G. Zaichnevsky, represents a most important event in the tradition of Russian Jacobinism.

Young Russia was ostensibly written to oppose the viewpoint presented by most other proclamations of the time, in particular that of *The Great Russian,* which was distributed from July to September 1861 and supposedly drafted by Chernyshevsky.[63] This earlier proclamation, *The Great Russian,* which came out eight months after the Tsar's Emancipation Decree and was one of the first products of the Russian clandestine press,[64] was a pamphlet advising the Russian radical intelligentsia to pressure Tsar Alexander II for a constitution. In spite of the fact that this peaceful approach was accompanied by a threat of future violence from the peasantry if the Tsar did not grant the constitution, M. N. Pokrovsky, the Bolshevik historian, notes the "Menshevistic tone" of *The Great Russian,* "because it views the peasants as dependent upon the educated classes, whom the Tsar cannot shoot, to bring peaceful pressure to bear upon the government, eventually winning any concessions it can."[65]

Indeed, by contrast, *Young Russia* displays more Bolshevism than it does Menshevism. *Young Russia* was issued by "The Revolutionary Committee"[66] in May 1862. It read in part:

We have not studied Western European history for nothing. It was studied for a definite reason. We will henceforth not be the pitiful revolutionaries of 1848, but rather the great terrorists of 1792. We are not afraid if we see that for the overturning of the contemporary social order it will prove necessary to expend twice as much blood as was expended by the Jacobins in the 1790's. We firmly assert that the revolutionary party, which will stand at the head of the government if the movement will only prove success-

ful, must retain the present centralization of government—beyond all doubt politically centralized and not
merely administratively centralized. By this centralized power it can lay the foundations for economic and
social life in as short a time as possible. It must take
the dictatorship into its own hands and not stop
at anything. *Elections for a national assembly must
take place under the surveillance of the [revolution-
ary] government which will at once make sure that
no partisans of the old order—that is, if they are still
alive—make up the composition of this new assembly*
[my italics—A. L. W.].[67]

The proclamation continues with a discussion of the tasks of
the revolutionary government:

We demand the establishment of socialized factories, the administration of which must be elected
from society and be held responsible for a prescribed
length of time to give a total accounting of things [to
the public]. We demand the establishment of shops in
which goods will be sold at prices which they actually
cost to produce and not at that price which insures to
the seller the quickest possible profit. . . . We demand the complete liberation of women, the awarding
to them of all those political and civil rights enjoyed
by the men. . . . The properties of all churches must
be confiscated on behalf of the state for the payment
of foreign and domestic debt.

There is a great deal that is perhaps typically Russian:
the instruction which the eclectic Russian receives from events
abroad in the West; the naïve statement about prices being
equal to the costs of production (elimination of profit along
with the surplus funds necessary for investment and for the
expansion and development of the nation's economy); demands
of socially conscious women, who played an increasingly great
role in the revolutionary activity in Russia throughout the
nineteenth century; the anticlericalism which has characterized revolutionary movements from the highest to the lowest
strata of Russian society for centuries. But there is also much
which is typical only of the Jacobin tradition in Russia. Some
of the principles embodied in this extraordinarily prophetic

proclamation have persisted up to and including the advent of Bolshevism to power in 1917. In the seventies it was Peter Tkachev who endorsed them, refurbished them, and made elaborations upon the Jacobin theme with impressive thoroughness, inner consistency, and above all, candor.

At the time of their appearance these Jacobin ideas are reported to have displeased Bakunin, onetime leader of the Russian Section of the International in Geneva whose views had become anarchist after passing through a brief Jacobin phase. Furthermore, the Zaichnevsky proclamation obviously enjoyed little fame in its own day in Russia. As L. F. Pantaleyev, a contemporary, records in his memoirs:

> Among the Petersburg youth, *Young Russia* did not meet with great enthusiasm or sympathy. True, it was disseminated, but only because the youth at that time considered it their duty to distribute any proclamation.[68]

In addition to Bakunin, as both Kozmin and Venturi demonstrate, Chernyshevsky and Herzen were hostile to Zaichnevsky's theories of revolution.[69] Herzen and the members of the newly-formed Land and Liberty circle all expressed themselves negatively on *Young Russia*.[70] The consensus among *Young Russia's* critics is perhaps best summed up by Kozmin as follows:

> It was the product of an immature mind [which] could only bring harm to revolutionary activity in Russia and drive away broad social circles.[71]

But of course some did support Zaichnevsky's ideas and kept them alive, as the very existence of the *Young Russia* circle and of a subsequent proclamation, *To The Russian People*, written by Leonid Olshevsky, testify.[72]

Even the most radical offshoot of Land and Liberty, the People's Will group (*Narodovol'tsi*), believed unanimously, or nearly so, throughout its career in the late seventies and early eighties, in the convening of a postrevolutionary constituent assembly to determine, on the basis of a democratic franchise, the political and social structure of the new society.[73] But Russian Blanquists and *Narodovol'tsi* did see eye-to-eye on one important point at least: political revolution must come first, or at least simultaneously with social revolution; the autocracy must go. This radical political view represented a new philosophy in the midst of Land and Liberty's emphasis on the priority *social* questions and their solution. Tkachev introduced this new seize-the-political-power-first philosophy in well-argued form, as Lenin noted in *What Is To Be Done?* The necessity of terror against the autocracy and the Tsar in particular became the keystone of the *Narodovol'tsi* program. Ivanov-Razmunik notes, "Tkachev preached in his *Nabat* a political revolution employing terror as the weapon of struggle, but his voice had an alien ring at this time [early seventies]."[74]

With the eighties and the formation of Marxist study groups, Marxist ideas on the necessity of the dictatorship phase, the class struggle, and the necessity of preventing counterrevolution by means of the proletarian dictatorship began to impress some of the radical intelligentsia. While Plekhanov deplored the Blanquist tradition of the Tkachev circle in Geneva[75] and had no desire, he said, to continue this heritage, Lenin and his cohorts at the turn of the century began grafting Marxism onto the nearly century-old Russian Jacobin and Blanquist tradition and, by so doing, revitalized and strengthened Tkachev's thought, imbuing it with the more elaborate "scientific" socialism of Marx and Engels. Tkachev's writings in *Nabat*, Lenin advised revolutionaries in 1900, should be required reading.[76]

NOTES

1. Martin Malia, "What Is the Intelligentsia?," *The Russian Intelligentsia,* ed. Richard Pipes (New York: Columbia University Press, 1961), p. 1. Malia derives the Russian word *"intelligentsiya"* from the Latin adjectival substantive *intelligens-intelligentis,* having the approximate meaning of "intellectual," "discerning." This direct Latin derivation of the Russian word seems more likely than any indirect French derivation since the French word *intelligent* does *not* connote "intellectual," as do both the Latin and Russian terms.

2. Richard Pipes, "The Historical Evolution of the Russian Intelligentsia," *ibid.,* p. 47.

3. Michael T. Florinsky, *Russia, A History and Interpretation* (New York: The Macmillan Company, 1953), I, 483, 497.

4. Arnold Toynbee, *A Study of History* (New York and London: Oxford University Press, 1947), one-volume abridgement, p. 11, where

Toynbee defines the term: "The word 'proletariat' is here and hereafter used to mean any social element or group which in some way is
in but not *of* any given society." And, "Wherever we find an intelligentsia, we may infer . . . that one of the two [civilizations] is in
the process of being absorbed into the other's internal proletariat. . . .
An intelligentsia is hated . . . by its own people because its very
existence is a reproach to them." (pp. 393–94).

5. Pipes, *op. cit.*, p. 48.

6. Florinsky, *op. cit.*, I, 600–601.

7. N. O. Lossky, *History of Russian Philosophy* (New York: International Universities Press, Inc., 1951), p. 47.

8. *Ibid.*, p. 13. Compare Franco Venturi, *Roots of Revolution—
A History of the Populist and Socialist Movements in Nineteenth Century Russia* (New York: Alfred A. Knopf, 1960), pp. 20–21.

9. Franco Venturi, *Roots of Revolution* (New York: Alfred A.
Knopf, 1960), p. 20.

10. Lossky, *op. cit.*, p. 47. Compare, Venturi, *op. cit.*, p. 19.

11. Venturi, *op. cit.*, pp. 19–20.

12. S. V. Utechin, *Russian Political Thought* (New York: Frederick A. Praeger, 1963), p. 117.

13. Baron von Haxthausen, Prussian State Counsellor, had added
the strictly nonsocialist idea that the landlord should act as protector
and supervisor of the peasant commune. Engels was sympathetic to
the view, prompted by Haxthausen and developed by Herzen, that
Russia's road to socialist reformation could be shortened because of
the tradition of collective use of the land prescribed within the
obshchina (see discussion below, pp. 94–95).

14. Some of the older intelligentsia vacillated in their opinions on
this matter. Herzen, for example, seemed to revise his thinking later
in his life, for he welcomed the Polish rebellion of 1863 and predicted
that the "awakened giant" (the Russian peasantry) would soon take
matters into its own hands in the wake of the unsatisfactory Emancipation Decree of the Tsar in 1861, a decree that he had first welcomed.

15. For a thoroughgoing treatment of this abortive revolt, see
Anatole Mazour, *The First Russian Revolution: 1825* (Berkeley:
University of California Press, 1937).

16. The insurrection was ignited prematurely by a succession crisis brought on by Tsar Alexander I's sudden death in Taganrog, a
port on the Sea of Azov, on November 19, 1825; the Decembrists had
originally planned the revolt for the year 1826. During the ensuing
three weeks, Constantine, Alexander's brother and heir to the throne,
refused the throne and thus opened the way to another brother,
Nicholas, an exacting disciplinarian who was most unpopular with
the St. Petersburg military. Constantine delayed making an official
statement to abdicate until December 12th. On December 14th the

Senate met to take the oath to Nicholas before the arrival of the rebellious troops. Artillery units loyal to the new Tsar Nicholas I crushed the insurrection which had begun to be assisted by a crowd of civilians who mixed with the soldiers and pelted government troops with stones and even logs. Having begun near dawn, the insurrection ended as daylight was draining out of the short winter day.

17. Malia, Pipes, *op. cit.*, p. 9.

18. An event of considerable importance anticipating the approach of a new, more radical and revolution-minded generation was the famous letter written by the *raznochinets* Vissarion Belinsky to Nikolai Gogol in 1847, the year before Belinsky's premature death, and distributed in handwritten copies. Another noteworthy event was Bakunin's conversion to revolutionary ideas by 1842, a somewhat atypical development in the pre-Emancipation period of the 1840's and 1850's; it was, however, a highly auspicious event. By the late 1850's, the left-wing elements of the Westernist intelligentsia led by Chernyshevsky and Dobrolyubov had first begun to manifest itself (cf. Venturi, *op. cit.*, pp. 106–107).

19. See Vladimir L. Burtsev, *Za sto let* (London: Russian Free-Press Fund, 1897), for texts.

20. *Ibid.*, II, 74. Burtsev's book contains detailed records of revolutionary groups, their clandestine literature, members' arrests and exiles, and instances of censorship of revolutionary and Western literature by the Tsarist government. Hobbes's work was put on the censor's index in 1868, undoubtedly because of its materialism.

21. F. I. Dan, *Proiskhozhdeniye bol'shevizma* (New York: Izdatel'stvo Novaya Demkratia, 1946), p. 171. On the intellectualistic character of Russian revolution, Nicholas Berdaev once observed: "In Russia revolution was a religion and a philosophy, not merely a conflict concerned with the social and political side of life" (*The Origins of Russian Communism* [New York: Charles Scribner and Sons, 1937], pp. 124–25).

22. Bernard Pares, *A History of Russia* (New York: Alfred A. Knopf, 1939), p. 355. Compare Geroid T. Robinson, *Rural Russia Under the Old Regime* (London: Longmans Green and Company, 1957), pp. 86–87.

23. John Stuart Mill once cautioned: "The abuse of intellectual power is only to be dreaded when society is divided between a few highly cultivated intellects and an ignorant and stupid multitude" (J. S. Mill, *Auguste Comte and Positivism* [Ann Arbor: University of Michigan Press, 1961], p. 171).

24. *Raznochinets* or *raznochinstvo* is difficult to define except loosely. The *raznochinstvo*, whom detractors called "black students," were generally intellectuals from non-noble ranks of peasants, petty tradesmen, merchants, teachers, clergymen, and other professional and middle-class people who, under conditions of widespread illiteracy,

tended to form an independent stratum whose principal work consisted of "work with the brain." Although the *raznochintsi* were an expression of the retreat of feudalism in Russia, they could not ally themselves with a bourgeois class because no sizable bourgeoisie existed at that time in Russia. Therefore, these mixed-rank intellectuals were without social roots, a factor which tended to isolate them.

25. Dan, *op. cit.*, p. 38.

26. *Ibid.*, p. 39.

27. V. Ivanov-Razumnik, *Istoriya russkoi obshchestvennoi mysli* (St. Petersburg: M. M. Stasyulevich Tipografiya, 1908), II, 34.

28. Nicolai G. Chernyshevsky, *What Is To Be Done?* (New York: International Book Store, n.d.).

29. See discussion below of Tkachev's review of a work by Mill, p. 130. Like other revolutionary intellectuals of the sixties and seventies, Tkachev concerned himself with a great range of topics and problems. A partial list of them would include Russian prisons, American prisons, family relations, criminal law, education, revolution, economic determinism, constitutionalism, anarchism, individualism, the woman question, psychiatry, development of capitalism in the village, and so on, plus reviews or discussions of such thinkers as Bentham, J. S. Mill, Comte, Adam Smith, Ricardo, Marx and Engels, Blanqui, Malthus, Girardin, Machiavelli, and many others.

30. Mikhail N. Pokrovsky, *Ocherki po istorii revolyutsionnovo dvizheniya v Rossii XIX y XX-kh vv* (Moscow: Krasnaya Nov' Izdatel'stvo, Gosudarstvennoye Uchebno-pedagogicheskoye Izdatel'stvo, 1945), p. 57. Masaryk makes the same assertion upon the authorship of *To the Russian Peasants*, which he claims was "written, at least in part, by Chernyshevsky." Compare Thomas G. Masaryk, *The Spirit of Russia* (New York: Macmillan and Company, 1919), I, 39. See below, pp. 121–24.

31. Ivanov-Razumnik, *op. cit.*, II, 11.

32. *Ibid.*, II, 15.

33. *Ibid.*, II, 11, Marx wrote to the members of the *émigré* committee of the Russian Section in Geneva, March 24, 1870: "Such works as those of Flerovsky and those of their teacher, Chernyshevsky, really do the Russians honor and prove that their country is also beginning to participate in the general movement of our century." *Karl Marx and Frederick Engels Correspondence (1846–1895)*, trans. Dona Torr (New York: International Publishers, 1934), pp. 284–85.

34. Masaryk, *op. cit.*, II, 5.

35. *Ibid.*, II, 6.

36. N. G. Chernyshevsky, *Izbranniye ekonomicheskiye proizvedeniya* (Moscow: Gosudarstvennoye Izdatel'stvo Politicheskoi Literatury, 1948–1949), II, 617.

37. N. G. Chernyshevsky, *Polnoye sobraniye sochinenii* (Moscow: Gosudarstvennoye Izdatel'stvo, 1939–1951), XIV, 505 (Letter of January 12, 1871).

38. *Eugene Onegin* was frequently the subject of discussion among the men of letters of the older generation of the thirties and forties. It was a symbol of the times that Chernyshevsky took Pushkin's place in the 1870's.

39. Ivanov-Razumnik, *op. cit.*, II, 55.

40. *Ibid.*, II, 53.

41. What Chernyshevsky and Dobrolyubov are saying in fact is that the real or concrete tree is more beautiful than the artist's tree; and that life in general is more beautiful than its depiction in art. For Plato, too, the material embodiment of the idea of form is superior to its representation in art, which is twice removed from the Idea or Form.

42. Ivanov-Razumnik, *op. cit.*, II, 56.

43. The current epithet among the radical youth of the time for the Russian peasantry was "the simple folk."

44. Masaryk, *op. cit.*, II, 21; below, pp. 141–47.

45. N. A. Dobrolyubov, *Polnoye sobraniye sochinenii* (Moscow: Gosudarstvennoye Izdatel'stvo, 1934–1939), IV, 138.

46. Venturi, *op. cit.*, p. 192.

47. Dobrolyubov, *op. cit.*, II, 30. One is reminded of a statement once made by Tkachev about thoughts becoming actions: "To be forever carrying about in one's head ideas which are not permitted to be put into practice is in itself tormenting, a dreadfully excruciating torture."

48. Venturi, *op. cit.*, p. 187.

49. Dobrolyubov, *op. cit.*, II, 211.

50. Venturi, *op. cit.*, p. 195.

51. Quoted by Rene Wellek, "Social and Aesthetic Values in Russian Nineteenth-Century Literary Criticism (Belinsky, Chernyshevsky, Dobrolyubov, Pisarev)" in Ernest J. Simmons, ed., *Continuity and Change in Russian and Soviet Thought* (Cambridge, Mass.: Harvard University Press, 1955), p. 394. In this way Pisarev sought to popularize science amongst the superstitious peasantry after they had first been taught to read. Compare V. S. Kruzhkov, ed., Preface to *D. I. Pisarev: Izbranniye filosofskiye i obshchestvenno-politicheskiye stat'i* (Moscow: Gosizdat, 1944).

52. Quoted in Ivanov-Razumnik, *op. cit.*, II, 69.

53. *Ibid.*, II, 69–70.

54. Kruzhkov, *D. I. Pisarev . . . stat'i*, p. 386; Dan, *op. cit.*, p. 99.

55. Below, pp. 86–87, 92–97.

56. Masaryk, *op. cit.*, II, 35; Kruzhkov, Preface to *D. I. Pisarev stat'i.*

57. The founding meeting of the society and subsequent proclamations, including Stepniak's famous March 1881 proclamation to the Tsar, all proclaim the necessity of the calling of a postrevolutionary constituent assembly which will determine democratically the specific political action that is to be taken in making reforms. Herzen's anti-Jacobin position is found well stated by the venerable member of the old generation in *My Past and Thoughts,* reproduced in A. I. Herzen, *Polnoye sobraniye sochinenii i pisem* (Petersburg: Gosudarstvennoye Izdatel'stvo, 1919–1925), XIV, 495 ff; Bakunin took his position against Zaichnevskian Jacobinism in his *The People's Cause: Romanov, Pugachev, or Pestel?,* published in 1862; Chernyshevsky, bitterly criticized by the Jacobin Zaichnevsky for being a pedant, is quoted in B. Kozmin, *P. G. Zaichnevsky i 'Molodaya Rossiya'* (Moscow: Gosizdat, 1932), p. 125, in an anti-Jacobin vein.

58. The term Jacobinism, used henceforth in this paper, refers to a party in the French Revolution that favored postrevolutionary one-group rule and revolutionary violence against those who opposed the new order or who would make counterrevolution and establish a different order. During the dictatorial rule of the revolutionary group, the opposition is forbidden by the Committee of Public Safety to express itself against the new regime in writing or speech. Blanquism is the latterday expression of Jacobinism, the revolutionary class by the middle of the nineteenth century being the factory proletariat or, as Blanqui himself was ready to accept, *déclassé* professional revolutionaries recruited from mixed ranks of the bourgeoisie—lawyers, teachers, students, etc. Zasulich, Figner, Axelrod, Plekhanov, Dan, and many others personally familiar with revolutionary circles of the seventies and eighties, all asserted—and Tkachev admitted as much, too—that Jacobinism appears to have been a *bête noir* even to some of those (like Plekhanov) who were somewhat tainted with it themselves. Certainly the word "Jacobin" was very often used pejoratively in Russia to describe someone who wanted to take over and boss a movement—a term somewhat akin to "dictator" or "tyrant." Lenin was one of the first twentieth-century writers to attempt to give the words "Jacobin" and "dictator" respectability.

59. Alexander I. Herzen, "La conspiration Russe de 1825," Burtsev, *op. cit.,* II, 3. Much of Pestel's *Russkaya Pravda,* his revolutionary program, is reproduced in *Vosstaniye Dekabristov—materiali po istorii vosstaniya Dekabristov,* ed. Mikhail N. Pokrovsky (8 vols.; Moscow: Institut Marksa-Engelsa, 1925–1929), Vol. IV.

60. Venturi, *op. cit.,* p. 87. See "Speshnev," *Bol'shaya Sovetskaya entsiklopediya,* ed. A. Y. Vyshinsky, K. E. Voroshilov, *et al.* Nikolai A. Speshnev is described here as a left-winger of the *Petrashevtsi* circle who was familiar with Marx's *Poverty of Philosophy* and believed in nationalization of land and industry.

61. Venturi, *op. cit.*, p. 87.

62. The literal translation is *Young Russia,* but it is sometimes translated *The Young Russian.*

63. Authorship of this proclamation is attributed by most authorities to friends of Chernyshevsky, if not to Chernyshevsky himself. Pokrovsky claims that Chernyshevsky is the author on the authority of Lemke, researcher of Russian political trials and documents of the Third Section before 1917.

64. See an interesting discussion of this in Paul Miluikov, *Russia and Its Crisis* (Chicago: University of Chicago Press, 1905), 385–86.

65. Mikhail N. Pokrovsky, *Ocherki russkovo revolyutsionnovo dvizheniya XIX–XX vv.* (Moscow: Krasnaya Nov' Glavpolit Prosvet, 1924), p. 59.

66. Masaryk, *op. cit.*, p. 83. Masaryk may be referring to the Zaichnevsky circle consisting of university students. See Vladimir Y. Bogucharsky, *Aktivnoye narodnichestvo semidesyat'nikh godov* (Moscow: Izdatel'stvo M. i S. Sabashnikovikh, 1912), X, 49.

67. Note the proposal that the revolutionary government should take the elections under its "surveillance." G. A. Kuklin, *Itogi revolyutsionnovo dvizheniya v Rossii* (Geneva: Biblioteka Russkovo Proletaria, 1903), pp. 2–3. Lenin later explained that the Constituent Assembly, which the Bolsheviks disbanded on January 19, 1918, after its short thirteen-hour life, had had to give way to the principle of dictatorship. The problem of the democratic Constituent Assembly, Lenin said, was solved "forcibly" by the Bolsheviks because the Bolsheviks had established their dictatorship *before* the Assembly convened and that, in any case, the bourgeois peasant masses could only be "won over" (as he put it) to socialism through the *power* of the Bolshevik dictatorship and *not* by tabulating votes (see Lenin, *Sochineniya* [4th ed.; Moscow: Gosudarstvennoye Izdatel'stvo Politicheskoi Literatury, 1950], XXX, 315, and his "Thesis on the Constituent Assembly," *op. cit.*, XXVI, 34–44). Lenin, Stalin, Trotsky, Sverdlov and other Bolsheviks all offered elaborate rationalizations for disbanding the democratic Constituent Assembly, Russia's last since 1918.

68. Kozmin, *P. G. Zaichnevsky,* p. 31.

69. *Ibid.,* p. 31; Venturi, *op. cit.,* pp. 298–99.

70. Bogucharsky, *op. cit.,* pp. 49–52. Herzen's commentary on the evils of Jacobinism is quoted here.

71. Kozmin, *op. cit.,* p. 31.

72. *Ibid.,* p. 32.

73. See David Footman, *Red Prelude: The Life of the Russian Terrorist Zhelyabov* (New Haven: Yale University Press, 1945), for a discussion in English of the progress and activity of the *Narodovol'tsi.*

74. Ivan-Razumnik, *op. cit.,* II, 108.

75. George V. Plekhanov, *Nashi raznoglasiya* [Our Differences], first published in 1884 (Moscow: Novy Mir, 1906), pp. 45–62, which anticipates the later Menshevist-Bolshevist schism. Plekhanov, by his own admission, was not always himself free of Jacobinism. Jacobinism had crept into his earlier thought through several avenues. At first, Plekhanov had stressed the importance of bringing socialist consciousness *to* the working class from the outside, describing the role of the socialist intelligentsia as teacher and preparer of the working class in terms resembling those of several of his predecessors, Dobrolyubov, Pisarev, and especially Tkachev (see G. V. Plekhanov, *Sochineniya,* ed. D. Ryazanov [2nd ed.; Moscow: Gosizdat, 1923–1927] II, 84). However, Plekhanov had been fully aware, apparently, of the problem of cultural and economic lag in illiterate Russia and disdained the employment of a postrevolutionary authoritarian state to lift up the masses suddenly to a higher level. He likened such an attempt to employ what he called "Peruvian 'Children of the Sun'" acting as a socialist caste (Plekhanov, *op. cit.,* II, 81, 294). On the other hand, anticipating Lenin and owing a debt to many of his predecessors, Plekhanov, in his early writings, speculated on the possibility of shortening or even eliminating the capitalist phase of development in Russia by the voluntaristic alteration of the historical process by the revolutionary party—a concept which did not fit in well at all with his rather rigidly held scheme of economic determinism. In his famous admission of Jacobin guilt, his letter to Paul Axelrod, Plekhanov wrote: "And my Jacobinism? It is essential that you should restrain me. You have every right to check my centralistic, Jacobin tendencies. It is indeed true that I have sinned in this respect" (from *Perepiska G. V. Plekhanova i P. B. Axelroda,* ed. P. A. Berlin, P. B. Nikolayevsky, and V. S. Voitinsky [Moscow: Gosizdat, 1925], I, 21).

76. See quotation from Bonch-Bruyevich's memoirs above, pp. 4–5.

CHAPTER III

The Life of Peter Tkachev

It is unfortunate that more is not known of the short, forty-two year life of Peter Nikitich Tkachev. However, a biographical sketch of sorts can be pieced together by the use of a variety of source materials.[1]

Tkachev was born of landowning parents of modest means on June 29, 1844, on his parents' estate near Velikie-Luki in Pskov Province. His father died when Peter was very young; the surviving family consisted of Peter, his two brothers and two sisters, and his mother.

While still quite young, Peter enrolled in Petersburg *Gymnasium* No. 2. This occurred near the end of the despotic reign of Tsar Nicholas I, and Tkachev, like many of his contemporaries, loathed the regimen and atmosphere in the *gymnasia* of the day. He wrote of them:

> Crude despotism, ignorance, and pigheadedness of both teachers and administrators; floggings without end; senseless learning by rote; arbitrary, oppressive despotism of older students over the younger.[2]

At the end of his *gymnasium* matriculation in 1861, Tkachev decided to enter upon a law career and began studies in the law faculty of St. Petersburg University. It was here in the feverish and restive atmosphere of the University (the institution was nearly engulfed with student unrest in the spring of 1861) that a revolutionary temperament began to express itself. As early as the first autumn after his admission into the University, Tkachev was arrested along with a hundred other people, mostly students, for carrying on agitation against the government-appointed educational administrators and for demanding the right of assembly to air purely academic grievances. Of course, the government officially forbade any corporate student action on Russian university campuses. Particularly stringent measures had been instituted at Tkachev's university because of the unrest there the preceding spring. Since that time several rules had been established by a special *ukaz* dated May 18, 1861: 1) compulsory attendance by all students at all lectures; 2) all meetings or gatherings of students were forbidden; 3) new regulations provided, among other things, that a special uniform be worn by all students.[3] These new rules amounted to the abrogation of the earlier procedures established during the liberal phase of the reign of Tsar Alexander II.

When the University opened for the new school year on September 17, 1861, its auditoriums became noisy and unruly gathering places. The government thereupon took the extreme measure of closing the University for a time. As part of its price for reopening the school, the officials ordered that "matriculation certificates" (*matrikuly*) show the student's behavior record during his entire stay in the institution.

This order immediately divided the students into two distinct camps—those who agreed to comply with the new regulation and those who did not. When the University was reopened, vociferous arguments took place on the campus between the anticertificatists and those who chose to go along with the format of the new certificates. On October 12th a large crowd gathered near the gates of the University, which had now become surrounded by the police and military. All persons in the crowd were arrested and booked. The total number reached three hundred.

Among those arrested was Peter Tkachev. Since there was insufficient room to detain them all in the Peter and Paul (Petropavlovsk) Fortress, a large part of the group, including Tkachev, was dispatched to Kronstadt. After this episode the University resumed its classes, but its classrooms and lecture halls were practically empty. Large numbers of the October demonstrators had been expelled from the University. On December 20th, the government once again ordered the closing of the University.

During the unrest at St. Petersburg University, ordinary residents of the city began to show their sympathy with the demands of the students and to collect money and sign petitions in their behalf.

With this mass roundup of students in 1861, Tkachev's "education" in Kronstadt Prison and later in the Peter and Paul Fortress began. During his two months' prison experience Tkachev became acquainted, sometimes at first hand, with various revolutionaries and their programs. The word "education" is no exaggeration, Kozmin writes:

> Even in the Petropavlovsk Fortress and in Kronstadt the students availed themselves of their free time during which they were allowed meetings with their relatives, walks, possession of newspapers and journals, appointments for voice lessons, the staging of plays, singing of Russian and Polish revolutionary songs, reading and writing of revolutionary poetry, and, above all, endless debates on social and political topics. Many future opponents of the government became known here. The main group of participants in future revolutionary circles and secret societies came from the midst of the students who had been confined to Petropavlovsk and Kronstadt. The sojourn in prison became for many a political school.[4]

In another place Kozmin writes:

> Young people, who were earlier little interested in the political affairs of the nation, came out of the Petropavlovsk Fortress and Kronstadt dedicated opponents of the contemporary order.[5]

Although Tkachev and other ex-political convict-students were allowed to attend a few lectures pertaining to fundamental courses in their particular fields, the expelled Tkachev's formal education was, in fact, at an end in the winter of 1861, that is, after his release from prison. A turning point had been reached. Tkachev had been allowed to take his final examinations for admission into the law school and had passed them,[6] but this illegal agitational activity precluded full-time attendance at the University. A combination of the government's policy of intolerance toward student agitation, the awakened and restive spirit of the times, and Tkachev's own restless temperament[7] had resulted in his pursuing henceforth the career of a revolutionary and writer on social and political themes.

LITERARY ACTIVITY IN RUSSIA

As we shall see later in the discussion of the Nechayev affair, before his escape abroad Tkachev had been engaged in active, illegal revolutionary work, a veteran of some ten years of such activity. But like revolutionaries before and after him, Tkachev presented to the general Russian public only a "legalist" side in which no more of the current phase of his own philosophy was revealed in print than the watchful government censor would permit. Because of this censorship we are unable to ascertain how far Tkachev's thought had developed before his later *Nabat* (*Alarm*) period abroad. This much can be said: Tkachev's writings of the sixties for the journals *Russkoye slovo* (*The Russian Word*), on which one of Tkachev's co-workers was Dmitri Pisarev, and *Delo* (*The Cause*) betray some aspects of his later, fully developed world outlook and his intense yearning and literary ability.

After the arrest of Pisarev and another popular writer on *Russkoye slovo*, V. F. Sokolov, this famous journal, sharing with *Sovremennik* (*The Contemporary*) the greatest popularity among the reading public of the day, found itself without its renowned literary critic and its authority on economics.[8] The wealthy and radical publisher, G. E. Blagosvetlov, had already been familiar with Tkachev, for the latter had published off and on in two somewhat less important publications, *Vremya* (*Time*), closed in 1863, and *Epokha* (*Epoch*), both of which were founded by the great writer F. M. Dostoyevsky and his brother. These articles concerned mostly juridical questions. In them Tkachev had displayed more interest in the social and economic causes of crime than in formal law. Blagosvetlov decided to hire Tkachev. Tkachev thenceforth worked on *Russkoye slovo* until intensification of the censorship in 1866 and the resultant permanent closing of the famous journal.[9]

For a time, before joining *Delo*, Tkachev contributed to *Zhenskii vestnik* (*Women's Messenger*), for which he wrote an article entitled "The Influence of Economic Progress on the Position of Women and the Family."[10] Meanwhile, Blagosvetlov was having no luck in bringing *Russkoye slovo* back to life. Finally, however, at the end of 1866, Blagosvetlov met a former fellow-worker on *Russkoye slovo*, N. I. Shulgin, and in partnership with him received permission from the government to open a new legal journal to be called *Delo*.[11] Although Shulgin was the official editor and publisher, it was Blagosvetlov who exerted the real influence on the journal's policy. The talented Tkachev was immediately hired as a staff writer.

As with the last years of Pisarev's former radical journal, *Delo* in the post-Karakozov period of reaction was almost completely emasculated of truly radical articles, which were carefully lopped off the proofs by the government censor. Consequently, this new journal won little favor among the revolutionary youth, who by now had resigned themselves to illegal activity and illegal publishing of proclamations and pamphlets.[12] *Delo* had in Tkachev its chief editorial force, that is until he was arrested in the Nechayev affair in 1869. He was to appear in print again in his own Blanquist organ, *Nabat*, published in Geneva, Switzerland, 1876–1886, in the French Blanquist newspaper, *Ni Dieu ni maitre*, and in his contributions sent to *Delo* in Russia under various pseudonyms—e.g., P. Nikitin, P. N. Nionov (literally "P. N. Not-him"), *Postnii* (the "Pious"), *Vse tot-zhe* ("*Ibidem*"), and others.

THE NECHAYEV AFFAIR

The year 1861 saw the issuing of several important proclamations concerning the insufficiencies of the Emancipation Decree. Some of these were smuggled illegally into the country from abroad, as was the case with copies of Herzen's *Kolokol* (*Bell*), while others were printed or disseminated illegally at home. By the summer of 1862, a secret organization put in an appearance bearing the name Land and Liberty, the platform of which was largely taken from the important illegal proclamation written by Nikolai P. Ogarev and N. N. Obruchev entitled *What the People Need*, which had appeared for the first time in 1861 in the form of an article in Herzen's *Kolokol* (No. 107). The first publication, *Svoboda* (*Freedom*), issued by the new organization asserted that "the primary source of all the evils now preying on Russia is autocratic despotism—or in other words, the *political* order.[13] *Svoboda* preached the necessity of calling a totally representative constituent assembly "which would decide the specific lines of the newly-liberated social structure of Russia."[14] And this became a fundamental viewpoint of the Land and Liberty society and its successor, the Social-Revolutionary Party, until and even after the closing of the Constituent Assembly by the Bolsheviks in January 1918.

Meanwhile, as Land and Liberty got under way and its principles began to win supporters among the intelligentsia, the Zaichnevsky proclamation (which preached violence, the futility of educating or being educated by the peasants or waiting for their spontaneous revolt, and the necessity of an authoritarian revolutionary and postrevolutionary leadership by a single party of radical intellectuals) won few supporters (discussed more fully below, pp. 56–57). Meanwhile, too, Tkachev was working out (on *Russkoye slovo* and *Delo*) some of the departure points[15] for his later world view. Before the Nechayev affair, Tkachev seems to have participated in two other affairs—the Ballod and Olshevsky cases, the trials of which revealed the existence of the first revolutionary proclamations to be issued and disseminated in Russia.

Peter Ballod, a student of comfortable means, was successful in establishing in Russia in 1862 a small printing press capable of printing leaflets.[16] Among the various items published on Ballod's press was an appeal addressed to Russian army officers which had been originally drafted by Ogarev and his collaborators in London and sent to Ballod from there. Another Ballod pamphlet defended Herzen from attacks by Tsarist critics. Still another publication carried Chernyshevsky's attack against Zaichnevsky's Jacobinism. At one time Ballod had asked Pisarev to write an article for him but Ballod was unable to publish it because of his (Ballod's) arrest. The Tsarist police finally caught up with Ballod and his press, sentenced him to fifteen years' hard labor, and banished him to the Siberian gold fields.

In the 1862 trial of Ballod which was to bring Pisarev's

arrest as well, evidence was brought forward of collaboration between Ballod and the eighteen-year-old Tkachev. And although Tkachev was apparently not directly involved in the Ballod affair, the same tribunal formulated a second case against both Tkachev and another young man, Leonid Olshevsky.

In the spring of 1861 Olshevsky had written one of the first proclamations ever issued in Russia, *To the Russian People*, which depicted a going-to-the-people conversation between two rustic peasants about "a youth who is neither *barin* nor merchant, is dressed just like us in a red shirt and our *plisoviye sharovari* and who speaks just like us . . . [and] listens to everything we say."[17] This youth who has approached the peasant is a description of a type of going-to-the-people pre-*Narodnik* (or Populist, a term which one begins to hear around 1870) of the seventies and eighties, advising the peasants to "take axe in hand and scatter all the evil-doers." The whole proclamation was cast in the simple, ungrammatical speech of the peasant. The police discovered and traced the pamphlet to Olshevsky. When the authorities found a note among Olshevsky's belongings which read, "was at your place—did not find you home (signed) P. Tkachev," they apprehended Tkachev as well, later sentencing him to two months in prison. At the trial, Tkachev denied any implication in the affair. But police had found among his belongings many revolutionary poems and the Ogarev proclamation. Tkachev himself admitted visiting Olshevsky; after all, he said, he had known him previously in the Peter and Paul Fortress. Evidence was also presented at the same trial implicating Tkachev in the writing in 1862 of another Olshevsky leaflet, a manifesto entitled *What We Want*.[18] Its essential point was that revolutionary ideas should be spread among the peasant masses to convince them of the need "for a speedy revolution."

Tkachev himself claimed, however, that Olshevsky's views were moderate and had made no impression on him, any more than had those of Ogarev.[19] But Kozmin notes that Olshevsky himself "candidly points out that he saw in Tkachev not only a man who might be trusted but who to a great extent was a fellow-thinker."[20]

The Olshevsky affair surely points at least to the possible

existence of a kind of early *Narodnik* tendency in the thinking of young Tkachev. The Nechayev affair illustrates this more clearly.

After the Christmas holidays of 1868, student unrest was manifest on an even larger scale than it had been in the stormy year of 1861. Demonstrations, arrests, and closings of the universities occurred not only in the capital, but also in Moscow.[21] Secret meetings were held in which fiery disputes raged between the radical nonconformist student element on the one hand and the moderate or conformist element on the other. The moderate wing came out against resorting to any illegal publishing and wished to confine student complaints and demonstrations to grievances affecting only students and student problems. The radical wing sought to merge the narrow student grievances with the broader discontents of the Russian population at large; their slogan was, so to speak, "Citizens first, students second." These radicals held their meetings in students' and ex-students' apartments and were strictly illegal. One of these ex-students was Peter Tkachev. And at the head of the student movement at this time stood the "Eagle," Sergei G. Nechayev (1847–1882).[22]

It is not known precisely under what conditions Tkachev became acquainted with Nechayev. The latter was undoubtedly familiar with Tkachev's articles in *Russkoye slovo* and *Delo*, and Nechayev's quickly emerging fame among the revolutionary university youth was undoubtedly well known to Tkachev.

> What we know about the personality and views of both these people [Tkachev and Nechayev] is sufficient to establish the fact that even though there were divergencies of opinions on questions affecting the tasks and tactics of the revolutionary struggle of that time, the personality of Nechayev could not help but exert a great influence on Tkachev.[23]

Nechayev—fiery, explosive, murderously (literally) intolerant of unbelievers—was unceasingly optimistic about Russia's readiness for revolution and overconfident about the size and the thoroughness of organization of his circles. The revolutionary temperament of Nechayev is typified in his famous Catechism (*Katekhizis*) of ascetic revolutionary behavior, which appeared in the illegally published and disseminated *Program for Revolutionary Action* (winter, 1868–1869) on the writing of which Tkachev is believed to have cooperated; the Catechism, which interestingly *had been anticipated by an article written earlier by Tkachev in* Delo *(Nos. 4, 5) in 1868*,[24] exemplified some of the concurrent viewpoints of both the "Eagle" and Tkachev. Among the provisions of the Catechism were:

> In comradeship there is nothing else but the aim of liberating the people and bringing them their welfare.
> The *Nechayevets* revolutionary is engrossed in just one thing: the exclusive interest, the single thought, the single passion—revolution.
> The revolutionary, to the depths of his very being, not simply in words but also by his deeds, must break off every tie with the contemporary civil order, with the whole organized world, with all laws, conventions, generally accepted conditions of life in this society. He is mercilessly hostile to society; he continues to live in the society only so that he may eventually destroy it.
> He despises public opinion. He despises all the pretensions of contemporary morality. Everything that glorifies revolution is moral to him; everything that interferes with it is immoral and unjust.[25]
> All delicate and effeminate feelings of kinship, friendship, love, gratitude, and even honor must be crushed by the single, cold passion of the revolutionary Cause.
> The nature of the revolutionary excludes any romanticism, all sensitivity, rapturousness, and uncontrolled passion.
> All friendship, subordination, and other responsibilities in the relationship of one revolutionary to another is measured against the single standard of utility in the cause of practical revolution.
> Every comrade must have at hand any number of revolutionaries of second and third rank. He must consider them as so much revolutionary capital at his disposal.
> He who feels pity for anything in this society is not a revolutionary.[26]

Tkachev had *earlier* laid down almost identical rules in his "People of the Future," the article written in 1868 for *Delo*. But another concurrence of opinion between the two illustrates an early ambiguity in Tkachev's thinking, which we have already noted in the Olshevsky affair.

The *Program for Revolutionary Action* contains evidence of *Narodnik*-like thinking. For example, it went so far as to predict a spontaneous peasant revolt which would start in the Volga region and spread to the rest of Western Russia. Even the exact date of the insurrection was predicted, the ninth anniversary in 1870 of the Emancipation Decree of February, 1861. The revolutionaries of Nechayev's "Organization" (*Organizatsiya*) were confident of its success, as the daring propagandistic activity in the late sixties shows. Before 1869, said the *Program*, propaganda should be confined to university cities and communities and to the provincial capitals. But from May, 1869 to February, 1870, a vast army of revolutionary partisans were to "go to the people," invading the provinces, particularly the restive Volga region, and flood the peasants there[27] with propaganda calling for immediate revolt. During the spring of 1870, civil war was to be waged along both the Volga and Dnieper Rivers with thousands of peasants leaving their work in the fields and hiding in the forests. As we shall see, all these plans essentially contradicted Tkachev's later ideas on revolutionary tactics.

Later, in his *Nabat* articles in the seventies and eighties, Tkachev was to point out that the revolution could be made and state power effectively seized "by about a thousand well-organized revolutionaries."[28]

The *Program's* reliance on what Tkachev was to call later "the ignorant, uncivilized crowd" was clearly irreconcilable with Tkachev's later revolutionary elitism.[29] Populism (*Narodnichestvo*) tended to place great faith in the native ability and readiness of the Russian peasant to make revolution and by means of a constituent assembly to work out the new social structure by following democratic procedures.[30] It is curious, therefore, to find Tkachev in his early days involved in this movement; we must attribute it either to opportunism or to an actual but transitory phase in Tkachev's thinking.

When the police began closing in on the center of the Nechayev movement in St. Petersburg, Nechayev decided to skip abroad, to meet with Bakunin, leader of the Russian Section of the International. Tkachev might have carried on the propaganda activity preparing for the proclaimed and anticipated 1870 revolution but for the fact that he got into serious trouble. He and his wealthy wife and co-worker, Alexandra Dmitriyevna Dementyeva,[31] decided to issue a proclamation in March 1869, during a mass protest by students in St. Petersburg, a few days after Nechayev left for the West; it was Dementyeva who supplied the printing press. The proclamation was entitled *To Russian Society* and served as agitation to win the general population over to the cause of the students.[32] The police traced the pamphlet to Dementyeva's press; this led to Tkachev's arrest on March 26, 1869.

By the summer of 1871, so many *Nechayevtsi* (including the well-known Volkhovsky) were rounded up that the ambitious plans of the Program now had no organization or leadership. On July 15, 1871, the famous Trial of the Eighty-seven took place. Nechayev, who had returned from abroad in the autumn of 1869, was largely responsible himself for the arrest of his supporters following the Tkachev-Dementyeva affair. For meanwhile, Nechayev had committed murder in the name of the Cause against one Ivanov, who was supposedly guilty of betrayal of the "Eagle."[33] Nechayev was extradited from Switzerland to Russia.

Tkachev, found guilty of printing the student proclamation, was sentenced to one year and four months' exile—at first to Siberia; when his mother (a widow) intervened and asked for an appeal, Peter was permitted to live under police surveillance on his mother's estate in Velikie-Luki in Pskov Province.

THE *NABAT* PERIOD ABROAD

The exile on Mme. Tkacheva's estate lasted until December, 1873. At that time the St. Petersburg supporters of Lavrov and of his propagandistic Populism (then called the *Chaikovtsi*) answered their leader's call in Zurich for more *émigré* writers and organizers to work with the movement's headquarters abroad. They arranged for Tkachev's escape from the estate, unknown to his mother or his guards. Tkachev's wife, Alexandra Dmitriyevna, was evidently informed of Tkachev's plans. Like many of the feminine companions or wives of Russian revolutionaries, Alexandra Dmitriyevna was undoubtedly psychologically prepared for long absences from her husband. In this case, the separation lasted from 1873 until Tkachev's death in Paris in 1886. During that period Alexandra lived a good deal of the time in Novgorod (see n. 31) and Tkachev continued to write to her.

Soon Tkachev was in Zurich working on the Lavrovist organ *Vpered!* (*Forward!*). The fact that the Populists sought the services of Tkachev tends to substantiate the ambiguity which seems to have characterized his early thought; the Populists obviously considered Tkachev to be a comrade in arms or they would scarcely have risked carrying out such an escape. But it was soon evident after his arrival abroad that Tkachev could not adjust himself to the philosophy of *Vpered!* in spite of the aid Lavrov had given him in his escape enterprise. In fact, Tkachev soon began calling the Lavrovists "reactionary revolutionaries."

Vpered! preached the peaceful road of propaganda, of "going-to-the-people," of enlightening the people first. In the distant future, after the continuous spread of socialistic ideas among the peasantry, "the preparedness of the Russian people for revolution will disclose itself (*obnaruzhit'sya*) and political events will point to the calling of the people to revolt."[34] Tkachev could not reconcile himself to this point of view. In a pamphlet which he and some Polish *émigrés* (including Kasper Turski) with whom he had been associating issued by way of anti-Lavrovist propaganda, Tkachev wrote:

> The very difference between a violent revolution and a so-called "gradual evolution" lies precisely in the fact that in the case of the former, a revolutionary minority is no longer willing to wait but takes upon itself to force consciousness on the people.[35]

Another clash between Lavrov and Tkachev finally caused an irreparable breach in their relations.

Tkachev penned an article which satirized, in an unsubtle manner, the Lavrovist tactic of going-to-the-people. Tkachev painted a hyperbolized picture of an "ideal" future peasant life, but one full of greed and satiation. He wrote:

> Peasants will have in their personal possession so many cattle and poultry that they won't be able to count them. Everyone will have all the meat he could possibly eat, sweet wine to consume every morning, noon and night. . . . Everyone will work only as much as he desires, eat as much as he desires, and take a nap on the stove whenever he desires. A most extraordinary way of life![36]

According to Lavrov's own testimony, the article caused an uproar among members of the staff of *Vpered!* Whether Tkachev in his article had a bitter tongue-in-cheek and was satirizing the opportunistic and (to him) demagogical inclinations of the Lavrovists, or whether on the other hand he was himself writing a demagogical piece as a mere Machiavellian tactic directed to an illiterate peasant audience, Lavrov and his associates found the article offensive and refused to publish it.

In the final analysis, Tkachev's break with Lavrov appears to have been the result of Tkachev's disdain for Lavrov, whom he never seems to have considered worthy of editing a revolutionary journal. Kozmin hypothesizes that Tkachev saw in Lavrov a person who, being fourteen years his senior, was "alien to the new revolutionary movement," at best a liberal, but surely not a revolutionary.[37]

In collaborating with Lavrov, Tkachev had evidently expected that Lavrov would listen to a veteran revolutionary like himself. But this was not the case. Lavrov was an editor who was most jealous of his prerogatives—few editors are not, after all! And it became apparent to Tkachev that what Tkachev called a "one-man-leadership" policy (*yedinonachaliye*—his word for it) should definitely apply to the editorship of a journal, indeed, in *any* affair or activity:

> A single person should act only with complete authority in any undertaking. Only he alone should have the final say, while other persons merely offer advice, but no more.[38]

In this rare and revealing statement about one-man leadership, Tkachev had himself, not Lavrov, in mind.

Tkachev finally left *Vpered!* in 1874. He began to help the *Cercle Slave* group translate into Russian the French Blanquist Eduard Vaillant's brochure, "The International and Revolution." Throughout 1874, a number of pamphlets critical of Lavrov—and, incidentally, also of Marx's International—were issued by this circle. Finally, Tkachev and his Polish friends decided to start a Russian Blanquist journal of their own.

Thus, at the end of 1875, *Nabat*,[39] its name connoting a shriller ring than Herzen's *Kolokol,* got under way in Geneva with Tkachev as its editor.

This opened the most productive period in Tkachev's writing career, a period during which Tkachev, according to Lenin, Pokrovsky, Bogucharsky, Gorev, Mitskevich, Plekhanov, Kozmin, and others of various faiths, exerted a noticeable influence upon the split in the Land and Liberty society, which in turn led to the formation of the terrorist People's Will society. Anticipating such an influence in a general way, Tkachev himself wrote:

> I know very well that in Russia there are few who have *Nabat* at their fingertips. But almost all circles in Russia are familiar with its existence, progress, and principles. In a disorderly manner discussing this progress and these ideas, slandering and perverting them, the anarchists and Lavrovists have spread them among the youth. But nevertheless this has resulted in a final triumph for these ideas . . . now, in the form of the organization of the People's Will, in the form of a great number of "Executive" and other committees, and in the program undertaken at the Lipetsk meeting [June, 1879]. Finally, the great number of successful revolutionary plots reflects *Nabat's* influence.[40]

Paul Axelrod, who was in Geneva at the time of *Nabat's* foundation there, tells of a case of a *Nabatovets* who turned out to be a police spy:

> I do not recall all the persons who made up the *Nabat* group. But for a time, one Molchanov replaced Tkachev as chief editor of *Nabat*. Molchanov turned out to be a Tsarist police agent, however, and was exposed and expelled from the organization, only to crop

up later as a co-worker on *Novoye vremya* (*New Times*), edited by Suvorin.[41]

Axelrod then went on to describe the two-way split in the ranks of the Geneva Russian *émigré* colony in the late seventies. This was best typified, he wrote, by the *Nabatovtsi* and Bakuninists (or *Obshchinisti*, from the name of the Bakuninist-anarchist publication *Obshchina* [*Commune*]):

> *Nabat* had existed since 1875. In this journal Tkachev showed the development of those concepts which in the history of Russian revolutionary thought goes under the name of Tkachevism or as we have chosen to call it, Jacobinism.
>
> Tkachev's main point was that progress—having in mind, obviously, the progress of bourgeois society—consisted in the increasing application of force hostile to the people. *"Progress,"* he said, *"strengthens enslavement that much more, sharpens the weapons of oppression, strengthens the ruling classes, and complicates the struggle against these classes."*
>
> *In line with this, Tkachev considered that economic development of Russia is a most unhappy prospect, the destruction of all hope of revolution.*
>
> "The time has come to sound the alarm," he exclaimed. "Look at what is happening! The fire of economic progress is already consuming the foundations of our national life. Under its influence the old forms of *obshchina* existence are being wiped out. . . . New forms of bourgeois life are taking their place. Each new day brings new enemies for us to fight. . . . Economic progress will lend to the forces of government still greater strength and power than have hitherto ever existed."
>
> In the face of the growing danger, Tkachev called on revolutionaries to make haste. Revolution in Russia must be made immediately, before capitalism developed any further, otherwise revolution would be made impossible. . . . "Power must be seized and the conservative state transformed into a revolutionary state" [Tkachev asserted]. . . . But were the people capable of making such a revolution? Tkachev answered this with a resounding "No!" [Axelrod then briefly describes Tkachev's views on the revolutionary minority.]

Tkachev did not confine himself to recommending conspiratorial tactics for Russia alone. He hoped that the European workers' movement would develop conspiratorial methods as well. Legal workers' organizations were considered by Tkachev to be mere laughing stocks.

Tkachev, in all his various theories, remained a dedicated *étatiste* [*gosudarstvennik*] and, as a result, a bitter opponent of anarchism. . . . Tkachev believed that the immediate destruction of the state apparatus would be a measure which would lead directly to chaos. The state should not be destroyed, he said, but rather by means of the state and with the help of the state power there must be created the necessary conditions for putting into effect economic equality.

This was the essence of *Nabat's* line.

The *Nabatovtsi* considered the Alpha and Omega of revolutionary politics to be the merciless elimination of all enemies of the revolution, the use of terror and physical annihilation. In this, they made frequent favorable reference to Robespierre and Saint Just, and with pride called themselves *Yakobintsi* [Jacobins].

Once, in a dispute with a Tkachevist, I asked him: "Do you, as the member of a minority, consider it right that you force the people to be happy?"

This question greatly animated my co-debater.

"Why, of course!" he answered. "Since the people themselves do not understand their own good, thus what is truly good for them must be forced upon them."

In the history of the Russian revolutionary movements one often encounters the attempt to link up the practice of the *Narodovol'tsi* with the theories of Tkachev. However, this alleged resemblance is confined only to the application of conspiratorial tactics in the revolution. The most revealing link may be found between the two darkest pages in the history of our revolutionary movements . . . first, between the Nechayev and Tkachev movements on the one hand and the Bolshevist movement on the other. . . . Is not the Tkachevist theory of the "revolutionary minority" as opposed to the popular masses who are considered incapable of revolutionary creativity suggestive of the Bolshevist theory of the "bearers of revolutionary consciousness," which is likewise opposed to the masses who are viewed as being capable only of "spontaneity"?[42,43]

Another Geneva *émigré* personally acquainted with Tkachev in the late seventies period of *Nabat* and who has thrown light on the personality of Tkachev is Vera Figner. She wrote in her memoirs:

> In Geneva, on a vacation from school, I met Tkachev who had recently immigrated there from exile in Pskov Province. He and I soon became involved in discussion on political themes. His dedicated Jacobinism decidedly sickened us, and when he later tried to carry out business-like discussions with the "Frichists" about revolutionary activities in Russia, he had no success. The first issues of *Nabat* not only evoked no sympathy but appeared laughable to us. Despite his political theories, we considered him in no way to be a really serious figure in the revolutionary movement—his personality made no impression. However, he was very cheerful and a pleasant debater, with whom one could carry on a discussion in a comradely fashion. I always felt personally cheerful and comfortable in his company. We often spent our time boating on Lake Geneva, hiking along the shore in the evening, or sometimes matching wits and playing little games with each other.[44]

In establishing *Nabat,* Tkachev had not the slightest expectation or even desire that his journal should enjoy popularity with the masses (to whom it was not addressed in any case), nor with many of the *émigrés* whom he had already met abroad. As Tkachev himself explained:

> I had no thought of distributing *Nabat* inside Russia. *Nabat* was not intended to be an agitation-type publication; its task consisted merely of swaying revolutionaries to naturally practical views and principles of revolutionary activity, for which, under the influence of reaction, of the anarchists and Lavrovists and their harmful notions, they had ceased to have any respect whatsoever. These ideas and principles had nothing new about them, after all, but it would be a good idea not to forget them! And *Nabat* was able to fulfill (and actually did fulfill) this function, although

it was not distributed throughout Russia. It was enough that merely a handful of revolutionaries would become familiar with its program and basic principles, that it would provoke a lot of talk among the revolutionaries; it would be sufficient to recall the forgotten ideas of a small number of revolutionaries and then, by means of revolutionary activity itself, prove the rationality and practicability of these ideas and disseminate them among the majority of revolutionaries.[45]

Tkachev and his *Nabat* followers were not satisfied, evidently, with writing articles alone; they began to close ranks and to seek followers not only abroad but also inside Russia as well. For this purpose, several members of the *Nabat* circle traveled to Russia. These trips led to no significant results, mostly because their plans were frustrated by the hostile attitude of other revolutionaries toward their Jacobin ideas.

An example of a modicum of success was the formation in Russia of an avowedly Tkachevist organization calling itself Society for the Liberation of the People (*Obshchestvo Narodnovo Osvobozhdeniya*). There is scarcely any information available on this organization, beyond some data that Kozmin was able to unearth; other Soviet historians are silent about its very existence.[46]

The Society appeared in 1877, after a merger with other Russian Jacobins (mostly Zaichnevskian in origin, undoubtedly) inside Russia. Illustrating how difficult the situation was for Jacobins at that time was the fact that only one viable Jacobin circle was known to exist in Russia in the 1870's—the so-called Orel circle, named for the Russian city in which it was situated. It was composed of followers of Zaichnevsky, author of the *Young Russia* proclamation of 1862. Since the proclamation had called for a one-party seizure of power and establishment of a postrevolutionary dictatorship, the members of the Orel circle had little difficulty in seeing eye-to-eye with the Tkachevists of Geneva. (As early as 1862, it should be mentioned, Thachev had made the acquaintance of several members of the Zaichnevsky circle which then existed in St. Petersburg.) Kozmin speculates that Tkachev had undoubtedly given orders specifically to establish whatever links could be made with the followers of Zaichnevsky inside Russia, particularly in Orel.

However, no great assistance could be forthcoming in this effort from the Zaichnevsky circle itself, for by 1877 this group had ceased to exist; in August of that year Zaichnevsky himself was exiled from Orel to Olonets Province in Siberia, and some of the other members of this circle had been arrested.

Tkachev's Society, if it can be termed such, displayed an extremely conspiratorial, one might even say ultra-conspiratorial and clandestine character. Its Statutes (or bylaws) contained a provision which read in part: "A member of the Society is compelled to hold secret the very existence of the Society as well as the identity of anyone belonging to it." Moreover, with the permission of the Central Committee of the Society, the Statutes continued, agents of the Society would be ordered secretly to penetrate other revolutionary organizations, hiding from these organizations their membership in the Society, and conducting clandestine work so as eventually to bring the given organization under the total influence and control of the Society.

The conspiratorial and arcane character of the Society has, in fact, contributed to our present-day ignorance of most of its activity conducted by those few revolutionaries who were not arrested along with Zaichnevsky. At the same time, it is clear that many revolutionaries were aware of its existence and that some of them were quite possibly as Tkachev had hoped, influenced by the Society.

Federative links between various local, minute Tkachevist organs of the Society were also known to have existed—for example, in Southern Russia. The well-known revolutionary, I. M. Kovalskii, sentenced for revolutionary activity in Odessa in 1878, was a co-worker on *Nabat,* and at the same time a member of the Society for the Liberation of the People.[47]

The Society played an interesting role in the history of Russian revolutionary movements in another respect. Attempts were made in the spring of 1880 by the *Narodovol'tsi* N. A. Morozov and Gerasim Romanenko to form links with Tkachev's Society.

Early in 1880, this famous member of the People's Will Executive Committee, Morozov, found that he differed from many of his comrades in the Committee on a number of important theoretical issues. Even before this, at the time of his first trip abroad, Morozov had sympathized with certain of the ideas expressed in *Nabat*. Being personally acquainted with Tkachev and having once collaborated with him on *Zhenskii vestnik* (*Women's Messenger*), Morozov showed no animosity toward the chief editor of *Nabat*, as had any number of other detractors of *Nabat* who had never even met its editor. Rather, Morozov saw in Tkachev a most talented and informed intellectual, a revolutionary who stood head and shoulders above the general run of revolutionary *émigrés*. Returning abroad in 1880, Morozov was thus able to renew his former links with the *Nabatovtsi*, which he promptly did. The result of this re-acquaintance was a plan whereby federative relations would be established between the People's Will circles (which were impressively widespread throughout Russia) and the Tkachevist Society. This idea naturally appealed to the Tkachevists, since the People's Will enjoyed far more renown, had many more members, and was far better organized. Morozov declared his readiness to provide Tkachev's Society with funds and a printing plant belonging to the People's Will organization. However, the hostility of most of the other members of the People's Will Executive Committee toward the Tkachevist-*Nabat* revolutionary tactics and strategy was so strong that Morozov's own ambitious plan was nipped in the bud.

From that day on Morozov, joined now by Romanenko, carried on in their own names, calling themselves "Socialist-terrorists." Their brochures stressed the need for naked terror and violence in order to disorganize the government and force it to make concessions.[48] However, in introducing the element of individual terror as a tactic to be recommended to Russian revolutionaries, Morozov and Romanenko *could not*—and in fact, *did not*,—point to Tkachev and his *Nabat* articles for support or authority. Tkachev *strongly condemned* individual acts of terror as ineffectual, warning that they could only lead to the breakup of revolutionary organizations by the police and to the overall weakening of the revolutionary movement.[49] At the same time, Tkachev did not rule out the application of terror *against spies and informers; he did not condemn mob violence under all circumstances* but, in fact, endorsed it when that proved useful to the overall cause.

It was, in fact, the issue of terror which finally led to a breach in the relations between Tkachev and Kasper Turski, and a majority of the *Nabat* editorial staff followed the latter. Turski, evidently influenced by his sympathies with the *Nechayevtsi*, openly advocated the widest use of terror and violence, both of the mass and individual varieties. Tkachev, to repeat, regarded this tactic as ineffectual and harmful to the cause of revolution. When Turski made overt attempts to publish articles advocating terror, Tkachev tried to stop him, but was not always successful (an event which in itself testifies to the rather delicate situation then existing on the staff of *Nabat*). Finally, Turski, who appealed to the rank-and-file of the staff and won them over to his view, presented Tkachev with what amounted to an ultimatum—either accept the tactic of terror and assassination or leave *Nabat*. Tkachev retreated (we have no reason to believe for any other reason than that of principle), and, as a result, after 1879 began to relinquish more and more of his authority over *Nabat*'s editorial policy. *Nabat* soon began to reflect the opinions of Turski and his fellow-travelers. One result of his reduced authority and responsibilities on *Nabat* was Tkachev's freedom to travel —for example, from Geneva to Paris where after 1879 he began to take up residence.

Although Tkachev continued to contribute articles to *Nabat* from Paris, his name rarely appeared in the pages of the journal. When in 1880 a daring plan was hatched at *Nabat* headquarters in Geneva to transfer the printing of the journal to Russia, Tkachev too indicated his desire to go to Russia, specifically to St. Petersburg. However, the trip never materialized; the most important reason for its failure was the seizure of *Nabat*'s press and matrices for a forthcoming issue of the journal, which were all confiscated upon their arrival in the Tsarist capital.

During his residence in Paris, where he spent the rest of his life, Tkachev also collaborated on the French Blanquist journal, *Ni Dieu, ni maître*, from 1880 to 1882.

By the winter of 1881–1882, Tkachev showed the first signs of the illness described in several sources as a physiological "paralysis of the brain" that was to worsen to a point where Tkachev could no longer write and had no power over his extremities.[50]

In 1883 he was arrested by the Paris police when he was behaving strangely in the street. When taken to a nearby hospital, he refused to divulge his name until a Russian woman doctor arrived at the hospital. Soon several of Tkachev's relatives living in Paris came to see him. He remained under a doctor's care for three years. His condition worsened so that he could only answer questions, by first showing initial excitement, then lapsing suddenly into a stupor. Three weeks before he expired, according to those who visited him at the Hôpital Psychiatrique Ste. Anne in Montparnasse, Tkachev was a "living corpse" who could barely move about or speak.

He died at 12:15 A.M. on January 5, 1886. The next day a funeral was held at which twenty to thirty friends and acquaintances paid their respects. An attempt was made, according to a report in the newspaper *Obshcheye delo*,[51] to postpone the burial so that time could be found to inform all those who would be interested in attending the funeral. But the hospital regulations (pertaining to persons dying on hospital premises) prevented the postponement. As a result, only a small group of people trailed out of the hospital on January 6, the day Tkachev's body in its wooden casket was carried out to a waiting carriage and borne to the cemetery in the town of Ivry on the southeastern outskirts of Paris (Cimètiere Parisien d'Ivry).

The day of the funeral was cold and rainy. At about 9 A.M. the funeral cortege was moving along the streets in the rain. Waiting at graveside were two floral displays, one consisting of red *immortelles,* donated by cousins of the deceased, the other consisting of entwined yellow ivy tied together with red ribbon on which appeared the following words: *"ancienne redaction du Tocsin,"* donated by P. B. Grigoryev, one of the former editors of *Nabat.* When the cortege had approached the grave and the body had been interred, Lavrov, Tkachev's former opponent,[52] delivered a eulogy in French in which he spoke mainly of Tkachev's former literary activity in Russia and the influence which it had exerted on the young generation of that time. The second eulogy, which was Grigoryev's, went into Tkachev's activities after he left Russia, a favorable and flattering description which was given in Russian. Part of it ran as follows:

> He was one of the outstanding figures in our stormy epoch, one of the brilliant thinkers and most talented writers on terror [*sic*]. . . . All of us who stand here at his grave still traveled the path of peaceful propaganda and still recommended peaceful means of struggle against the government at a time when he alone appealed to us to leave purely economic soil and go over to political soil. And he spoke about organizational questions and so on. In a word, he indicated the way to terror.

A third eulogy was delivered by the French Blanquist, Eduard Vaillant.

The burial plot had been rented for a period of five years. Over the temporary grave lay a small tablet made of wood on which was inscribed "Pierre Tkatscheff." According to the obituary in *Obshcheye delo,* an attempt was made to collect the sum of 500 francs for the purchase of a permanent plot in the cemetery, which was to have been marked with a marble stone "capped with a sculptured crown of thorns, a monument suitable for an *émigré.*"[53] In fact this was never accomplished —records at the cemetery show that, because the plot was not purchased, Tkachev's bones were exhumed in 1892 and placed in an ossuary.

Like many figures in history, Tkachev, his life, and his work, were the subject of little interest in his own day, when compared to such famous names as Chernyshevsky, Pisarev, Dobrolyubov, and Lavrov. Tkachev's renown was to come later when, to cite a well-known example, Plekhanov leveled his attacks against the alleged neo-Tkachevism of Lev Tikhomirov in the former's monumental work, *Our Differences* (*Nashi raznoglasiya*), written in 1884, just two years before Tkachev died but after Tkachev had reached the point where he was mentally incapacitated and unable to make a reply. Tkachevism appeared again when Lenin delved deeply, according to Bonch-Bruyevich, into the writings of Tkachev, recommending them to others and developing concepts strikingly similar to those of Tkachev; and it appeared again after 1917 when postrevolutionary Russian historians (Pokrovsky, Kozmin, Gorev, Mitskevich, Nicolaevsky, *et al.*), published their findings and comments in Soviet journals and elsewhere and began to show a renewed interest in Tkachev's life and thought.

As will be shown later, various articles appearing in Russia in the 1920's made comparisons between Lenin's Bolshevist theory and Tkachev's theory. Today one finds that the interest in the life and work of Tkachev is in a depressed state in the USSR, at least as far as what is permitted to be published is concerned. Tkachev has evidently run afoul of two major contemporary policies of the Khrushchev and post-Khrushchev regimes in the USSR: first, the effort to detach from Bolshevism whatever extreme radicalism and terrorism used to be embodied in it (part of the current anti-Maoist campaign commending a peaceful path of revolution under certain circumstances, even the parliamentary route); and, second, the overall effort to glorify Lenin, his life and work, and above all his alleged originality. A most recent example of this type of utterly silent treatment of Tkachev (but at other times, brief and critical evaluation of Tkachev's concepts) was the total silence with which Soviet scholarly journals, newspapers, and, as far as could be determined, all Soviet media treated the 120th Anniversary on June 29, 1964, of the birth of Peter Nikitich Tkachev.[54]

Other developments in the foreign and domestic policies of the CPSU have caused an evident disinclination to refer to Tkachev, Tkachevist Blanquism, or Jacobinism. These include, besides the Sino-Soviet conflict, the current quasi-Lassalleist philosophy of the Soviet state as "an all-people's state," not a mere "workers' state," which does not fit well into the whole Tkachevist-Leninist elitist heritage; the same applies to the much-vaunted campaign toward "popularization" and "democratization" of the government which, as currently explained in the USSR, denotes increased "autonomy of the whole Soviet people"—all this is quite out of place with reference to the prerevolutionary authoritarian and centralist revolutionary tradition.[55]

What the future may bring may be a different story. Indeed, if freedom of expression within the social sciences field were to continue to broaden in the USSR,[56] relatively objective discussions like that of the 1920's about the roots of Leninism in prerevolutionary Russia could re-appear, despite the possible consequent detraction from Lenin's originality, a covenant which is today so closely and jealously guarded by the Party oligarchy. Leninism would thenceforth appear in its true dress rather than in the official robes of absolute originality and uniqueness in which it is so unwarrantedly attired in the USSR.

NOTES

1. Biographical information on Tkachev is contained in the following: M. Lemke, "K biografii P. N. Tkachev (Po neizdannym istochnikam)," *Byloye*, No. VIII (1907), 156–72—most important source of biographical material on Tkachev, some fifteen pages including interesting photographs of the revolutionary and his family; B. P. Kozmin, *P. N. Tkachev i revolyutsionnoye dvizheniye 1860–kh godov* (Moscow: Novy Mir 1922)—Kozmin's most extensive work on Tkachev, both his life and his writings; P. N. Tkachev, *Izbranniye sochineniya na sotsial'no-politicheskiye temy* (Moscow: Izdatel'stvo Politkatorzhan, 1932–1937), with a long preface in Vol. I written by Kozmin; B. P. Kozmin, *Ot devyat'nadtsatovo fevralya k pervomu marta* (Moscow: Izdatel'stvo Politkatorzhan, 1933); Boris Nicolaevsky, "Pamyati poslednevo Yakobintsa, G. M. Tursky," *Katorga i ssylka*, No. II (1926); references to Tkachev in the memoirs of Axelrod, Zasulich, Figner, *et al.*, cited throughout this work.

2. Kozmin, *P. N. Tkachev*, p. 11; quoted from Tkachev's "Unthinkable Thoughts," *Delo*, No. 2 (1872).

3. Kozmin, *P. N. Tkachev*, p. 13. For a fuller account of schools at this time see S. G. Pushkarev, *Rossiya v XIX–om veke* (New York: Chekhov Publishing House, 1956), pp. 105–11 and Venturi, *op. cit.*, p. 220.

4. Kozmin, Introduction to Tkachev, *Sochineniya*, I, 17.

5. Kozmin, *P. N. Tkachev*, p. 20.

6. Tkachev, a good student, was proficient in German, French, and English. Like Lenin in his early days, Tkachev earned some money for the family by doing translations.

7. An example of his youthful fire was his rash assertion that "for the rejuvenation of the country, all people older than twenty-five should be liquidated" (quoted from his letter to his sister in Kozmin, *P. N. Tkachev*, p. 19). It is interesting to note that while many of Tkachev's ideas were unacceptable to his contemporaries, some of them found Tkachev, the person, charming and affable. Vera Figner described him as "a cheerful person and an agreeable fellow-worker" (Vera Figner, *Studencheskiye gody*, [Moscow: Golos Truda, 1924], p. 119). All who read his works, including his detractors, agreed that he was a talented writer possessed of a keen intelligence (see the description of Tkachev in the prerevolutionary Brockhaus-Efron encyclopedia, *Entsiklopedicheskii slovar'*). A contemporary, P. P. Suvorov, described Tkachev as "a small and slender man, modest but smooth-talking, secretive, with a smiling face . . . clever, who never spoke loud his dearest thoughts." A fellow-writer, P. D. Boborykin, called him "a terrifying conspirator—a quiet, placid type, whom neither I nor my closest friends could picture as an *émigré*—this quiet and smiling youth the leader of a whole party?" But Tkachev's brother-in-law emphasized that he could become a fiery antagonist in an argument with others. See Kozmin, *P. N. Tkachev*, pp. 134–36.

8. Kozmin has noted the pre-Blanquist tendencies in the articles published in *Russkoye slovo* at this time. Venturi (*op. cit.*, p. 768), disagreeing with Kozmin that these tendencies are traceable to Pisarev, considers that they are more recognizable in Varfolomei A. Zaitsev (1842–1882). Zaitsev found the whole Populist movement of the age of reforms "steeped in useless illusions" (Venturi, *op. cit.*, p. 329), a position to be taken soon after by Tkachev.

9. The year 1866 saw the terrorist Karakozov's notorious attempt on the Tsar's life and the resultant unleashing of a new government reaction.

10. In Tkachev, "The Women's Question" ("Zhenskii vopros"), *Sochineniya*, I, 370–402.

11. The closing of *Russkoye slovo* left Tkachev a temporarily "unemployed proletarian [sic]," to use Kozmin's expression. Tkachev had then planned to come out with a collection of volumes on scholarly literature of various types under the title *The Beam (Luch)*, but the project never went beyond the first volume, which itself was confiscated by the censor (see Kozmin, *P. N. Tkachev*, pp. 47–48).

12. Blagosvetlov's statement on the course of action which *Delo* should take under conditions of censorship was: "Be crafty as a snake and innocent as a dove" (Kozmin, *P. N. Tkachev*, p. 49). By 1865, *Nechayevtsi* illegal revolutionary circles were already getting under way; they soon won the favor of Bakunin abroad (see Masaryk, *op. cit.*, II, 82, and Miliukov, *op. cit.*, p. 393). By comparison with the radical Nechayevtsi, *Delo's* line *was* as "innocent as a dove." It should be noted that Tkachev's literary activity at this time included translations and popularizations. For example, he translated Ernst Becher's Lassalleist book, *The Labor Question in Its Contemporary Significance and the Means to Its Solution* into Russian and acted as one of the earliest popularizers of Marx (on both *Russkoye slovo* and *Delo*). Because of his translation or popularization of Marx, Tkachev has been called, perhaps somewhat exaggeratedly, "the first Russian Marxist." Kozmin commented that those who call Tkachev the first Russian Marxist err; instead, Tkachev expressed, according to Kozmin, better than anyone else the Russian Marxism which existed in his time. He

shared this position, says Kozmin, with N. N. Ziber, regarded by Soviet spokesmen as the "forerunner of Legal Marxism."

13. Kozmin, *P. N. Tkachev*, p. 26.

14. *Ibid.*, p. 27. Other planks in its program included: intellectuals should spread propaganda for land nationalization among the peasants; they should stir up the peasants against their proprietors and creditors and also against the nobility and officialdom generally; the founding of schools, associations, and workshops (for bookbinding, sewing, and so forth) as the means for getting in touch with the pesantry and training new members; all these activities were to be directed by a central society located in Moscow; the spread of propaganda throughout the Volga region using river communication, since there was only one railway at the time, the St. Petersburg-to-Moscow line. (See Miluikov, *op. cit.*, p. 393.)

15. Tkachev's subsequent economic determinism was formulated in the early sixties, as cited below in this study, pp. 134–38.

16. Venturi, *op. cit.*, p. 251. See also Burtsev, *op. cit.*, p. 63. Another young man, one Pechatkin, was also involved, but apparently only in the Olshevsky case. Burtsev gives no first name or patronymic for Pechatkin nor is any further information on him available.

17. Kozmin, *P. N. Tkachev*, pp. 36–37.

18. Venturi, *op. cit.*, p. 251.

19. Kozmin, *P. N. Tkachev*, p. 39.

20. *Ibid.*, p. 41. Kozmin hypothesizes that Tkachev, in order to be exonerated, may well have underestimated and concealed his role in the Olshevsky affair. The same may also apply to the Nechayev affair where Tkachev's involvement seems more obvious.

21. Miliukov, *op. cit.*, p. 389.

22. Kozmin's Introduction to Tkachev, *Sochineniya*, I, 17. Sergei Gennadievich Nechayev was born in 1847 in the village of Khomutovsk in Vladimir Province. In 1867 he began his studies at the Sergeyev Trade School in St. Petersburg and began immediately to carry on agitation among the students. Nechayev escaped abroad in 1869, after being implicated in the unrest of the spring semester of that year at the trade school. Once abroad, Nechayev began to send inflammatory leaflets to the student youth of Russia; he also joined the International with Bakunin appointing him organizer of the Russian Section. Early in September 1869, Nechayev returned secretly to Moscow, restoring his links with student-protest organizations. He became acquainted at this time with such active revolutionaries as Volkhovsky, Dolgushin, Tkachev, Pryzhov, and others. Nechayev became the model for the revolutionary character Verkhovensky in Dostoyevsky's novel, *The Possessed.* A biography of Nechayev in English may be found in Michael Prawdin's *The Unmentionable Nechayev* (New York: Roy Publishers, Inc., 1961), which, however, quite inaccurately describes Nechayev as the spiritual father of Bolshevism.

Picture of Tkachev in his late teens, taken about the time of his first arrest and imprisonment in the Peter and Paul Fortress in the mid-1860's. Collection of the Institute of Russian Literature, Leningrad, USSR.

A photograph portrait of the Tkachev family shortly after the death of Peter's father in the 1860's. Tkachev is shown with his two sisters, A. N. Annenskaya and S. N. Kril'. His mother, M. N. Tkacheva, is seated in the center. Photograph in the collection of Russian Literature, Leningrad, USSR.

Envelope containing a letter written by Tkachev to his wife, just after his escape abroad, postmarked Königsburg, December 20, 1873. Second postmark indicates that the letter was received at the Velikie-Luki post-office on December 24, New Style. The date December 11 is according to the Old Style Julian Calendar. Central Archive, Moscow.

The December, 1873, letter from Tkachev to his wife, Alexandra. It opens "Dearest Sasha" and apologizes for his sudden departure from Russia, begging his wife to forgive him and suggesting that she might want to join him at some later date. "Therefore, I've found it prudent to say nothing about my departure." (She never saw him again.) The letter closes with: "Keep well and don't be angry with me. I kiss you firmly. Yours always, Petya." The postscriptum says he will send her further details soon.

L'ANARCHIE DE LA PENSÉE

Par Pierre TKATCHEFF.

АНАРХІЯ МЫСЛИ

СОБРАНІЕ КРИТИЧЕСКИХЪ ОЧЕРКОВЪ

П. Н. ТКАЧЕВА

Изданіе Журнала „НАБАТЪ"

ЛОНДОНЪ

Типографія журнала „НАБАТЪ."

1879

Cover of an important essay by Tkachev, *Anarkhiya mysli: "Sobraniye kriticheskikh ocherkov"* (Anarchy of Thought: "A Collection of Critical Remarks"). The work attacks Bakuninist anarchism and argues the case for a strong postrevolutionary dictatorship. It was republished in Geneva in 1904 by M. K. Elpinin Publishing House. Pamphlet and photograph courtesy of Butler Library, Columbia University.

23. Kozmin, *P. N. Tkachev*, pp. 153–54.

24. *Ibid.*, commenting on Tkachev's article entitled "People of the Future," pp. 90–98. There is a dispute over the authorship of the Catechism itself. Kozmin asserts that Bakunin is the probable author; Boris Nicolaevsky agrees, as he once informed me. Michael Prawdin asserts that despite the fact that Bakunin denied authorship, the Catechism appears to be the result of the joint efforts of Bakunin and Nechayev. Soviet investigators make the same allegation (B. P. Kozmin, *Russkaya sektsiya pervovo internatsionala* [Moscow: Izdalet'-stvo Akademii Nauk SSSR, 1957], p. 155). *The Program for Revolutionary Action* is reproduced in Burtsev, *op. cit.*, pp. 87–89.

25. Bakunin, Tkachev, and Nechayev called themselves dedicated Machiavellians.

26. Quoted in Kozmin, *P. N. Tkachev*, pp. 96–97. Some of these stipulations were repeated almost word for word some fifty years later by Lenin. The text of the Catechism may be found in Kuklin, *op. cit.*, pp. 202–203. At the time he drafted the Catechism contained in "People of the Future," Tkachev is reported to have remarked, "We should kill everyone over 21 years of age to make a new start" (Kozmin, *P. N. Tkachev*, p. 19).

27. The fertile but climatically capricious Lower Volga region was notorious in Tsarist days for high rent in kind (*barshchini*) and unrest. Rumors spread throughout Russia that the tenth anniversary of the Tsar's Emancipation Decree would see the benevolent cancellation by the Tsar of the peasants' redemption payments; these rumors abetted the spread of the peasant unrest of 1870–1871 and a new wave of radicalism among the intelligentsia, which had also been aroused by the Nechayev affair (see *Istoriya SSSR*, No. 5 [1964], p. 115, an article entitled "Revolyutsionniye narodniki 70-kh godov-ideologi krestianskoi demokratii"). Successive bad harvests and famine (1867–1868, 1873–1874; 1880, etc.) also aggravated the situation. For a discussion of this, see Sh. M. Levin, *Obshchestvennoye dvizheniye v Rossii v 60–70-e gody XIX-ovo veka* (Moscow: Izdatel'stvo Sotsial 'no-ekonomicheskoi, 1958), p. 398.

28. Bogucharsky, *op. cit.*, p. 454.

29. See chap. IV below, pp. 72–97.

30. The revolutionaries of the seventies dreamed of a grassroots' social revolution "which would destroy the whole existing social and political order replacing the contemporary government apparatus with a union of free communes" (Kozmin, Introduction to Tkachev, *Sochineniya*, I, 25).

31. Dementyeva has been described as witty and sophisticated to the point of superciliousness. She was, indeed, a forerunner among Russian woman revolutionaries including such more famous figures of later times as Vera Figner, Vera Zasulich, Sophie Perovskaya, *et al.* She graduated from the *gymnasium* in 1867 and participated in 1869

in a fictitious marriage to a member of the Nechayev circle, one Nikolayev (a bit of intrigue arranged by Tkachev to gain rights to an inheritance to be spent for revolutionary purposes). It was around this time that she became engaged to Tkachev. She was indicted in Tsarist courts for implication in the distribution of the *To Society* proclamation written by Tkachev and was put under police surveillance for this in the city of Novgorod. Her charm and beauty and dedication to the cause soon made her the darling of Novgorod revolutionaries— to such an extent, in fact, that Tsarist authorities sent her still further away to Kaluga where she spent her time in the company of N. P. Shelgunov. Shelgunov's diary became a source of much of the information about her. See also Kozmin, *P. N. Tkachev*, pp. 176–79, for additional material.

32. The proclamation was apparently part of Phase One of the propaganda plans outlined in the *Program;* it was to win over the population of the capital not only to the student cause, but the general cause of revolution. For involvement with Tkachev and Dementyeva, thirty-eight students were expelled from a technical institute in Petersburg and fourteen others jailed.

33. Ivanov, who was found in 1869 by police in the pond of Petrovsky Razumovsky Park on the outskirts of Moscow with rocks tied to his body, had, it seems, demanded of the "Eagle" that he prove that a gigantic network of Nechayev circles actually existed in Russia, as he had told his comrades (including Bakunin) living abroad in Geneva —Bakunin naïvely believed as a result that an effective "World Revolutionary Alliance" had been established between the Nechayev circle and other circles abroad. The betrayal was largely the crime of incredulity and insubordination. (See David Footman, *Red Prelude: The Life of the Russian Terrorist Zhelyabov* [New Haven: Yale University Press, 1945].) Nechayev, sentenced to a long prison term, died of tuberculosis in 1882; his term in prison was in part devoted to establishing links with revolutionaries on the outside; among these were members of the People's Will secret society of which Lenin's brother, Alexander, was a member.

34. E. Selskii, *Po puti k svobode* (Moscow: F. Y. Burche, 1907), p. 53.

35. Quoted by Mikhail Karpovich, "A Forerunner of Lenin: P. N. Tkachev," *The Review of Politics* (July 1944), p. 342. Tkachev's other enemies were the anarchist Bakuninists, who believed any central political authority to be oppressive and unnecessary, and the official Marxists, who, to Tkachev's mind, were obsessed with economic determinism and historical materialism. Tkachev's differences with Marx and Engels anticipated Lenin's later differences with Plekhanov. See the discussion in chap. V below.

36. Kozmin, Introduction to Tkachev, *Sochineniya*, I, 22.

37. *Ibid.*, p. 23.

38. *Ibid.,* p. 23. One-man leadership was restored to prominence by Lenin in the immediate postrevolutionary period. In the prerevolutionary editorial squabbles between Lenin and others, Lenin frequently demanded one-man editorial powers for himself.

39. The Russian word *nabat* has the following etymology, according to A. G. Preobrazhensky, *Etymological Dictionary of the Russian Language* (New York: Columbia University Press, 1951), p. 588: "N A B A T (hard sign): Genetive-case meaning is a bell with a special sound signifying some sort of general calamity; *nabatnii* (bell); '*bit*' *v nabat*' ('strike the alarm'). Old Russian meaning, a large copper drum—from which comes the expression 'strike the alarm.' . . . Probably from the Arabian *naubet* through some Turkic source. . . . Its original meaning is not known; it is understood to mean: a ringing as of warning and awakening (arousing). . . . Dal maintains, not completely convincingly: 'thundering and banging . . . blows against a board' could never be termed a *nabat.*" One may encounter the term occasionally even today in the USSR. For example: the character *Krasnii Nabat* in a play by A. Shtein, which was reported and reviewed unfavorably during the Khrushchev period in *Pravda*, July 12, 1964. The review describes the character's nickname, the Red Alarm, as "loud and pretentious." Valery Tarsis, the anti-Soviet expatriate author, in his writings in the USSR, frequently used the metaphor of an alarm to denote the "battle for freedom." In *Ward No. 7*, Tarsis wrote: "The time had come to sound the alarm (*nabat*), to call for the struggle for freedom, for the fight against the new fascist [i.e., communist, as Tarsis had explained earlier—A. L. W.] destroyers of souls" quoted in "In Russia's Insane Asylums," *Problems of Communism* (September-October, 1965), pp. 66–71, an article by Laszlo M. Tikos). Tkachev's publication *Nabat* has been translated *Tocsin* and *Alarm Bell*. *Alarm*, a sometime name of radical publications in English-speaking countries, seems to be an adequate translation of *Nabat*.

40. In *Perezhitoye i peredumannoye* (Berlin: Izdatel'stvo Z. I. Grzhebina, 1923), pp. 162–63, Axelrod, writing as a memoirist, recalled: "Soon after his [Tkachev's] arrival in Geneva, he visited me and invited me and several others to come to his apartment to discuss a certain essay. I do not remember the topic of the essay, but its central idea, if memory does not fail me, concerned the fact that 'progress' was not desirable from the standpoint of the people's ultimate welfare but, on the contrary, 'progress' should be understood as the worsening of the situation of the masses, the increase in inequality, and, as a result, intensified oppression of the masses. The essay was quite modest in length and I recall that it did not stir any particular controversy or create any particular interest. It seems strange to me now that an essay containing such an idea of progress should not have evoked a greater response from its listeners. Can this perhaps be attributed to the fact that by the word 'progress' we understood 'bourgeois progress,' attaching to this latter expression the idea of the growing poverty and misery of the people?" Axelrod seems to be describing an interesting parallelism between a Tkachevist idea and a later Social-Democratic-Marxist concept. Tkachev's description of the reputed influence of his *Nabat* is quoted in Bogucharsky, *op. cit.*, pp. 454–55. See below, pp. 124–28.

41. From Axelrod, *op. cit.*, pp. 194–98.

42. Axelrod, *op. cit.*, pp. 197–98.

43. Boris I. Nicolaevsky informed me of his discovery that Turski, a well-read Polish intellectual, had provided Tkachev with a good deal of background on such revolutionaries and their ideas as Saint Just, Mably, and the Babeuvists, although it would be most difficult to ascertain just how much Tkachev had absorbed of these influential writers and active revolutionaries from his own rather copious reading. Nicolaevsky quoted from a pamphlet written by Turski in 1877 entitled *Idealizm i materializm v politike,* published under the *Nabat* imprimatur (see *Katorga i ssylka,* No. II (1926), for an article by Nicolaevsky entitled "Pamyati poslednevo yakobintsa," which includes some excerpts from Turski's essay).

44. Vera Figner, *Studentcheskiye gody,* pp. 118–19.

45. Kozmin, Introduction to Tkachev, *Sochineniya,* I, 26–27.

46. The description of this society is taken from *ibid.*, I, 26–28. For some unknown reason, these facts are completely ignored by Venturi in his otherwise excellent book.

47. Kovalskii was sentenced to death by the firing squad; the sentence was carried out on August 2, 1878. Eight persons in all had been implicated in the dissemination of Jacobin propaganda in Odessa. Copies of *Nabat,* among other revolutionary publications, were seized upon Kovalsky's arrest.

48. Kozmin, Introduction to Tkachev, *Sochineniya,* I, 29.

49. Lenin had the same negative opinion of individual terror, as represented, for example, by the needless and fruitless tactic of assassination, a tactic the application of which resulted in the most tragic consequences for those who participated in such plots (as in the case of Lenin's own brother) and which led to destruction of secret revolutionary organizations and their dismemberment by the police courts.

50. Kozmin, Introduction to Tkachev, *Sochineniya,* I, 30; Lemke, *op. cit.*, p. 156. Close examination of the sources shows that the condition was brought on by physiological disease, possibly a blood or glandular disease. No simple derangement theory fits in with accounts given by Tkachev's contemporaries. Moreover, none of Tkachev's enemies ever called him a madman (*sumashedshii*) which they might well have done if there had been any suspicion Tkachev had literally become insane.

51. *Ibid.*, p. 156.

52. Lavrov himself died in 1900 at the age of seventy-seven.

53. *Obshcheye delo,* No. 83 (1886); quoted in Lemke, *op. cit.,* p. 158.

54. No such silence has greeted other 120th or 150th anniversaries which have occurred from 1963 to 1968—e.g., in 1963 the 150th birthday anniversary of N. P. Ogarev (1813–1877). See Albert L. Weeks, " The First Bolshevik," *Problems of Communism,* November-December, 1967, pp. 96–102.

55. On the anti-Tkachevist bent of the current anti-Chinese line of the CPSU, see *Kommunist,* No. 4 (1964), pp. 48–49, 53, in an article entitled *"I Internatsional i sovremennost'."* *Buntarstvo and Blankizm* are used pejoratively. The wording of the contemporary Program of the CPSU, adopted in 1961, contains numerous phrases of a Lassalleist nature, with respect to the "all people's state."

56. Two Soviet historians, with whom the author had a long discussion in New York in 1962, made just such a prediction, as have others with whom he has spoken inside the USSR.

CHAPTER IV

Tkachev's View of the State
and Revolution

To trace the alleged influence of one thinker on a later one in some direct, linear fashion is a most questionable enterprise since it is often doomed to indefiniteness from the start. Who could possibly isolate all the psychological, intellectual, and accidental factors which have controlled the line of development which a given thinker's philosophy has taken?

Still, several Western authorities on prerevolutionary and Soviet history have implied or stated that Tkachev strongly and undeniably influenced Lenin and that Leninism was a direct offshoot from Tkachevism. A few examples of such assertions follow.

Leonard Schapiro has stated in *The Communist Party of the Soviet Union:*

> An ideology for revolutionary activity was evolved by P. N. Tkachev . . . , the first Russian to teach that the revolution should be made by a small conspiratorial body of professionals, acting in the name of the people. . . . The resemblance to bolshevism, such as it was eventually to become, is in some respects very striking, and it is with justice that Tkachev has often been described as the originator of many of Lenin's ideas. Lenin himself would later closely study Tkachev, and insist on Tkachev's articles as required reading for his own followers.[1]

Stefan T. Possony states in *Lenin—The Compulsive Revolutionary:*

> It is evident that Tkachev's ideas impressed Lenin; he later required his followers to read Tkachev carefully. We do not know at what time Lenin himself read Tkachev, but he may have done so while in Switzerland. When he returned to Russia he possessed a clearer vision of the tasks ahead.[2]

Alan Moorehead in *The Russian Revolution* has stated:

> Tkachev indeed is a predecessor to Lenin, for he envisaged a communist state on utopian lines which would be created by a small resolute group of these supermen.[3]

John S. Reshetar in his *Concise History of the Communist Party of the Soviet Union* writes:

> It was at this time [1873] that Tkachev asserted the views which Lenin was to expound later. . . . Lenin's debt to Tkachev is indicated in the program of the latter's journal, *Nabat* . . . , which began to appear in Geneva at the end of 1875. . . . Lenin's debt to Tkachev is a substantial one. If Lenin was hesitant in acknowledging the debt, as he was also in the case of Nechayev, this can be explained in terms of anxiety to make the Bolsheviks appear to be the party of the masses—as contrasted with Nechayev's and Tkachev's concept of the minority conspiratorial party. Lenin was not opposed to conspiracy—he recognized it as a necessary element in combatting an autocracy—but he felt impelled to mask it as the "vanguard" of the future.[4]

The German scholar, Werner Scharndorff, has written in *Die Geschichte der KPdSU:*

> Nechayev and . . . Tkachev, far more than Marx or Engels, are the spiritual and ideological fathers of the CPSU. . . . Lenin's later concept of the "vanguard of the proletariat" can be found earlier in Tkachev.[5]

Finally, occasionally a rare dissenting opinion, denying the influence of Tkachev on Lenin, can be found, as in Louis Fischer's *Life of Lenin:*

> There is no evidence that Lenin was a follower of Tkachev, whom he mentions once—unfavorably— or that he was influenced by Sergei G. Nechayev.[6]

One may find in the writings of Tkachev any number of concepts which are similar in nature to those which were later devised and advocated by Lenin and his Bolshevik faction within the Russian Social-Democratic Party. In describing, as we have above in the Introduction, the repeated reading of Tkachev by Lenin in 1900 and perhaps at other times and his recommendation that revolutionaries master the works of Tkachev, we are inferring from this evidence that Lenin appears to have learned from or at least to have been inspired by Tkachev's proto-Bolshevism. This is stated with the caveat that to gauge the influence on one man of the reading of another's books is a most delicate task. Nevertheless, the fact remains that in the writings of Tkachev there may be found certain significant concepts which can be described as proto-Bolshevist. And, as we have seen, Lenin gave them almost unqualified endorsement.

TKACHEV'S VIEW OF THE MASSES

One of the most important—perhaps even key concepts— in Tkachev's whole thought is his exposition of the relationship between the masses and the revolutionaries and the revolutionaries-become-rulers. This is one of Tkachev's major contributions to the Russian revolutionary heritage, to the "revolutionary *Geist*," which was passed on to future revolutionary movements and exerted an influence over revolutionary movements in his own day.

Tkachev had very few illusions about the masses; in regard to his antidemocratic attitudes, he stood practically alone in the democratically inclined era of the 1870's when Populism was ascendant. For him, the masses, at least in their prerevolutionary unregenerate form (and also for a protracted period

after the revolution), were not only illiterate and factually
ignorant but stood in dire need of the most profound mass-
psychological reconditioning, re-education, and regeneration.
Not only that, but the masses were often profoundly lacking
in revolutionary courage and passion. In their unreformed, corrupt state in contemporary half-feudal, half-bourgeois Russia,
they were shot through, said Tkachev, with conservatism and
venality, caught helplessly in an increasingly vicious circle
from which by their own efforts they could not possibly escape.
In an important early writing, when he was beginning to show
the influence of Pisarev, Tkachev described the Russian masses
in the following antidemocratic terms in "Destroyed Illusions"
("Razbitiye illyuzii") written in 1868:

> . . . psychological poverty . . . monotonous char-
> acter . . . moral immaturity . . . a man of the
> masses is above all else an egotist. The course of his
> egotism may be found not only in his intellect, in his
> stupidity or immaturity, but in his material poverty.
> . . . Although he may feel a common interest and
> solidarity with his brothers, nevertheless he refuses to
> stick up for his comrades knowing that this might
> threaten him with a loss of work or his piece of
> bread. . . . The result is that the general interest
> [*obshchii interes*] will always be lost sight of, while
> each behaves strictly according to his own interests,
> each scrapes only for himself, and each loses out in the
> end.

> If you leave the people to themselves, they will
> build nothing new. They will only spread the old way
> of life to which they are already accustomed. The peo-
> ple, so long as they are without leaders, cannot possi-
> bly build a new order upon the ruins of the old . . .
> or progress in the direction of realizing communist
> ideals.[7]

The people by their own efforts cannot liberate themselves. Also, as we recall from Tkachev's superciliously demagogical promises to the insatiable peasant (the satirical article
for Lavrov's *Vpered!* cited above, which so infuriated Lavrov),
one may detect Tkachev's contempt for the uncultured insati-

ability of the peasant, the glutton to whom the pie-in-the-sky
and the tongue-in-cheek promises were directed by Tkachev.[8]
Tkachev also employed the most pejorative terms to describe
the Russian *demos:* e.g., "the uncivilized crowd . . . half-
educated many . . . untamed, crude, undeveloped inarticulate
masses . . . the naïve masses," and so on.

As long as the "uncivilized crowd itself is too crude
[*gruba*] and ignorant," Tkachev wrote, "to discern the causes
of its hardpressed condition and itself to find the road to its
amelioration,"[9] who or what stratum in Russian society *could*
lead the masses out of their vicious circle? Would a protracted,
gradualistic process of education of the masses to enable them
to liberate themselves and establish a better order be the best
solution? Or are the masses incapable of being educated within
the existing social and political order?

As early as the mid-1860's Tkachev took a firm stand on
this crucial issue and never seemed seriously to waver from it,
despite his various associations with Populists or pre-Populists.
Perhaps reflecting both his sympathies with Pisarev's writings
as well as the native inclinations existing within his intellectual
makeup, Tkachev revealed himself even in his youth to be of
elitist persuasion. In such early writings as "Destroyed Illusions," "Rising Forces," and "People of the Future and the
Heroes of the Petty Bourgeoisie" (all three of which were written for *Delo* in 1868 when Tkachev was only twenty-four years
old), as well as in later writings in *Nabat* and in attacks on
Bakuninist anarchism, Tkachev put a high premium on what he
called the "civilized crowd . . . the articulate minority . . .
the best folk in our midst . . . the new intelligentsia"—the
elite-revolutionaries before the revolution and the elite-revolu-
tionaries-become-rulers after the revolution.

Tkachev wrote of this minority:

> The [intellectual] minority will impart a consid-
> ered and rational form to the struggle, leading it to-
> wards predetermined goals, directing this coarse ma-
> terial element [the masses] towards ideal principles.
> In a real revolution, the people act like a tempestuous
> natural force, destroying and ruining everything in its
> path, always acting without calculation, without con-
> sciousness.[10]

Again:

> A revolutionary minority is no longer willing to
> wait but must take upon itself the *forcing of con-
> sciousness* upon the people [my emphasis—A. L. W.].[11]

It seems clear from this that the intellectual minority of
radical revolutionaries—by means of what Tkachev termed
their "socialist outlook"[12]—would provide the revolution with
its "form," leadership, and goal (formal, efficient, and final
causes, in the manner of Aristotle?) ; meanwhile, the masses
would provide little more than inarticulate destructiveness, or
even merely indifference.[13] In fact, Tkachev once wrote that
once the masses do act, they "can act only as a destructive
force, not as a creative force.[14] He further described the relationship between the revolutionary minority and the masses as
follows:

> The relationship of the revolutionary minority to
> the people and the participation of the latter in revolu-
> tion may be described in the following terms. The rev-
> olutionary minority, freeing the people from the op-
> pressive terror and fear of the contemporary rulers,
> opens the way for the people to apply their destructive
> revolutionary force. Relying on this force, the revolu-
> tionary minority ably [*iskusstvenno*—also "shrewdly,
> artfully"] directs this violence for the destruction of
> the immediate enemies of the revolution.[15]

Past and contemporary critics of Tkachev have seen in
Tkachev's recommendations of a minority-led revolution (could
any planned revolution be led by any other than a minority?)[16]
an advocacy of a mere palace *coup*, infantile, left-wing *buntarstvo* and *putschism*.[17] Contrasting this with what present-
day Soviet ideologues consider true Leninism, critics of Tkachev
have detected what they regard to be sheer "petty-bourgeois
Blanquism" and inattention to the popular base of revolution.

In the light of this kind of criticism, it is important to
become acquainted with Tkachev's *own* explanation of the manner in which revolution was to be best organized. Was it to be
an isolated *coup d'état* in the capital, "strangulation of the
Tsar with an officer's scarf," as it were? Or was it to have a

substantial popular base? Tkachev stated his position on this quite clearly:

> An attack at the *center of power* and seizure of power in revolutionary hands without at the same time a popular uprising (even if merely local) could lead to positive, lasting results *only under the most favorable of conditions* [italics mine—A. L. W.].[18]

Thus, "only under the most favorable of conditions" could a *coup* at the "center of power" (say, in the capital) "lead to lasting results," *unless the* coup *were accompanied by popular uprisings.* Blanqui's position was evidently similar (see n. 19).

Furthermore, Tkachev was sensitive about what effect this or that programmatic goal or tactic would have on the psychology of the masses, and therefore indicated his concern for the attitude of those masses once the programs were disseminated throughout the population. Also, Tkachev would not have emerged as a mere *putschist* even if the totality of his Blanquism had consisted merely in the reading or observation of Blanquism and Blanqui; Blanqui himself disavowed *putschism* and cannot be called an advocate of the isolated *coup d'état*.[19]

Finally, in the way in which Tkachev conceived of the precise organization of revolution, it is clear that he never for a moment excluded the destructive force of the masses, although he was willing to accept passive acquiescence on the part of the masses. On the contrary, Tkachev pointed out that one of the most important tasks of the organized revolutionaries was to impart to the masses "the feeling [at least] of united force":

> The masses must feel that effective force has been gathered in the name of their cause. . . . Only this assurance can unite them and once united, they will be able to feel the force in themselves.[20]

TKACHEV'S EVALUATION OF FORCE, THE STATE, AND REVOLUTIONARY ORGANIZATION

It has been apparent from the discussion in the section above that Tkachev was impressed by the efficacy of force, or even the *appearance* of force. In the preceding quotation, Tkachev is speaking of the popular awareness that "effective force has been gathered in the name of their cause." Beyond this feeling of united force which the masses should have in order to make the revolution possible, the concrete expression of force, whether in the old state or the new, is given strong emphasis by Tkachev. Concepts of the efficacy of force and organization vs. the inefficacy of weakness (powerlessness) and chaos (anarchy or polyarchy) were carefully canvassed by Tkachev when he wrote of revolutionary organization, the postrevolutionary state of "permanent revolution," or even when he described political power in general.

Whether from familiarity with the ideas and writings of Hobbes and Machiavelli[21] or for a possible multitude of other reasons (including his own early elitist inclinations evident at a very early age), Tkachev had the greatest appreciation and respect for the might and efficacy of centralized authority— what it was able to accomplish and how it could overwhelm even a disgruntled population, to say nothing of class enemies. Tkachev was impressed with the manner in which the government apparatus under certain circumstances *could stand above all classes* asserting its authority universally, almost in total disregard for any narrow, class interests and often only for the purpose of retaining its political hegemony. (This insight constituted one of many non-Marxist concepts in Tkachevism.) As we shall presently see, this appreciation of the weapons and tangible power available to the modern state is a rather striking anticipation of a modern, twentieth-century point of view and its totalitarian potentialities.

Tkachev, like many other philosophers and revolutionists, was silent about his own preferences among the philosophies of the past which may have exercised an influence on him. One may only speculate rather fruitlessly on what the sources of his ideas on force may have been. Tkachev developed at some length in two of his works his theory of force, law, and the state, but unfortunately without making any attribution to thinkers of the past. "Bards of the French Bourgeoisie" and "The Utopian State of the Bourgeoisie," both early works,[22] are vehicles for revealing a good deal of Tkachev's political theory.

As we have already noticed, Tkachev emphasized that the state possessed enormous power, for both good and evil. The state, he once wrote, "is the only force which by the might of its hand can alter the unprofitable contemporary situation of labor and curb the avarice of capital." Beyond the sphere of economics, it is *public law*, Tkachev continued, which "provides the standard of our behavior and the dictates of our conscience" (a statement resembling Hobbes's "law is the public conscience").[23]

Somewhat in the manner of Rousseau, to whom he does refer several times in these two cited writings,[24] Tkachev expresses concern lest the supernatural character of religion, with its address to the *individual* conscience, "allow an individual to choose his own, separate road of moral action, which by satisfying his own individual conscience would meanwhile cause law to lose its universal obligatoriness and its universal applicability."[25] Law might then become, Tkachev warned, "subjective, personal, individualistic . . . law which would be one thing for Ivan and another for Peter, and which would spell the end of law as an obligatory norm for human action in general"; public law would thenceforth cease to function as "the common regulator [Tkachev uses a participial form of the Russian verb-cognate *regulirovat'*—A. L. W.] of human relations."

Tkachev, the former law student and writer on jurisprudence, emphasizes the point that law is not only based on force ("law without sanctions is no law at all," he writes, complimenting Spinoza for his insights in this connection), but law should be constantly supported and conserved in its effective application. Moreover, application of force in civil society—by means of law, police, and courts—must be viewed as an abettor of human progress, and not the opposite as the anarchists of Tkachev's day asserted. The law must, however, be applied forcefully and for good ends.[26]

Tkachev then launches into a discussion of descriptive and normative law. Note here, too, how loosely Tkachev applied the words "natural" or "natural laws" which, in the light of his other theories, seem to have little resemblance to the concepts of the Stoics or St. Thomas; in this respect, Tkachev writes more like a man of the eighteenth-century Enlightenment.

A fact constantly reiterated by history and which
has become an eternal and irrevocable law [in the
sense of principle—A. L. W.] is that there is a distinction between citizens as members of a given society
and their, so to speak, universal-human status—that
is, the distinction between their social relations and
their relations with others *qua* members of the universal human family. The first type of relationship is
ever changing, inconstant, at any one time dependent
on this or that contingency more than on any single
unchangeable law. Relations of the second sort have
the character of permanence and definiteness [deter-
minateness] and are dependent on general, unchang-
ing natural laws governing all animal life and regu-
lating the mutual relations between all living things
on this planet. . . .

We have the right to ascribe certain facts in
human social life to the action and regulation of the
universal and changeless laws of nature . . . i.e., to
regard the facts as inevitable and irrevocable in any
kind of social system whatsoever. We know, to give one
example, that all living creatures die, that they have
sexual relations with each other, and so forth. We
know that these facts are encountered in any kind of
social organization . . . and we assign to them irrevocable laws which regulate their activities.

On the other hand, history confronts us with the
fact of the unequal distribution of wealth and so on.
These are facts which pertain only to a certain type of
social organization. Outside the given system there is
no basis for their existence; they are mere products
of a given social system, not products of universal
relations, of man *qua* universal human being.

But there is one fact which is constantly observed in human social relations, as well as in the
relations governing all living things on earth. *This is
the constant supremacy of the strong over the weak*
[my emphases—A. L. W.].[27]

Tkachev then expands on the relationship between the strong
and the weak and how force is distorted in bourgeois society:

This supremacy and its omnipotent application of
force which oppresses the weak is the ground for the

progress of animal organisms and the rule of animals over each other. A stronger organism, an organism which cannot live in harmony in the world with less strong organisms seeks ever to improve itself. . . . The same general law of nature applies to relations among men outside society. . . . The powerful seek to subdue the weak and by this action the human organism constantly improves. . . . We can observe the same process within human society, but only here may force and powerlessness assume an entirely different importance. Force and weakness cease to have any meaning in the sense of physiological perfection or physiological imperfection of the human organism. Instead, by force and weakness are meant those external attributes which give to certain people the ability of employing their great resources . . . for satisfying the demands of their organisms. These attributes have nothing to do with physiology; organisms of less physiological development may be able to exercise supremacy over the physiologically stronger.[28] Although from this we must admit that social organisms experience the action of the general laws of nature which ascribe to force the unconditioned and natural (and, consequently, also just—i.e., supremacy by right)— dominance of the weak by the strong. . . . This law, however, can be considered irrevocable when applied to social relations where, at the same time, it can also lose its rationality. It can lose its rationality here and its character as a motivator of progress and social improvement because this conception of force has ceased to express itself as an idea of true, individual force, individual improvement and perfection; in social relations, we mean by the strong not people who are "more perfect" than the others, more intelligent, or closer to the human ideal, but rather people who merely possess a greater quantity of the material means for existence. The consequence of this view is that . . . material wealth [in bourgeois society—A. L. W.] is exploited in such a way as to bring harm to development and progress. Thus, if we admit that such an arrangement is not the best possible one, that in many cases it is unsatisfactory, then we must also admit that its unsatisfactoriness did not consist in the fact that force has everywhere become right, that it everywhere reigns supreme, but, rather, that the *meaning of force has been distorted and perverted* so that so-called social force is nothing more than a fiction [*fiktsiya*], that it is not really based on force, that it does not lead to improvement of man, and applies only to purely external and peripheral matters. *Force has always reigned and always will*—this is a universal principle governing the relations of all living organisms. To go against it is unthinkable. Whoever wishes to go against it is foolish. Progress is unthinkable without it; to exclude it from life is to exist in a desert or to fall into a deep sleep. *Rather, what is needed is to make force real force.* What is considered to be force today is not true force. What is needed is to reform social force, to alter both its character and its form [italics are Tkachev's].

Why should punishment then, Tkachev asks, "that is, physical compulsion applied to individuals, be considered such a terrifying encroachment on man's freedom, allegedly bringing harm to the general welfare—and, oh, terrible world!—bringing harm to *communism*."[29]

Government and law, expressing themselves as force, have always existed and always will exist, asserts Tkachev, and they can be harnessed for good as well as for evil. In bourgeois society, what force there is—and Tkachev regards it as mainly fictitious, at least as far as economics is concerned—is used merely to support the given bourgeois type of social organization. In the last quotation above, Tkachev says that despite critics' pejorative use of the word "communism" to suggest something evil, i.e., connoting force being applied through public law for the general welfare, such a good application of force (by means of dictatorship as we shall see presently) is exemplified precisely by communism. In this connection, Venturi reproduces an interesting elaboration of this concept of the positive use of strong political power found in a pamphlet written by Tkachev's collaborator on *Nabat*, Kasper Turski:

The anarchist section of the International wants the complete destruction of the bourgeois order and wants to set up in its place the principle of absolute individual liberty—a principle purely bourgeois in its essence, on which the present order is founded. But there metaphysics does not limit itself to this sort of

mess: while proclaiming the principle of absolute individual liberty, they also want equality. But if to obtain this equality, it is indispensable that individual
liberty is curtailed, it is obvious that there must be
some force capable of setting that limit. Whether this
force arises from a mutual contract, or whether it is
imposed by a minority, will depend on the circumstances that accompany the revolution. But in one way
or another it is still necessary to have force capable of
maintaining equality between the strong and the
weak.[30]

In at least one instance Tkachev saw the very origin of
civil society and the state as the result of war and a contest
of power, of opposing increments of force: "Basically, the state
has grown out of war and the principle of war has become
imbedded in it."[31] In another place, Tkachev asserted that "war
and the application of force can solve any problem, not only
social but also religious, moral, metaphysical, or whatever."[32]

In the above quotation, it would appear that Tkachev displays a somewhat Spinozist view of the state,[33] but he emphasizes that the factor of force is a most effective agent
(through law) for bringing about a total reformation and regeneration of the old, corrupt society in which the majority
profits, languishes or suffers, as the case may be, *unconsciously
and with no means in itself for correcting the situation.*

Tkachev's characteristic emphasis on authoritarianism was
extended to his theory of *revolutionary organization* as well
as to the postrevolutionary dictatorship, both of which were
to be led by the socialist intelligentsia.

In propounding his theories, Tkachev ran into much opposition from those same intellectuals to whom he directed
most of his appeals. To those holding out-and-out anarchist
positions and to those of the more subtle democratic point of
view of Lavrov, Tkachev's ideas were "dangerous." On one occasion, Lavrovists, in the manner of Lord Acton, warned the
Nabatovtsi that power is likely to corrupt its users, especially
if that power approaches the absolute. Tkachev countered:

What are you frightened of? What right do you
have to think that this minority—partly due to its
social position, partly because of its ideals, and com-

pletely dedicated to the people's interest—by seizing power in its hands would suddenly be transformed into a popular tyranny [*narodnovo tirana*—literally, popular tyrant]?

You claim: All power corrupts men [Tkachev is referring to Lavrov—see n. 34—A. L. W.]. But where do you get the idea that leaders, in seizing power, are better men before they seize power than afterwards? Read their biographies and you get the opposite impression. Robespierre, a member of the Convention, the omnipotent ruler of the destinies of France, and Robespierre, the unknown provincial lawyer, were one and the same person. Power in no way made the slightest change in Robespierre's moral character or his ideals and intentions, or even in his conduct in his own home.[34]

Referring to any strong government, past or contemporary, which oppressed its citizens, Tkachev said that it was of utmost, crucial importance that the power of that regime be destroyed and humiliated. This would be a prerequisite for any subsequent unleashing of the destructive force of the people; otherwise, popular unrest or outright rebellion would have no effective result. At the same time, Tkachev had the profoundest appreciation of the power of an absolutist, inegalitarian regime to perpetuate itself indefinitely and intimidate its subjects (but not successfully to intimidate the truly conscious, revolutionary minority!). This appreciation of absolute power was extended by Tkachev to include the Tsarist state:

> The most powerful, the mightiest enemy against which we must struggle—this is our government, with its military forces and its enormous material resources.[35]

The masses rise up effectively, Tkachev said, "only when they see that the strength of the regime is not as great as it appears to be." Power is pitted against power, as Tkachev viewed the problem in terms reminiscent of certain earlier political philosophers. Weakness fails; strength wins.

What could help bring on this impression among the populace that the state had grown or was growing vulnerably weak?

Revolutions of the past in Rome or in Paris in 1871, Tkachev wrote, had taken place only when "the supreme ruling strata had exhibited chaos, lack of order, anarchy or polyarchy [*poliarkhiya*], the regime beginning to waver and falter."

When this occurs, the organized revolutionaries must strike at the *centers of power*, removing, and above all publicizing the removal of, the power over sanctions and reprisals —the state's effective power—once held by the old regime so that:

> . . . the removal of the knout and the other types of severe punishment will cause a reaction in the people to this disorganization, a popular feeling of no longer being afraid while all the latent dissatisfaction and their pent-up loathing of unrestrained force will be unleashed.[36]

Speaking of the old regime (the Tsarist state), Tkachev stated further: "People fear its possession of material force. But once it loses this force, not a single hand will be raised in its defense."[37] Among the factors which could help bring about this weakness in the government—a domestic application of Lenin's later weakest-link theory—would be "two or three military defeats."[38]

The revolutionary striking force, consisting of dedicated professional revolutionaries, must be tightly organized and centralized and at the same time totally committed to the socialist ideology. They and their obedient followers must be disciplined and obey orders coming from the top. As Tkachev wrote in *Nabat:*

> The success of revolution depends on the formation and organized unity of the scattered revolutionary elements into a living body [*zhivoye telo*] which is able to act according to a single, common plan and be subordinated to a single, common leadership—an organization based on centralization of power and decentralization of function.[39]

The revolutionary organs, Tkachev added, must act together like "a revolutionary army."[40]

Conscious of the relatively small number of professional

revolutionaries that would be involved, Tkachev emphasized most strongly the necessity of their disciplined organization:

> If organization is necessary for any large or strong party, it is without any question even more necessary for a weak or small party, for a party which is only at the beginning of its formation. Such is the position of our social revolutionary party. For it, the problem of unity and organization is a matter of life and death.[41]

The utopian revolutionaries, on the other hand, "rejected any kind of subordination or centralization recognizing only a federative tie between autonomous revolutionary groups acting independently. . . . Such an organization is not equipped for quick and decisive action; it merely opens the way to mutual animosities, wrangling, all kinds of wavering and compromises. . . . It is unable to follow any kind of common plan with strict consistency; its activity will inevitably lack form, harmony, and unity."[42]

In addition to possessing superior knowledge (or consciousness [*soznaniye*])[43] and intellect, a member of Tkachev's revolutionary organization would have to embrace with his total being the "socialist world view." He must be the carrier of the new ethos of positive utilitarianism which is to unite all members of society into an altruistically-inclined, harmonious whole. The revolutionaries must be men who "are the most honorable of men and who are therefore sympathetic to the interests of the workers."[44] The revolutionary must adhere to the catechism for revolutionary behavior and morality—to wit:

> He is no revolutionary if he pities anything in this society. . . . It is even worse for him if he has any kindred, intimate, or amorous relationships. He is no revolutionary if relationships are able to check his hand. . . . The necessity of attachment to females for the completeness of life's happiness and harmony is only complete rubbish invented by some medieval mourners over the heavenly Virgin, by those same perverse knights who were themselves tied to women like workhorses. . . . The revolutionaries know too that no matter how warm or beautiful a woman's body may be, no matter how sweet the music of her

voice or how heavenly to look into her eyes, they will
not tolerate all the same even the slightest competition
with the irresistible strength of that ideal which fills
their lives and actions. So much joy and grief are in
their memories, so many hopes and plans, so many
other thoughts and considerations that to renounce the
ideal in the slightest would mean suicide—this ideal
which is so closely bound into their whole internal
being.[45]

Tkachev sketches two lines along which the revolutionary
organizations and their propaganda should develop:

1. *Propaganda addressed to the majority of the
educated and to the privileged stratum:* the same relationship as with the people—exploit the tactic of
agitation. Feelings of dissatisfaction and contempt for
the existing regime must be stirred up, at the same
time giving great attention to whatever facts may
exist which would best kindle these feelings. In the
selection of these facts, revolutionary propaganda
must interpret the facts not so much in the light of the
principles governing the present regime as in the degree they bring about the suffering of the people
in this or that stratum;

2. *Propaganda addressed to the revolutionary
youth and their party [partiya]:* they must pay particular attention to organizational questions in carrying out their goals. The youth must be convinced of
the present necessity for immediate, practical revolutionary activity; it must be explained to the youth that
the principal condition for the success of this activity
depends on the lasting organization of its revolutionary forces, on the unification of particular, individual acts into a single whole, a disciplined, harmonious
whole. Our revolutionary practice has worked out a
number of roads of revolutionary action: the avenue of
coup d'état-style conspiracy; the avenue of popular propaganda (namely what your journal [*Vpered!*] calls
"development in the people of consciousness of their
rights and demands"); the avenue of direct, popular
agitation [*agitatsiya*] (i.e., direct incitement of the
people to rebellion). This is not the place to argue
about which of the three types of action is most ex-

pedient and useful. All three avenues are equally expedient for the speediest realization of a national revolution. Let each choose whatever kind of action best suits the conditions. Whoever wishes to employ all three at the same time, let him—whatever is best for him. And whoever does not know which road of action he wants to follow, let him not waste time and energy in preliminary self-enlightenment and reeducation of the people.

It is not the time now for protracted discussion. Let each make his own selection as quickly as possible and speedily take action along his chosen road. As to the question, "What is to be done?" let us not preoccupy ourselves with that any longer. That has been settled long ago. Make the revolution. How? However you may, however you are able to. Given a rational organization of forces, no single attempt, no single application of force can prove useless. Therefore, the question of organization is the most pressing problem to be conveyed by revolutionary propaganda addressed to our youth. Because of its extraordinary importance, no other question should be given more attention, especially in the case of practical revolutionary activity for the present time; no attention should be given those questions which have no direct connection with practical revolutionary action or which are concerned mainly with the future—questions which can lead only to further divisions and disunity within the circles of our revolutionary youth.

I have in mind here those questions concerning the construction of a better social order in the future and the practical measures for bringing it about once the revolution has completed its destructive mission. For now, the present must occupy our attention.[46]

Tkachev used a considerable lexicon and all manner of verbal weapons in his "Tasks of Revolutionary Propaganda in Russia" (or "Letter to the Editor of *Vpered!*"), as elsewhere, to condemn the "gradualist," "demagogic," democratic methods of popular revolution and going-to-the-people propaganda of Lavrov's program. In the letter he gave four reasons why he thought Lavrov's democratic Populist approach was "false and pernicious":

First, it is harmful because you are foisting upon the youth [the young intelligentsia] the notion of revolution by means of peaceful progress. You defend the idea of revolution while at the same time recommending peaceful progress. You attack the attempts at unleashing deliberately the revolution, and in this fashion you discredit revolution in general in the eyes of our youth.

Second, it is harmful because the road which you have indicated for the youth as the only road which is expedient for preparing the revolution is by no means the only road. If the youth were to follow only this road, not only would the revolution as a forceful overthrow not be brought closer but would be postponed into the far future. The youth would not be working for revolution in the present but working only for peaceful progress in the future.

Third, your propaganda is harmful because instead of arousing the youth and inciting them to immediate practical revolutionary action, it only distracts them from it by preaching to revolutionaries not so much the real necessity for revolutionary action as the necessity "for strict and concerted preparation for it." All your advice about the youth having to "enlighten themselves" or "reeducate themselves" has nothing to do with either the social situation presently existing among our revolutionaries or their present attitude. Instead, it only sharply contradicts those sacred responsibilities which the suffering of the people have laid on the shoulders of each and every revolutionary.

Fourth, it is harmful because it undermines the faith of the youth in their own strength, in the possibility for their immediate revolutionary action, and in the possibility of revolution in the near future.[47]

Tkachev continues, describing the manner in which Lavrovist propaganda "paralyzes revolutionary energy" with its compromising proposals for peaceful evolution. Tkachev's scorn for compromise and peaceful progress was also extended to German Internationalist theory about economic progress bringing increased proletarianization and chances for revolution—continued economic progress under Russian conditions, Tkachev thought, would only complicate revolution. He ridiculed the Lavrovist concept of progress, adding that the word progress was used by Lavrov "to cover up all manner of philistine-philosophical rubbish . . . all kinds of gradualists [postepenovtsi], all shadings [ottenki] of the progressive movement, from the bourgeois-liberals to the revolutionary socialists. . . . We need a banner inscribed with greater detail, clarity, and definition, defining the aims and ideals of a revolutionary party."[48] The Lavrovist program, Tkachev wrote, "was reactionary [reaktsionnaya] and utopian."[49]

Tkachev further condemned the Lavrovist organizational scheme of decentralized, federated revolutionary organizations and circles as "bourgeois," a word frequently used by Tkachev not only in the economic sense but in the sense which Lenin and others were to use it later: implying excessive respect for bourgeois civil liberties and "democratism." It was a bourgeois scheme, Tkachev said, because it was an example of "putting the particular interest above the general interest, the partial above the whole, egoism above altruism." Any non-centralistic form of revolutionary organization, Tkachev continued in his letter to Lavrov's Vpered!, "would mean a hodgepodge of independent, autonomous revolutionary groups which would thereby open the way to all kinds of wavering and compromise."[50] Tkachev had scorn for "confederate, federal, or non-centralistic" forms of bourgeois government and administration in general. Such a point of view, he said, is merely one other form of "bourgeois individualism" and outworn "legalism," formalism, and "preaching of bloodless revolution."[51] Tkachev compared Lavrov's peaceful evolution line to the "German program of the International."[52]

Speaking of bourgeois democracy and universal suffrage in that system, Tkachev wrote:

> Universal tabulation of votes, which is attained by the workers as a majority in the state, proves always to be a mere fiction, a fantastic right and from this right flow benefits to those whose interests have nothing to do with those of the workers. Only force can give meaning to right.

Workers can have no rights where the total force brought to bear by the state and the socialist dictatorship is not applied in the name of the workers; "economic slaves must remain political slaves."[53]

THE POSTREVOLUTIONARY "WORKERS' STATE"

Just as "the *muzhik* . . . , the uncivilized crowd is too crude and ignorant to discern consciously the causes of its hard-pressed condition,"[54] so also, Tkachev wrote, are the people incapable of instituting a new order. Indeed, as Tkachev expressed it, "They are to be given no crucial or determinant role.[55] . . . If you leave the people to themselves, they will build nothing new."[56] Instead of relying upon public opinion (which is mostly unformed and uninformed, according to Tkachev) and the ascending mode of grassroots democracy—division into political parties, pressure groups, etc.—the radical minority of socialist intellectuals do not wait for the people to make the revolution themselves; they establish a new political order, leading the mostly ignorant masses up the road to a new social order and to the reeducation of those masses. For this purpose, the philosophy of Tkachev's "men of the future" is crucial:

> Their distinctive merit lies in the fact that all their activity, even their whole way of life, is dominated by just one ambition, one passionate idea: to make the majority of men happy and to invite as many as possible to the banquet [*pir*] of life. The realization of this idea will become the sole aim of their activity because this idea is completely fused with their concept of personal happiness. Everything is sacrificed for this idea—if one may use the word sacrifice—although it would be impossible, of course, to say how the idea, or better the conception, of the means by which this ordered brotherhood could be realized. There are many different approaches to this.[57]

The background for Tkachev's recommendation for a post-revolutionary authoritarian state was his dispute with the Bakuninist anarchists and their articles in *Obshchina* (*Commune*). In Tkachev's important collection of notes entitled "Anarchy of Thought," published in four numbers of *Nabat* in 1876 and issued as a separate pamphlet in England in 1879, he contended that Bakunin's concept of "revolutionary instinct of the masses" simply ignored the significance of a dominant ideal and focused undue attention on the mere reputed *narodnost'* contained within the ideal, in other words, on the democratic element from which the ideal supposedly sprang. No, Tkachev replied, the socialist intellectual minority understood the people's suffering and the relief from it better than the people themselves. After guiding and terminating the "destructive phase" of the revolution, the radical intelligentsia-leadership would thence proceed to the "constructive phase" of revolution, to the establishment of the "permanently-revolutionary state."[58] Tkachev describes the role of the radical minority in this state:

> The revolutionary minority, having freed the people from the yoke which had oppressed them and from the fear and terror of the old regime . . . directs [force] shrewdly [*iskusstvenno*] toward the destruction of the enemies of the revolution. In this manner, the minority can deprive the enemies of all means of resistance or counterattack. Then by making use of its force and its own authority, it can proceed to the introduction of new, progressively communist elements into the conditions of national life and free the life of the people from their age-old chains and breathe life into its cold and dead forms.[59]

"This formula," says Tkachev self-assuredly, "is a logical necessity derived from an evaluation made by us of the character and extent of true revolutionary force lodged in our people at the present time."[60]

Just as the revolutionary minority, in making the political revolution, would have to count on either popular disaffection (toward the old regime) or popular indifference (toward the revolution), so also after the first phase of the revolution the minority should also be able to count on at least "passive support" by the people. Apropos of this, Tkachev wrote:

> Putting revolutionary ideals into effect not only does not contradict the true needs of the people but engenders them with the spirit of communal solidarity which will, in turn, interpenetrate the whole social structure. This will occur in such a way that there

will not be the slightest basis for assuming that the people would refuse their passive support for the revolutionaries.[61]

At this point, Tkachev introduces what he calls the "conservative ideals" existing in national life, more specifically in the Russian people, which strike a contrast with the usual monotonous conservativeness of the people. These ideals, he wrote in "The People and Revolution," aim at the "preservation of all or at least the most substantial elements in the national life which have developed historically." Here, as in his letter to Engels, Tkachev describes the Russian *obshchina* as a "substantial element" embodying (although by no means *at present* concretely expressing) the socialist ideal of the autonomous commune based not on private ownership and use of the land, but on "brotherly solidarity of all members of the commune—in other words, the ideal which was so clearly expressed in this communist legacy of the past."[62]

Tkachev had no illusions about the speed with which the regeneration of the Russian *obshchina* and of Russian life as a whole could take place:

> Of course, the road from the forms of life which have given the foundations for this ideal to the goal of full communism is a very protracted one; communism is embodied in these forms, so to speak, in seed form. This seed can grow and not be stifled only if our economic life is developed in a certain [socialist] direction.[63]

Contributing to the length of the road is cultural lag; Tkachev wrote, "[The peasant] loves traditional forms of his life and does not want to lay a finger on them." Tkachev often construes conservative tradition contemptuously; the masses display inertia, monotony, routine.

Tkachev strongly emphasized that the *obshchina* developing in Russia in the 1870's was *headed in the wrong direction* and "little-by-little" had to be set on a new course:

> If it continues to develop in this [a bourgeois] direction, as it has in Western Europe, it will suffer the same fate as the commune did in Europe: it will disappear as it did in England, Germany, Italy, Spain,

and France. But if the revolution dams the wave of the swiftly accumulating tide of bourgeois progress in time, if it stops this flood and leads it in a completely opposite direction, then without a doubt our present-day *obshchina* will be converted little-by-little into an *obshchina*-commune [*obshchina-kommuna*].[64]

At the present time, Tkachev wrote, the Russian *obshchina* is at a crossroads: one sign points to communism, the other to individualism.[65] The development in the correct, communist direction will take a long time. What is involved is:

> . . . [that] the entire reconstruction of society, of all the economic, juridical, social, private, and family relations, all ideas and philosophies, all the ideals and mores of society takes place in the revolution.[66]

Presumably, Tkachev thought that the state, by controlling the economic life of the people, could proceed more easily to the spiritual regeneration of the people. He once wrote: "Whoever wants to govern the soul of man must also rule over his body. This is as obvious as the simplest axiom of geometry."[67] "Are you afraid of the word 'state'?" Tkachev asked anarchists sarcastically. "It's a sign of childishness to fear words."[68]

Tkachev viewed the power of his postrevolutionary state as somewhat similar to that of the centralized revolutionary party before the revolution: centralization is a way to get things accomplished, not only rapidly but logically and in tune with basic socialist philosophy. The same applies to the postrevolutionary period. To decentralize after the revolution and to go over to democracy, confederative arrangements, and "influence from below" threaten to destroy the very aims of the revolution.

> The revolutionary minority, fragmented into separate, independent *obshchini* and towns, would willy-nilly and behind the backs of the revolutionary minority become subordinated to local influences— that is, to that very majority which is penetrated to the bone with routine traditions, which shows an instinctive yearning for the old and, by casting its glance into the past, seeks the signs and symbols which are to rule in the present as well. One can

imagine how quickly and successfully we could carry out socialist principles if the program depended on one-sided local wishes and the capricious arbitrariness of the routine-ridden majority! Even under the most favorable conditions the socialist program would move ahead at a snail's pace, constantly snagged by the vain desire to appease the old with the new and constantly detouring from the directly logical road of social reform onto the road of historical tradition. . . . Routine would conserve family relations [among other elements in national life] with intense stubbornness so that the only means by which these relations could be altered in the spirit of communist principles would be for the power of reform to stand above all local influences, above all historical tradition. To deny this obvious truth one would have to be a person totally lacking a practical outlook. It is not at all surprising, therefore, to find our opponents, the anarchists, denying it. It is surprising, however, to find them proposing that socialist ideals should be realized while at the same time proposing as the means for realizing them a road which would more quickly restore the old order than the new. . . . They are only the representatives of *gradual gradualism* [*postepennaya postepenovshchina*]. They criticize us in the strangest way . . . for having stated openly that we wish to eradicate from past society the traditions of private ownership, tear up by the roots the principle of marketing, reconstruct family relations, and indoctrinate [*perevospitat'*—also reeducate—A. L. W.] the people. They assert that all of this may be achieved by means of successive, gradual reforms![69]

Despite his great faith in the state's ability to change fundamentally the bases of Russian social life, Tkachev added a minor qualification to his authoritarian theory. Decrees alone cannot work miracles. He could imagine, he wrote in the same article quoted above, "people believing blindly in the decreeing power of the state," who could imagine that the state, merely by the superficial fiat of decrees, could realize the theoretical socialist program. These people are unrealistic, Tkachev commented, since they deny the necessity "of forcible interference of the developed minority into the business of reconstructing social and family relations of the underdeveloped majority."[70] Such a theory resembles, Tkachev said, the "hermaphroditism" of the anarchists who cannot quite make up their minds whether to deny the need for the state altogether or to let some of it in through the back door in the form of persuasive decrees, decrees not backed up with the force of the state, its police, and its "collective dictatorship" composed of the advanced minority.[71] The state must be fully authoritarian, Tkachev responded, holding in its hands total power over both the material and spiritual aspects of social life— controlling not only the economy and the formal law-making power but holding within its grasp control over the press, education, even relations within the family.[72] A socialist K.O.B., *Commission for Public Security* [*Komissiya Obshchestvennoi Bezopasnosti*] must be established to root out hostile elements, particularly among the older generation.[73]

NATIONAL IN FORM; SOCIALIST IN CONTENT

It was obvious to Tkachev that in the carrying out of the socialist program in the postrevolutionary workers' state, account would have to be taken of the numerous national differences within the Russian Empire. Moreover, there were different types of socialism already in evidence in the revolutionary movements of various nationalities. Both in the pre- and postrevolutionary periods, the problem of national differences and different roads to socialism would have to be faced.

In one of his last writings, Tkachev expressed alarm and scorn for the tendency which he observed in the mid-1870's for Russian revolutionary organizations to fall into autonomous, national groupings.[74] Somewhat in the manner of Marx and Engels but still more in anticipation of the attitude of Lenin and particularly Stalin, Tkachev emphasized that the national problem, including the status of the borderlands, *must always be subordinated to the aims of the revolution and of the postrevolutionary regeneration of Russian social life.* As he wrote in *Nabat* in 1878:

> The state, science, trade, industry all have the
> same general tendency—obscuring national differences

which once so sharply distinguished one people from another. . . . No matter how much we may deplore bourgeois progress, we must give credit to this tendency, in terms of our ideals and our interests, a tendency which is highly favorable to us. Bourgeois progress is leading to the triumph of our ideals: brotherhood and equality.

In striving for revolution in one or another region [of Russia], one is not working for the interests of one nationality alone, but rather for Russia as a whole and for all humanity. . . . Socialists do not regard nationality differences as eternal. . . . On the contrary, they believe that with the universal triumph of the principles of socialist revolution, all individual differences, particularly those of tribe and nation, will eventually disappear. . . . As long as individual inequality as well as tribal difference remain, the final goal of socialism—equality and brotherhood—cannot be fully realized. The nationality principle does not harmonize with the principles of socialist revolution; the former must be sacrificed for the latter.

One cannot have a Yakutsk socialism, a Little Russia socialism, Georgian socialism, and so on, any more than you can have Yakutsk, *et al.*, geometry.[75]

Tkachev adds that the *national form* of states will remain—along with the nations composing the old Russian Empire—until socialist (i.e., communist) society has been fully achieved.

Tkachev then introduces a modern-sounding socialist theory of "many-roads-to-socialism." He writes:

Just as it is impossible to teach geometry in the same way to people with different levels of attainment and knowledge . . . so is it impossible to alter the social relations of peoples with the same means, peoples whose civilizations have been developed along differing lines, customs, world outlooks, with differing economic, political, and juridical institutions. These are the ABC's of social science, the elementary demands of the political art, and no one with even a passing knowledge of the revolutionary world outlook of the Russian socialist-revolutionaries . . . could ever ignore these demands.[76]

Tkachev then modifies his qualifications:

> However, the carrying out of socialism with the
> aid of different tactics by no means equals any "na-
> tionalization" of socialism. On the contrary, socialism
> is everywhere and always multi-national in character,
> everywhere and always remains the same general
> formula equally applicable and compulsory for all
> "tribes, dialects, and strata." Therefore, no matter
> how variegated the means may be for the realization
> of socialism in practice, under its influence all tribal
> particularities, all nationalities must merge into a
> common human family [*slit'sya v odnu obshchechelo-
> vecheskuyu sem'yu*].
>
> To repeat, between the principle of socialism and
> the principle of nationality lies an irreconcilable an-
> tagonism. Either socialism must fall victim to nation-
> alism or nationalism to socialism. . . . To be true,
> dedicated socialists, the Ukrainophils must forever re-
> nounce their nationalistic utopias. There is no other
> choice. [The Ukrainians] have taken up an unclear
> and indeterminate position on this question. They are
> neither peahens nor crows [neither fish nor fowl—
> A. L. W.].[77]

WITHERING AWAY OF THE STATE

What was to follow the "permanently-revolutionary"
workers' state? In the manner of Lenin, Tkachev did not altogether annihilate the anarchist dream of a stateless and law-
less millennium. The communistic society in which obedience
would be voluntary, bureaucracy absent, true individuality-
within-the-community realized, and in which other fully-com-
munist ends would materialize was only rarely touched upon
by Tkachev and by Lenin.

Until the protracted period of the dictatorship had thoroughly reeducated the popular masses, talk of millennial communism was premature and harmful. It was especially premature to speak of individualism and reduced state power *within
the bourgeois period*. Multiparty parliamentarism in the presence of the "insurance-company-like" or reformist action of a

weakened bourgeois state (e.g., in the thought of Girardin) only contributed to the overall weakening of the bourgeois state.

In his description of the bourgeois state, Tkachev emphasized its "disharmony . . . reflecting the underlying antagonism of bourgeois social and economic life. The bourgeois state, he wrote, is like a body "possessing unequal strength on its one side so that until its strength is balanced, it will be unable to move. So also are bourgeois governments composed of parties reflecting various interests. Until one party is victorious over all the others . . . and the fuller that victory is, the more energetically will become that life of society which it can inspire with its strength, the more thought-out will be its acts."[78] Tkachev, as already indicated, assigned enormous tasks to his permanently-revolutionary state, both in the cultural and economic realms. But after society is set into harmonious motion, its institutions recast and socialized, its people reeducated (over a protracted period, he said), what will then become of the state?

Tkachev gives little attention to such a far-off goal, devoting most of his attention, understandably perhaps, to the preparation of the political revolution and the political means to be used after the revolution for realizing communism (the term "socialism" is used by him interchangeably with "communism"). As Kozmin has pointed out, Tkachev strikingly anticipated the position taken some forty years later by Lenin in *State and Revolution* (not to be confused with Tkachev's "Revolution and State") when Tkachev cast his eyes beyond the period of transition of state socialism into the distant future when the state would disappear:

> In Tkachev's opinion, the state will become useless and will wither away only when complete equality is attained between people. . . . In the transitional period state power is the most necessary weapon in the hands of the revolutionary party.
>
> At one time, Engels, in a polemic with Tkachev . . . designated Tkachev as an orthodox anarchist-Bakuninist. . . . However, Engels was not familiar with Tkachev's earlier writings (the articles "Rising Forces" and "Destroyed Illusions") . . . which illus-

trate how incorrect it was to label Tkachev an anarchist.

The manner in which Tkachev presents the eventual destruction of the state is a far cry from anarchism. Lenin in his work, *State and Revolution*, . . . showed how anarchists and socialists differed . . . and that the state would disappear only after the reconstruction of society had been completed. Therefore, Tkachev's conviction that in the future the state would be destined to wither away gives no one the right to call him an anarchist.[79]

Thus, Tkachev seems to have shared with certain other socialists of his time the idea of the eventual disappearance of the state—after a very protracted period. This is one of the few areas, in fact, where Tkachev found himself more or less in agreement with other socialists, whether Western European or Russian. Where he most differed with them, and where Tkachev placed most of his emphasis and displayed most of his originality, was in other areas: revolutionary organization, the elite-vis-à-vis-the-masses concept, the enormous power he assigned to the state and its capability to do good under a socialist dictatorship, *et al.*

Still another idea concerning the future society of nearly perfect equality, besides statelessness, was Tkachev's concept of regenerate, "true" individualism. There is a tendency for Tkachev to construe individualism as individual autonomy, a society of absolutely freely-willing individuals, which Tkachev terms anarchy. Anarchy means that individuals can do what they wish. But for anarchy to be anything but chaotic (as it must be in bourgeois society)[80] and a paralyzing struggle of human forces:

> In practice the principle of pure human freedom must be accompanied by the destruction of not only force but all kinds of state power, by the destruction of the domination of positive law—in other words, anarchy. But anarchy can come about only with the existence of complete and absolute equality. . . . In the absence of such equality, anarchy must inevitably develop into oligarchy, free competition into monopoly, and juridical equality into factual exploitation of man by man.[81]

For an individual to be *truly* autonomous and hence free, Tkachev takes the Platonic position that reason and the subjection of the appetitive to the rational intellectual element in man is the only means to attaining human freedom. But this becomes possible for society as a whole (beyond the small circle of revolutionary-socialist dictators) only after the long period of totalitarian reeducation of the mostly egotistical and egoistic "routine men" of contemporary (especially Russian) society carried out under the leadership of the "collective dictatorship."

NOTES

1. Leonard Schapiro, *The Communist Party of the Soviet Union* (New York: Random House, 1960), p. 4. One might question, however, Schapiro's statement that Tkachev was the first Russian to propose a Jacobin or Blanquist revolutionary technique. Certainly he was the first to develop it in any thoroughgoing way.

2. Possony uses Schapiro as his source for his statement that Lenin read the works of Tkachev in Geneva. He further states that when this took place is not known. This is not true (see above, pp. 4–5).

3. Alan Moorehead, *The Russian Revolution* (New York: Harper and Brothers, 1958), p. 33.

4. John S. Reshetar, *A Concise History of the Communist Party of the Soviet Union* (New York: Frederick A. Praeger, 1960), pp. 7–10.

5. Werner Scharndorff, *Die Gechichte der KPdSU* (Munich: Gunter Olzog Verlag, 1961), pp. 10–11. This book was subjected to strong criticism in the Soviet journal *Voprosy filosofii*, No. 4 (1964), for its having traced a lineage running from Tkachev and Nechayev to Lenin. More will be said of anti-Tkachev Soviet criticism below, pp. 176–87.

6. Louis Fischer, *The Life of Lenin* (New York: Harper and Row, 1964), p. 45. Lenin did not mention Tkachev "once" but several times, and never really unfavorably; in several places he speaks of the revolutionaries of the seventies (meaning especially the radical revolutionaries and terrorists) as "magnificent" heroes. The following passage from Lenin's *What Is To Be Done?* is sometimes *inaccurately* translated to indicate an alleged anti-Tkachev position held by Lenin: "The attempt to seize power on the basis of the teaching of Tkachev and carried out by means of 'what was terrifying' and what actually turned out to be terrifying terror was magnificent [*velichestvenna*], while the 'sensational' terror of Junior Tkachev [*obviously meaning Lenin's opponent, Nadezhdin*—A. L. W.] is simply laughable and especially ridiculous when the concept of organization is to include middle-size peasants" (Lenin, *Sochineniya* [3rd Ed.], V, 477. Lenin is

here *contrasting* Tkachev's views with those of Nadezhdin and unfavorably to the latter's ideas, but not to Tkachev's, whose ideals and activities Lenin calls "magnificent" in one place and "tragic" in another.

7. The article appeared in *Delo* and is reproduced in Tkachev, *Sochineniya*, I, 325–69. The quotation is on pp. 47–49 of the same volume in Kozmin's Introduction.

8. See above, pp. 51–52.

9. Tkachev, *Sochineniya*, III, 491–92. This Tkachev article, entitled "Teach the People or Be Taught by the People," was evidently evoked in part by L. N. Tolstoy's *Letters to the Fatherland*, which had appeared in 1874. Tolstoy had maintained that sufficient education of the people would consist of teaching enough grammar for them to read Orthodox Church texts. Also, if Tkachev thought that the oppressed toilers could not themselves become conscious of the means to liberate themselves and to build the new order, he could scarcely sympathize—and in fact did not—with Marx's *Communist Manifesto* or the tactics of the First International. Tkachev's own views on the nature of the class struggle, his rejection of the Hegelian dialectic and orthodox economic determinism caused a clash between him and the Marxists. See discussion below, pp. 118–24.

10. From "A Letter to the Editorial Board of *Vpered!*" (1874) in Tkachev, *Sochineniya*, III, 65. For Tkachev, the "formal" and "efficient" causes of revolution are the radical intelligentsia—i.e., they impart the form to and guidance of the struggle, while the "material cause" is the stuff of revolution, the inchoate masses.

11. *Ibid.*, III, 64.

12. *Ibid.*, I, 51.

13. Kozmin has pointed out: "Tkachev assigned to the [Russian] peasantry *an essentially passive* role while the active role went to the revolutionary minority (B. P. Kozmin, "Ocherki po istorii ratsionalizma," *Literaturnoye nasledstvo* [1933], No. 7–8 [1933], p. 116. Lenin, it will be recalled, in *Leftwing Communism—an Infantile Disease,* asserted that the indifference of the masses toward revolution *could* be one of the sufficient conditions for preparing to carry out the *coup d'état.* See below, pp. 77, 93–94.

14. Tkachev, *Sochineniya*, I, 49, where Tkachev employs the term *sotsialisticheskoye mirosotsertsaniye.*

15. *Ibid.*, I, 51. Tkachev described the modest *raznochinets* background of most of the young socialist revolutionaries of the type he idealized as follows: "A majority of them are the offspring of proletarian parents, or people who are not very far removed from being proletarians. . . . At each step they have felt their economic weakness and their independence. Just through the consciousness of their powerlessness, their inadequacy, and their dependence are they led to a feeling of dissatisfaction, hate, and protest" (*ibid.*, I, 71). Note here

the resemblance to Blanqui and Blanqui's very loose definition of "proletariat" (and Lenin's also) including in this category poor intellectuals and professional people ("unemployed lawyers," as Blanqui once expressed it), a condition which is "favorable for the development in their minds of a revolutionary outlook" unflawed by venality. A man of the revolutionary party (and Tkachev used the word party—*partiya*), Tkachev once wrote, "must be a politically inclined person, a man of the party who is absolutely unswerving, who holds steadily to the party banner and does not vacillate from one side to the other" (*Ibid.*, II, 5). A fuller exposition of Tkachev's basic theory of "force" and the "creative uses" to which it can be put is discussed above, pp. 78–85.

16. Compare Alfred de Grazia, *Politics and Government—The Elements of Political Science* (New York: Collier Books, 1962), I, 284; "The new forces of revolution cannot succeed without visible, organized, and permanent interests"; and p. 281, "The *coup d'état* is *part of all revolutions* and *exists also in a form sufficient in itself* to take over the government" (de Grazia's emphasis).

17. See *Kommunist*, No. 6 (1964), pp. 48–49, for the extensive use of such pejoratives and epithets. Similar articles have appeared throughout 1964–1967 in *Partiinaya zhizn'*, *Pravda*, *Izvestia*, and other Soviet publications in which these epithets are used to criticize the Chinese Communist leadership in Peking. In the *Kommunist* article, the CPSU ideologists have discovered Marx's rarely cited (in the USSR until recently) caveat that for certain countries like the U.S., England, or Holland, a "peaceful road to revolution" might prove possible (see text of Marx's statement in K. Marx and F. Engels, *Sochineniya* [2nd ed.; Moscow: Gosudarstvennoye Izdatel'stvo, 1928–1933], XVIII, 154).

18. Kozmin correctly rebukes a Soviet writer, I. A. Teodorovich, for having accused Tkachev of being contradictory on this point, that Tkachev had sometimes said seizure of power was possible without popular rebellion, at other times that it was not. Rather than falling into contradiction, Kozmin maintains, Tkachev had quite clearly emphasized that past and future revolutions were possible only when at least two conditions were present: 1) weakness or chaos within the government apparatus; 2) popular disaffection becoming overt in the presence of the powerless forces of the ruling circles (Tkachev, *Sochineniya*, I, 48, footnote by Kozmin).

19. See the discussion on this point in Alan B. Spitzer, *The Revolutionary Theories of Louis Auguste Blanqui* (New York: Columbia University Press, 1957), where Spitzer quotes Blanqui as follows: "If we seize power by an audacious *coup de main*, like robbers in the shadows of the night, who will answer for the duration of our power?" (Spitzer, *op. cit.*, p. 146). Venturi adds this footnote (*op. cit.*, p. 778): "It ought not to be forgotten that Tkachev himself on one occasion attributed the origin of his ideas to Blanqui, even if only in general

terms. But this claim was made on an occasion when historical exactitude is not customary—a funeral oration on Blanqui's death." Venturi keenly and correctly notes that *"Tkachev was a Russian Jacobin before becoming an exiled Blanquist"* (Venturi, *op. cit.*, p. 403).

20. Tkachev, *Sochineniya*, I, 48.

21. Tkachev occasionally made favorable references to Machiavelli, Hobbes, and Spinoza.

22. Both may be found in Tkachev, *Sochineniya*, II, 5–68. They appeared originally in *Delo* in 1869.

23. *Ibid.*, II, 19–20. As we mentioned above, Tkachev made reference to Hobbes, but we do not know which works, if any, he had read.

24. For example, *Ibid.*, II, 24. Rousseau's fears about individualization of religion and his generally Erastian mood may be found in *Social Contract*, Book IV, chap. viii, "Civil Religion," in which he largely endorses Hobbes's approach to the problem.

25. *Ibid.*, II, 22.

26. *Ibid.*, II, 23–26.

27. *Ibid.*, II, 23–26. It has been said of Marx that he thought more like an encyclopedist of the eighteenth century than a philosopher of the nineteenth century, a century which was, near its close, more obsessed with relativism, flux, protoexistentialism, and psychologism than with the enthronement of reason and the universal application of science characteristic of the men of the Enlightenment. The same might be said of Tkachev. At the same time, of course, there was in the nineteenth century a strong admixture of the preceding century's devotion to reason and self-evident propositions (as in Comtean positivism), and the same elements are evident in much of Tkachev's thought.

28. Tkachev in another place predicted that after the coming of the secular millennium, people would grow to resemble and equal one another *physiologically*—an interesting secularization of the Augustinian idea that resurrected souls and bodies in the heavenly city would be at the peak of their perfection, equally beautiful and unspoiled.

29. Tkachev, *Sochineniya*, II, 51.

30. Venturi, *op. cit.*, p. 780 (a long footnote). Venturi's source is Boris Nicolaevsky, *op. cit.*, p. 62.

31. Tkachev, quoted in Kozmin, "Ocherki po istorii ratsionalizma," p. 123.

32. Tkachev, *Sochineniya*, II, 65–66.

33. In the sense that Spinoza is keenly aware of the close association between effective supreme power of the state and its possession of the requisite force to make law effective. ("The soul and mind of the sovereign authority have as much right as that authority has power.")

Spinoza also assigned "public lands and everything connected with them" to the authority of public law.

34. From a later work, "Revolution and State," by Tkachev, published in Nos. 2, 3 of *Nabat* (1876); reproduced in Tkachev, *Sochineniya*, III, 246–57. The quotation above is from pp. 250–51. According to Kozmin, Tkachev was referring to Lavrov and a brochure written by Lavrov entitled "Russian Social and Revolutionary Youth" (published in London in 1874 during Lavrov's residence there) in which Lavrov stated: "History shows and psychology convinces us that any unlimited power, any dictatorship, corrupts even the best people. Could it be possible that our revolutionary youth would agree to the accession to the throne of certain dictators who, even for the best intentions, would only become new sources of social evils and who more likely than not would not be the dedicated fanatics as much as the passionately ambitious men who thirst for power for the sake of power?" (This is quoted in Tkachev, *Sochineniya*, III, 466, as a Kozmin-edited footnote.) Lenin and Trotsky and other Bolsheviks in 1917 compared themselves to the Jacobins of revolutionary France. Among the Bolsheviks the name Robespierre had no derogatory connotation.

35. From Tkachev's "Letter to the Editor of the journal *Forward!*" *Ibid.*, III, 69.

36. *Ibid.*, III, 244; from an article written by Tkachev for *Nabat* in 1876 entitled "Our Illusions." The word *illuzii* appears often in Tkachev writings. More will be said below of "centers of power."

37. From Tkachev's letter to Engels (discussed separately below, pp. 113–18), *Sochineniya*, III, 88–98. Quotation on p. 92.

38. While Lenin advised the Second International to strike at imperialism at its weakest links (where political power was weak), Tkachev advised Russian revolutionaries to strike at Tsarism when its political force was at its weakest.

39. Tkachev, *Sochineniya*, III, 84.

40. *Ibid.*, III, 74. Tkachev often used the term "army" to describe the organization and discipline of revolutionary forces of the type he recommended. Even today—to cite one of many examples, in the slogans for the forty-sixth anniversary of the Bolshevik Revolution published in *Pravda*, 1963—the term army is used to describe communist-led revolutionary forces.

41. *Ibid.*, III, 286, in the 1868 *Delo* article, "Rising Forces."

42. *Ibid.*, I, from Kozmin's Introduction. Kozmin notes that Tkachev's recommendations for a disciplined, centralized revolutionary organization was "of enormous historical service" (p. 52).

43. Alfred Meyer (*Leninism* [New York: Frederick A. Praeger, 1962]) is one of the few authors dealing with Leninism and communism to probe deeply into Lenin's elaboration of the Marxist (and Tkachevist) theories of class consciousness and the purest form of this consciousness in the minds of intellectuals (this point is driven

home by Lenin in his *What Is To Be Done?*). See Meyer, pp. 28–36.
Lenin pointed out in *What Is To Be Done?*: "It is neither very easy
or imperative to bring workers up to the level of the intellectuals."
And, "The theoretical doctrine of Social-Democracy arose quite independently of the spontaneous development of the workers' movement.
It arose as the natural and inevitable outcome of the development of
ideas in the revolutionary socialist intelligentsia." Also, "The ignorant worker is unable to recognize his enemies." Tkachev: "The uncivilized crowd is too crude and ignorant to discern knowingly the
causes of its hard pressed condition and to find the means of its
amelioration." As we shall see later, Tkachev says that the masses,
when left to their own devices, will develop only petty-bourgeois and
peasant private-property-mindedness, a development which Tkachev
observed in his own day; Lenin added the gloss that the ignorant
worker, when left to his own devices, develops "spontaneously" only
"trade-union consciousness," or the materialistic pursuit for more
money represented by the political doctrine of Economism. The positions of Tkachev and Lenin are both vaguely reminiscent of Plato's
scorn for the followers of Pericles, a demagogic leader, according to
Plato, who played upon man's appetitive nature (cf. *Gorgias*, 515)
instead of seeking to improve men's souls.

44. Tkachev, *Sochineniya*, V, 441–42, from an article entitled
"Preface and Notes to Ernest Becher's book, 'The Worker's Question
at the Present Time and the Means to Its Solution,'" published in
Delo, No. 7 (1869).

45. Tkachev's own catechism (evidently predating Nechayev's
more famous one) appeared in *Delo*, Nos. 4, 5 (1868) reprinted in
Sochineniya, I, 173–233, "The People of the Future and the Heroes of
the Petty Bourgeoisie." Lenin too was fond of catechistic injunc-
tions, having once described Ya. M. Sverdlov as a "brilliant example of
a professional revolutionary, a man who had wholly broken away from
his family, from all feelings and conventions of the old bourgeois society, . . . a man completely and unwaveringly devoted to the Cause of
revolution and who for many years . . . forged in himself those qualities which have hardened revolutionaries for many years" (Lenin,
Sochineniya [3rd ed.; Moscow-Leningrad: Gosudarstvennoye Izdatel'-
stvo, 1932], XXIV, 80). See also Sophie Perovskaya's *Memoirs* and
Lenin's *One Step Forward and Two Steps Backward* and *What Is To
Be Done?* for examples of Lenin's sense of catechism.

46. Tkachev, *Sochineniya*, III, 84–85, from "Tasks of Revolutionary Propaganda in Russia" (1874). The words "propaganda" and "agitation" were used frequently by Tkachev and the distinction between
them drawn carefully by him. Centuries earlier, the word propaganda
had been used by the Roman Catholic Church (*propagandum*) in the
sense of propagation of the faith. Pope Urban VIII (1623–1644) established the College of Propaganda to educate priests in the faith to
prepare them for missions. Note in the Tkachev quotation how he

construes propaganda to mean the totality of revolutionary principles while agitation has the more immediate, opportunistic use of employing any means to incite the people.

47. *Ibid.*, III, 75–76. Tkachev coined a Soviet-sounding name for his revolutionary agitators, *bortsi-agitatori* (fighting agitators).

48. *Ibid.*, III, 78. In a footnote in his letter to Lavrov, Tkachev asserted: "I am speaking only for myself, since your other co-workers on *Vpered!* have refused those rights which I have demanded both of them and myself." An example of Tkachev's jibes directed occasionally at Lavrov in his letter is the following: "I forgot to mention that in personal conversations with me about this [about who is suited for membership in revolutionary circles] you made an important concession to me. You agreed with me that revolutionary action should not be denied to anyone, that anyone so wishing would be able to, and indeed should, participate in revolutionary action. This was very kind of you. But, pardon me if I say that I don't believe in it now. The fact is that it runs absolutely counter to one of the points in your program" (*Ibid.*, III, 75).

49. *Ibid.*, III, 74.

50. *Ibid.*, III, 66. The word "opportunism" was, as far as we know, not employed by Tkachev as it was later by the Bolshevik pamphleteers to condemn gradualism, formal democracy, autonomy of revolutionary organizations, etc. Many of Tkachev's other pejoratives and epithets *did* reappear later in Bolshevik literature—e.g., reactionary, philistine, petty-bourgeois, cretin, renegade, Judas, compromiser (close to the Bolshevik "opportunist"), legalism (resembling Trotsky's and Lenin's "formal democracy"), spontaneity, etc. The reader has undoubtedly noticed other terms coined or borrowed by Tkachev which reappeared in post-1917 Soviet ideology: permanent revolution, constructive phase of the revolution, kulaks, propaganda and agitation, collective dictatorship, state of the workers, revolutionary party, *et al.*

51. Compare Kozmin, *P. N. Tkachev*, p. 105.

52. Tkachev, *Sochineniya*, III, 458, in a footnote by Kozmin.

53. *Ibid.*, II, 40.

54. *Ibid.*, III, 401–402. The term "workers' state" is quoted by Kozmin, *P. N. Tkachev*, p. 105.

55. *Ibid.*, p. 265.

56. Tkachev, *Sochineniya*, I, 47–49. A fuller exposition of Tkachev's attitude toward the masses may be found above, pp. 00–00. Venturi (*op. cit.*, pp. 419–20) points out that just at the time of the seizure of power by the socialist conspirators, it would be necessary, according to a passage from Tkachev, to summon a National Assembly (*Narodnaya Duma*) which would then sanction (or be obliged to sanction) the impending actions of the permanently-revolutionary state which "must rely strongly upon propaganda" (*Sochineniya*, III, 226). An immediate task facing the dictatorship, Tkachev adds, is "learning

how to keep power and using it to carry out the socialist program, a program which must above all be expressed in clear, strictly defined, and consistent form. . . . Otherwise the dictatorship will destroy itself by its own contradictions and inconsistency" (*Ibid.*, III, 227).

57. *Ibid.*, I, 174.

58. By his conception of permanent revolution, Tkachev has strikingly antedated Trotsky's formula of the same name by some thirty-five years. He describes his postrevolutionary state in various ways: e.g., authoritarian-dictatorial (*avtoritarno-diktatorskoye*); revolutionary (*revolyutsionnoye*); permanently-revolutionary (*postoyanno-revolyutsionnoye*).

59. Tkachev, *Sochineniya*, III, 266, from "Rising Forces."

60. *Ibid.*, III, 267. This "formula" is best explained by Tkachev in the quoted article, "The People and Revolution," written for *Nabat* in 1876.

61. *Ibid.*, III, 266. Bakunin in his later period thought that the Jacobin approach would bring a counterreaction by bourgeois elements among the numerous peasantry. "Every act of official authority," Bakunin wrote of postrevolutionary authoritarianism, "necessarily awakens within the masses a rebellious feeling, a legitimate counterreaction." G. P. Maximov (ed.), *The Political Philosophy of Bakunin* (Glencoe: The Free Press, 1953), p. 398 (from "Letters to a Frenchman"). Tkachev is clearly aware of the problem of popular inertia after the socialist revolution. He makes a formulation of citizens' duty toward the state which as a Soviet historian has observed, amounts to the stricture: "He who does not toil, shall not eat" (Kozmin, *P. N. Tkachev*, p. 113). See also n. 68 in this chapter below and quotations, pp. 92, 96–97.

62. Tkachev, *Sochineniya*, III, 263.

63. *Ibid.*, III, 263, 265.

64. *Ibid.*, III, 263. The concept of a *preemptive* revolution—a revolution which stops the drift toward an increasingly entrenched and consolidated bourgeoisie—anticipated a similar Leninist idea that to wait meant to make socialist revolution all the more difficult, if not impossible.

65. Tkachev himself uses the metaphor of the crossroads and road signs in *ibid.*, III, 263.

66. Tkachev quoted by Kozmin, in his Introduction, *ibid.*, I, 53.

67. *Ibid.*, III, 254.

68. *Ibid.*, III, 263. "For your logic to be consistent," Tkachev wrote of the anarchists' position as he understood it, "you must abhor the power of the state as well as the authority over man's spirit—that is, you must inscribe on your banner that well-known bourgeois principle of political economy and market-place morality: *laissez faire, laissez*

aller, and then from your Olympian heights, look upon postrevolutionary chaos" (*Ibid.*, III, 254). It is interesting to find that when the Bakuninists criticized what they called Jacobinism of the Tkachevist type, they too, like *their* critics, used the epithet "bourgeois" to describe Jacobinism. Bakunin wrote: "Labor financed by the state—such is the fundamental principle of authoritarian Communism, of State Socialism. The State, having become the sole proprietor . . . , becomes the sole capitalist, and the distributor of its profits. . . . We should ruthlessly eliminate the politics of both bourgeois democrats and bourgeois Socialists [whose] . . . baneful theories can end *only with the workers being used once more as an instrument against themselves and being turned over again to bourgeois exploitation*" (Bakunin, *op. cit.*, pp. 293–94). Foreshadowing of Michels and Djilas!

69. Tkachev, *Sochineniya*, III, 256.

70. *Ibid.*, III, 257.

71. *Ibid.*, III, 257, where we find *kollektivnaya diktatura*.

72. *Ibid.*, III, 353, 355 ff. Tkachev makes an interesting anticipation of the later spirit of "Workers' Opposition" within his postrevolutionary workers' state. Socialist ideals, he writes, "will inevitably meet opposition from these same 'toiling masses'" (*Ibid.*, III, 371). The socialist-intelligentsia minority, he says in several places, frequently finds itself at odds with the majority of the population, which is basically, instinctively conservative. This is true of the working class, either of the city or village.

73. *Ibid.*, III, 350.

74. Tkachev's point is best summed up in his "Revolution and the National Principle," *Ibid.*, III, 405–24, from *Nabat*, 1878 (without issue number).

75. *Ibid.*, III, 421–22.

76. *Ibid.*, III, 424.

77. *Ibid.*, III, 424.

78. *Ibid.*, II, 41. Much of Tkachev's observations of organized political life took place in France. Thus, Tkachev seemed to reflect the mass-movement point of view as far as political parties were concerned. He ignored the two-party systems of either England or America, systems where, as Arendt points out (*On Revolution* [New York: Viking Press, 1963], pp. 273–74), "conditions of mass society do *not* lead to the formation of mass movements [or distrust of the prevailing representation in parliament]." He can conceive of no political party standing outside some specific economic or social interest; this in turn seems to lead him to the one-party concept, a route which is traversed not only in theory (see, for example, Maurice Duverger, *Political Parties, Their Organization and Activity in the Modern State* [New York: John Wiley & Sons, Inc., 1961], p. 419 *passim*) but also in practice—in the French Revolution, for example, the journey from multiparty rule to the dictatorship of Robespierre. Tkachev seems to

be cognizant only of the two extremes—multiparty rule on the one hand (which he calls *"poliarkhiya"*) and one-party rule on the other (which, when evil, is the dictatorship of the wealthy; when good, the socialist dictatorship).

79. Tkachev, *Sochineniya*, I, 54–55, from Kozmin's Introduction. The polemic against Engels is discussed below, pp. 113–18.

80. It is interesting to note the adjectives Tkachev uses to describe bourgeois society and the bourgeois state: it is, he wrote, inefficient, disharmonious, inequalitarian, chaotic, unjust, antagonistic, puffed up with pride and egotism, unenlightened (as a whole), rife with unhappiness, in which children are brought up brutishly, and so on. The opposite of all this would appear to resemble the Christian millennium.

81. Quoted in Kozmin, Introduction to Tkachev, *Sochineniya*, I, 19.

CHAPTER V

Tkachev's Sociology, Economics, and Psychology

There is, of course, an obvious interrelationship between Tkachev's views on politics, revolution, and the state and his social philosophy. An examination of his writings shows, however, that Tkachev's main interest lay in politics and revolution; his political philosophy determined—or predetermined—his outlook in almost every other field. This is true for the following reasons: (1) Tkachev places the strongest emphasis on and devotes most of his intellectual resources to describing the commanding position of politics over economics, over society and over the unregenerate psychology of the masses—in fact, to delineating the transcendent importance of politics in the whole life of a nation before, during, and after revolution; (2) Tkachev's somewhat superficial or biased treatment of ascendant-types of social philosophies and the subjectivist and democratic sociologies of Lavrov and Mikhailovsky, and also the criterion he used to test all social philosophies (are they useful to the political-revolutionary cause?) tend to politicize his total philosophy; (3) perhaps his own academic background as a student of law tended to stimulate a somewhat exaggerated respect for the omnipotence and efficacy of law, especially positive public law, and the wonders of reform which it could work from above for society below.[1]

At the same time, it would be a mistake to slight Tkachev's social philosophy or his overall sociological and psychological outlook. Concepts in these fields strongly influence many of his political ideas, as will become obvious from reading the succeeding parts of this chapter.

RUSSIAN SOCIETY: SPECIAL CASE

It is perhaps appropriate to begin a description of Tkachev's views on society and culture with an exposition of his treatment of Russia as a special revolutionary case. In proposing a special revolutionary road for Russia, Tkachev found himself at odds with what he considered to be the "untutored" views and "metaphysical" historiography of Marx and Engels. It was with the latter that Tkachev carried on open polemics. The polemics reveal a good deal of Tkachev's ideas on such Russian institutions as the *obshchina*, Russian rural life, the psychology of the Russian masses, as well as Tkachev's philosophy of history which he said was unlike the dialectical theory of Marx and Engels.

Tkachev began his "Open Letter to *Gospodin* Friedrich Engels":

You must be well aware of the fact that we Russians were the first to extend a brotherly hand to the great association of West European workers and that we have taken a most active part in its work, more active, in fact, than our own interests may have demanded. But, unfortunately, you have not been able to understand that, although we are in full accord with the basic socialist principles of a European worker's party, we are not in agreement on tactics and never will be or should be (at least with the faction in the movement headed by Messrs. Marx and Engels) in unison [*solidarni*] on questions concerning exclusively practical realization of principle and the revolutionary struggle in the name of socialism. The situation in our country is totally exceptional. It has nothing in common with the situation in any country of Western Europe. The means for struggle suitable to the latter are, at the very least, unsuitable in the extreme for our country. We need a completely special revolutionary program which is unlike the German program insofar as the social and political conditions existing in Germany differ from those in Russia. It would be just as absurd for the German program to proceed from the conditions existing in Russia as it would be for the Russian program to proceed from the conditions existing in Germany (from the standpoint of the social conditions of the German nation). You do not understand this; you cannot accept the Russian point of view; and yet you take it upon yourself to issue indictments against us and give us advice?

If it were not for the fact that all your wisdom and naïveté were directed to the discrediting of the Russian revolutionary *émigrés* and for the fact that the German public might believe in your facts, I would not bother you with my letter. But, unfortunately, such is the case. Therefore, I consider it my responsibility to come to the aid of your naïveté and somewhat restrain your self-assuredness.[2]

Much of the disagreement with Engels revolved about the question of the *obshchina*, the nature of Russian society as Tkachev understood it, and the way in which Tkachev viewed bourgeois progress in his largely nondeterministic view of history (Tkachev completely rejected Hegelianism, for example). Not a little confusion was introduced into the controversy by what appears to have been at times a confusion of identity, Engels mistaking Tkachev for a Bakuninist, a possibility that is sometimes overlooked in the small amount of literature available on the Tkachev-Engels correspondence.[3]

Tkachev was *not* guilty, as Engels evidently thought, of romanticizing the Russian *obshchina*. Quite the contrary. In his earlier years, Tkachev in fact had shown contempt for the Haxthausen-inspired and Slavophil adoration of the *mir*.[4] The "virgin" *mir*, Tkachev often pointed out, had long since ceased to be virgin and had begun, in fact, to take the road of bourgeoisation. He backed up this fear with large doses of statistical data, as Lenin was to do later in attempting to prove the spread of proletarianization in Russia. Tkachev's investigations led him to the conclusion that bourgeois phenomena of private property, exploitation of labor, growing inequality of wealth, and so on were becoming increasingly evident in Russia. If they were allowed to continue, the reconstruction of Russian society along socialist lines would be much harder to accomplish, if not altogether impossible. Moreover, Tkachev added, as bourgeois progress continued in Russia, powerful—more powerful than hitherto—weapons for oppressing the masses, under the aegis of the new bourgeois class, would come into the mighty hands of the bourgeois state. The Tsarist state, Tkachev wrote, has a tendency today "to hang in the air," but it will surely send down roots into the economic life of the country if the bourgeois state is permitted to come into existence and carry out bourgeois progress under its supervision.[5] Thus arises the need for a pre-emptive revolution before bourgeois development is allowed to proceed much further. The petty-bourgeois peasantry should be regarded as a reactionary element; especially under Russian conditions:

> Small, parceled property in land—that is the logical demand, the economic basis for bourgeois society. . . . Along with the aristocracy of the land and the factory aristocracy, this kind of property creates masses of restive village proletarians [N.B.!— A. L. W.].[6] Such volcanic soil is difficult for the bourgeois. It's best for the bourgeois to rely in all respects on the mass of petty peasant proprietors . . . that is, the cretinized, or to put it more delicately, conservative peasantry. With this kind of support among the petty peasantry, the hundreds of thousands of village proletarians need represent no danger . . . ; the bourgeoisie will always be able to hitch on to a Napoleon [a Napoleon III—A. L. W.] who will study the situation and support the cretinized peasantry who can continue unabated their control over the tranquil crowd of hungry people.[7]

This spreading bourgeoisation in the peasantry, if allowed to continue—and a bourgeois-style revolution would only accelerate the process—threatened to engulf the Russian *obshchina*, which despite all its faults, Tkachev regarded as a starting point for a socialist revolution in peasant Russia. The Russian peasants, Tkachev wrote to Engels in his famous letter, "if one can put it this way, are communist by instinct, by tradition." Tkachev continues:

> The idea of collective property is as deeply entrenched in the total world outside of the Russian peo-

ple that now, when the government is beginning to realize that this principle is incompatible with the so-called "welfare society" in whose name the peasants are supposed to be led to the awareness of private property, it will be able to make the people accept bourgeois property only by way of bayonets and whips.

From all of this, it is clear that our people, despite their naïveté, stand immeasurably closer to socialism than the peoples of Western Europe, although the latter are better educated than the people of Russia. . . .

We may therefore term the Russian people instinctively revolutionary despite its seeming apathy and the absence of consciousness of what it is doing.

Our intelligentsia-revolutionary party is quantitatively small, this is true. But it possesses no other than socialist ideas.[8]

Engels, both in his initial article, which stirred Tkachev to write his open letter, and in his reply to Tkachev's letter insisted that Tkachev was unduly exaggerating the role of the Russian peasant commune:

The Russian village commune has existed for centuries without having ever produced any stimulus to develop out of itself a higher form of communal property. . . . The initiative for such a possible transformation of the Russian village commune can only originate, not in the communes themselves, but solely in the industrial proletariat of the West. The victory of the Western European proletariat over the bourgeoisie and the corresponding replacement of capitalist production by the socially directed production—this is the necessary precondition for raising Russian village community to the same level.

Agrarian communism, in fact, a derivative of gentile society, has never developed anywhere by its own forces anything but its own disintegration. The Russian village commune itself was already in 1861 a relatively weakened form of this communism.[9]

Engels, later in his 1894 article, begins an important *qualification* in his theory that a proletarian revolution in the West must precede any significant change in Russian society, revitalization of the commune, etc.:

> On the other hand, it is not only possible but certain that after the victory of the proletariat and the transfer of the means of production to common ownership among Western European people, the countries which have just entered the state of capitalistic production and have still preserved will derive from the remnants of communal ownership and the corresponding folkways a powerful means for appreciably shortening their process of development to a socialist society and of escaping most of the suffering and struggle through which we in Western Europe have had to labor. But in this process the example and the active support of the formerly capitalistic West is an unavoidable prerequisite. . . . It will be relatively easiest for Russia [among countries in the precapitalist phase of development] because here a part of the indigenous population has already acquired the intellectual achievements of capitalistic development and it will thus be possible here, in a revolutionary period, to accomplish the social transformation almost simultaneously with the West.[10]

Marx himself had written the following to Zasulich in 1881:

> The special study that I have made [of the Russian peasant commune] from original sources has convinced me that this commune is the strategic point for the social regeneration of Russia.[11]

Further, in his letter to N. K. Mikhailovsky in 1877, Marx criticizes an overzealous Russian Marxist who, it appears, was performing a Plekhanov-like interpretation of Marx's historical materialism so that for this Russian:

> . . . it is absolutely necessary to change my sketch of the origin of capitalism in Western Europe into an historico-philosophical theory of Universal Progress, fatally imposed on all peoples, regardless of the historical conditions in which they find themselves, ending finally in that economic system which assures both the greatest amount of productive power of social

labor and the fullest development of man. This is to do me too much honor and too much discredit.[12]

Marx warns in the same letter that "if Russia continues to move in the path followed up to 1861, it will lose the finest occasion that history has ever offered a people not to undergo all the sudden turns of fortune of the capitalist system."[13]

All this was to a greater or lesser degree in tune with Tkachev's ideas. And yet, a polemic did take place between Tkachev and Engels. It appears that a good deal of the opposition between Engels and Tkachev was motivated by the complex politics of the First International more than by basic, ideological differences, although differences there were. Indeed, grounds existed for a much more profound disagreement between Marx and Engels on one side and Tkachev on the other than the issue of the precise role to be played by the Russian *obshchina*. This fundamental difference revolved about Tkachev's rejection of the Marx-Engels logic of dialectic as applied to history, although this issue was never debated with them by Tkachev.

TKACHEV SUBSTITUTES *SKACHOK* FOR THE RIGIDITY OF DIALECTIC

Tkachev's differences with the European Marxists, besides being based on a dispute over the proper tactics for Russia, were also derived in part from differences of a more profound variety. Tkachev, in fact, rejected the dialectical-materialistic description of historical progress which in attribution to the European Marxists, he condemned as a Hegelian, metaphysical perversion of socialism.

As much as their views differed sharply in other respects, Lavrov and Bakunin both agreed essentially that the social regeneration of Russia must largely proceed from below, from the popular masses. For Lavrov this involved the transfer to and assimilation by the people of "the moral ideal of socialism" through the *commune* and the *artel'*; for Bakunin, socialism must arise from below, out of the revolutionary creativity of the popular masses.[14]

Lavrov and Bakunin traversed only one of the roads that led from the milestones of frustration represented by the years

1848, 1855, and 1863—the road of continued hope placed in the people and their instinct and courage to make a revolution. A second road, however, led in an antidemocratic direction. The frustration of social revolution either before or after the emancipation of the peasants destroyed a second group's confidence in the Russian people and their willingness or capability to make the revolution and bring about the social regeneration of Russia. While Lavrov and Bakunin traveled the first road, the second group, composed of Tkachev and Russian Jacobins before and after him, had shown little confidence in what Tkachev sarcastically termed "God-the-People." Tkachev once wrote of the Russian people:

> The average representative of the people is a dispassionate person; this is particularly true of the Russian people. Slave-like impulses have been encouraged in the Russians by centuries' old slavery. Secretiveness, untruthworthiness, servility . . . have all served to atrophy the energy of the Russian people. They are phlegmatic by nature. It is impossible to place any hope in their enthusiasm. Their stoical passivity is like the encrusted shell of a snail.[15]

The late Cuban revolutionary, Ernesto (Che) Guevara, who was slain by army troops not far from the Bolivian capital in October 1967, had written in his diary: "They [the Bolivian peasants] are as impervious as stones; when you talk to them it is as if in the depth of their eyes they were mocking you."

Tkachev's reaction to the many failures to realize a popular revolution in Russia, when combined with his elitist Pisarevism, is illustrated by the Jacobinism of his teachings on revolutionary tactics. Authority for making the revolution and assuring that it would be carried out under the proper form and with the proper socialist goals must rest, Tkachev often emphasized, in the socialist intelligentsia and professional revolutionaries, not the people. Thus, Tkachev's revolutionism is deeply imbued with what might be called "voluntarism"—the emphasis upon the conscious actors and movers of history—intelligent leaders—rather than upon gradual impersonal forces of history on the one hand or the spontaneous movement originating in the popular grassroots on the other. Tkachev was just as contemptuous of historical determinism as he was of democratic romanticism both of which he called reactionary.

The elements of the writings of Marx and Engels which most impressed Tkachev, according to his own admission, were *not* those of a Hegelian nature. He scorned dialectical materialism and historical materialism with its assumption, at least in one possible interpretation of Marx's and Engels' writings, that a capitalist stage would *necessarily* have to be passed through before the proletariat and, indeed, all society would be prepared economically and socially to move to the higher phase of socialism. Of course, Marx and especially Engels, introduced various qualifications into their theory of the deterministic process of history, but not enough qualifications apparently to convince Plekhanov, for example, that Russia could voluntaristically bypass the bourgeois social and economic phase, although Plekhanov did toy with the idea of shortening the necessary bourgeois phase (a qualification later elaborated by Lenin).[16] Thus, Tkachev would have nothing of the Hegelian element in Marxism. He was in any case unsuited temperamentally to the essentially conservative, patient, scholarly spirit which permeated much of the thought of Hegel. Tkachev would have perhaps agreed with Marx that philosophers have talked enough about the world; it is now time to change it.

For Tkachev, the owl of Minerva flies at dawn, not at dusk. "Only when criticism and knowledge are in the very heat of the battle, when they create history, only then will they be accompanied by effects flowing from the real interests of people."[17] Of Hegel, Tkachev once wrote: "We have not the slightest reason, not a single rational basis for embracing Hegelian philosophy. . . . It is so much nonsense."[18]

Tkachev introduced his own position on the question of voluntarism vs. determinism in history in the following manner:

> Although a person and personal actions play an extremely important role in these historic metamorphoses, which are called historical progress, and although personal actions may destroy that which has existed for centuries, and lay out a new road for the future development of mankind—despite all this, personal action must be based upon certain real social

elements. It must find support and justification in the
given conditions of the economic life of the people.
Without this support and without this firm soil under
its feet, it is completely powerless and whatever personal action is carried out will only become ephemeral
having only transient importance. . . . Nobody takes
issue with this basic truth at the present time and
soon it will be copied into children's notebooks.[19]

From this, it would seem that Tkachev came close to Engels'
interaction concept, or at least does not go all the way over to
voluntarism, occupying a middle position between economic determinism in history and what Tkachev calls "personal action."
However, Tkachev admitted qualification of the theory that economic conditions are determinant; the "New Principle" of a
new order may permit transcending given economic conditions:

Sixteenth-century Germany saw movements of
two types—first, a purely democratic and peasant war;
second, a purely bourgeois uprising in the cities. The
first could have counted on success; the second was
doomed to failure . . . it would seem that we have
been inconsistent and are defending a paradox. In one
case, we indicate the possibility of historical jumps
while in the other we are basing ourselves on gradualism in historical development. . . . If a historical
leap is possible in the first case, why not in the second?
This is why: The peasantry was struggling for a
change in the very principle underlying its given social
order; while the bourgeoisie was leaving the principle
intact, being concerned simply about the acceleration
of some of its logical consequences. But insofar as the
first was possible, the second was impossible. Every
given economic principle embodied in a given social
order develops according to the laws of its own logic
and to change these laws is just as impossible as changing the law of human cognition, the laws of our physiological and psychological control centers. In the
sphere of logical thought, it is impossible to go from
one premise to the next skipping the middle premise.
It is exactly the same with a given economic principle
in a given social order—it is impossible to skip over
intermediate stages going directly from the first to the
last stage. Anyone who would try to accomplish this

kind of leap would be doomed to failure before he began; he would only exhaust his strength. . . . *But it is a completely different case if, in discarding the old principle of social order, he intends to replace it with a new one.* His aims will be crowned with success with extreme ease and his actions will have nothing whatever to do with utopianism. Thus, we come to a conclusion which appears to be an obvious paradox but actually is completely true, that those persons whose theories seem in most cases to be utopian are actually a good deal more practical than any of the most so-called farseeing statesmen. . . . The aims of the peasants were less utopian than the aims of the bourgeoisie.[20]

The *logical consistency* of the ideas on the one hand—as utopian as they may be reputed to be—and the *clarity of the purposes* for which they were to be put into action may assure their success, says Tkachev, *although an abrupt leap* (skachok) *might be necessary to put them into practice.* It is as though he were saying that the purpose or principle under which social change is to be guided by wise intellectual leaders is far more important and crucial—indeed determinant—than the inertia of the old order which is about to be replaced by a new one. Add to this idea Tkachev's psychological bent—"There is no greater torture than to carry around in one's head forever ideas which are not permitted to be put into practice,"[21]—and the amalgam contains a strong voluntaristic tendency. Tkachev, as might be expected, frequently pointed to outstanding figures in history, leaders who well understood what they were about or whose ideas were logical and essentially practical and purposeful. Failure often resulted, Tkachev said, from poor organization, inattention to the need for using force and violence, insufficient understanding of the Machiavellian principle of the ends-justifying-the-means,[22] or in some cases, purposelessness, weakness in the intellectual formulation of the "New Principle" which was to underlie the "New Order."[23]

Of course, Tkachev's preference for historical leaps over "sitting, arms folded, and waiting" was well-suited to the Russian situation as he understood it. Gradualism, under Russian conditions, meant that bourgeois development must go on, sink roots in Russian society, and eventually replace all the positive collectivistic elements in its national life with West European monopolism, encrusted bourgeois state, private farming, impossibility of revolution, individualism, and so on. Thus, the longer one waited, the worse Russian society would become from the standpoint of the suffering toilers, and the more remote, if not altogether impossible, revolution would become, the replacement of the old, illogical principle by the new, logical principle.

"The radical minority cannot wait for the people," Tkachev wrote; "the uncivilized crowd is too crude and ignorant to discern knowingly the causes of its hardpressed condition or to find the means of its amelioration." Meanwhile, "kulakization" was growing in the peasantry:

> Among the peasants, a class of kulaks [*kulaki*] is developing. They buy and lease out land which belongs to both the peasants and the gentry, and so constitute a sort of peasant aristocracy. The free mobility of the property in land from one owner to the other becomes easier with every passing day. The liberalization of agricultural credit and the spread of money transactions increase with each day. And so in Russia at this time, all the conditions are present for the formation, on the one hand, of a very strong, conservative class of peasants, landowners, and farmers; on the other hand, a bourgeoisie of money, trade, and industry—in fact, capitalists. As these classes come into being, the people's situation will become correspondingly worse, while the chances of success of a violent revolution will grow increasingly problematical. That is why we cannot wait. That is why we claim that in Russia a revolution is, in fact, indispensable, and indispensable for the present moment. Let us not allow any further postponement, any more delay. Now, or at the very least very soon—or . . . never. Circumstances are now acting in our favor. Within ten or twenty years, they will be acting against us. Isn't this clear? Don't you understand our true reason for making haste and for our impatience?[24]

If the leap (*skachok*) were not made soon, Tkachev wrote, the "village bourgeoisie" (*kulaki*) would become the natural allies of their bourgeois brothers in the cities. The result would be that the Tsarist state *might then sink roots* into the bourgeois class of town and country. Up to now, remarked Tkachev, the Tsarist state tended to "hang in the air," tended not to have social or economic roots.[25] Once the bourgeoisie and the force of the state had become a united front in Russia, the socialist-led revolution would be most difficult to effect.

It is perhaps not surprising to find that Tkachev was strongly opposed to spontaneity (*stikhiye*), as an example of reactionary theories of peaceful progress. Spontaneity, he said, is in fact all that the majority of the people are capable of; they are not equipped intellectually, like the radical socialist minority, with principles and direction. The people can be expected only to act spontaneously, "like a hurricane," when they are in a revolutionary mood; the people drift aimlessly and venally when they are not in a revolutionary mood.[26] Tkachev's view of the spontaneity and lack of knowledge of the overwhelming majority of the urban and village working class strikingly anticipates Lenin's similar concepts in his *What Is To Be Done?* Furthermore, like Tkachev before him, Lenin pointed out in his 1901–1902 work that only an enlightened minority of professional-revolutionary intellectuals, not the ignorant masses, could properly orient the coming revolution in its proper socialist direction. The latter, Lenin emphasized, were capable only of spontaneity and "trade-union consciousness"—meaning, as Lenin explained in *What Is To Be Done?* and later writings (in his attacks on Economism and Tailism), venal and acquisitive desires on the part of the toiler to make more money and imitate the bourgeois. It would be quite possible, Lenin indicated, even to find large numbers of workers assuming an *antirevolutionary posture* if they were permitted to fall under the spell of trade-unionism and Economism in the Social-Democratic program and tactics.

TWO TYPES OF PROGRESS—
NEGATIVE AND POSITIVE

Closely allied to his theory of the historical leap and his warnings against the spontaneous spread of bourgeois economic and social practices and institutions was Tkachev's own dialectic, or concept of progress as either negative or positive.

Tkachev viewed bourgeois progress—"development of the

principle of individualism, kulak agriculture, economic anarchy, heartless and greedy egoism"—as creating "new enemies and new social factors hostile to our cause with each passing day."[27] Far from viewing the spread of capitalism according to the gravedigger (you will bury yourselves) dialectic of the orthodox Marxists with its implicit or "chiliastic" optimism about the predestined future for socialism and the *Gotterdämmerung* for capitalism, Tkachev took a pessimistic view. As long as this type of bourgeois life developed, spread, and sunk roots in Russian life (or the life of any country), new complications and new opposition to the institution of socialism would be introduced. Adding to the reactionary influence of bourgeois social and economic progress, according to Tkachev, was the attitude toward this progress of various revolutionaries whom he called "reactionary advocates of peaceful progress." By reactionary revolutionism Tkachev frankly included the Marxists of the First International and the Lavrovists. They all simply misunderstood progress, said Tkachev. Economic progress, far from whetting the appetite for revolution or creating ever new opportunities for socialist revolution, "keeps alive and breathes new spirit into the dead and lifeless forms of our Tsarist state, giving them new strength and firmness which they have hitherto lacked."[28]

What, then, was *positive* progress? While negative progress could be summed up as drift, spontaneity, and revolutionary theories of peaceful progress, true positive progress consisted of subjective preparation for revolution, particularly by the socialist intelligentsia, and seizing upon those negative phenomena produced by negative, bourgeois progress and exploiting them at the proper revolutionary moment. Positive progress and positive revolutionism do not tolerate a posture of waiting —waiting for the people to become enlightened or for the majority of the population "to make up its mind."[29] The fate of Russia rested in the hands of the radical socialists; its fate can be determined if these revolutionaries know how to act and do act.

Paul Axelrod considered Tkachev's concept of the two types of progress to be as follows:

Tkachev's main point was that progress—having in mind, obviously, the progress of bourgeois society—

consisted in the increasing application of force hostile to the people. "Progress," he said, "strengthens enslavement that much more, sharpens the weapons of oppression, strengthens the ruling classes, and complicates the struggle against these classes."[30]

At the same time, Tkachev warned revolutionaries not to be intimidated (like the people) by the greater enslavement and "sharpened weapons" brought on by bourgeois progress:

> A revolutionary must know how to exploit and combine in a certain way all the elements of revolution developed by history . . . and developed thanks to the cowardice of the "preservationists" and the thoughtlessness of governments with their gendarmes and troops—thanks, finally, to the painstaking cultivators of retrogressive "peaceful progress" and their bourgeois science.[31]

Tkachev thus lumps in with other developers of revolutionary hatred the advocates of peaceful progress (*progressivisti*) ; they are in the same company with "exploiters, capitalists, landowners, priests, the police, bureaucrats, conservatives, [and] liberals."[32]

Tkachev ridicules those progressivists who regard any kind of progress as evidence of a change for the better.[33] Their argument, says Tkachev, is based on the assumption that as society develops in time it steadily improves itself. "Therefore, the progressivist is tranquil and self-satisfied. He is confident that everything happens for the best and that today is better than yesterday; tomorrow, better than today. At the same time he admits that 'the triumphant march of progress' is sometimes accompanied by slow-downs, stoppages, swervings off the main road, but he has no doubt that despite these aberrations, stops, and slow-downs, in the end progress will get back on the main road." For the progressivist, Tkachev continues, revolution is only a means for speeding up the process of improvement, not a means for changing the whole situation radically. This view inevitably recommends the spread of education, enlightenment, agitation, etc., among the people, but that is all. Force is not to be used; peaceful dissemination of truth is enough. Needless to say, Tkachev will have nothing to do with this concept of peaceful change through the spread of enlightenment. This brand of pseudorevolutionism, Tkachev answers, is:

> . . . a philosophy of compromise, a philosophy of progress which offers itself as revolution while being a philosophy which is harmful for the success of the revolutionary cause and is merely a philosophy of anarchy.[34]

It is strongly suggested in Tkachev's writings that Tkachev's jump theory (historical jumps instead of the slow-moving dialectic)[35] is closely tied in with the old Russian socialist idea (going back to Herzen) of skipping capitalism, with all its attending miseries, and passing directly into socialism, although not without a protracted period of dictatorial rule.[36] Thus, Tkachev's jump theory is the twin of his skip theory—the first an original idea, the second of some vintage in the Russian revolutionary spirit. To put it simply, the revolutionaries must execute the historical jump in order to bring about the pre-emptive skip to socialism.

This is a most interesting and important contribution, possibly one of those thought-provoking insights which so intrigued Lenin in his reading of Tkachev's works. Much follows from this core of the tandem jump-and-skip: the necessity for centralized revolutionary organization (how else can an historical jump be executed?); for firm, conscious direction of the post-revolutionary society toward the socialist ethos (how else can an old and evil concept be replaced by a new, truly progressive one?); for subordination of many other interests (national, private property, individualistic, etc.) to the commanding general interest of instituting socialism and the new altruistic principle (otherwise, the old idea and the old order may creep back in, a tendency mainly due to the conservative instincts of the masses).

Tkachev's prime-mover in history is the critically- and rationally-minded intelligentsia of radical socialists—or more specifically, of Tkachev-minded socialists, for many of his opponents also considered themselves to be as socialistic as he. Tkachev is voluntaristic, even "subjectivist," although he called himself an enemy of subjectivist literature and sociology.[37] As he once said: his party, his leaders with their socialist world outlook—all these can make Russia's destiny be whatever they choose it to be. It is clear why this kind of outlook found itself hostile to the Hegelian-Marxist dialectical approach, the latter gradualistic and reactionary.

These basically conflicting points of view have not ceased to afflict the communist branch of socialism since Tkachev's time—the Menshevik-Bolshevik split occurred along similar lines, as did the intra-CPSU(b) controversies in the 1920's and the Sino-Soviet conflict (at least as far as the ideological differences are concerned) of the present time. It is perhaps an affliction natural to *descendent* political systems—the holders of such extreme political power are beset with the crucial problem of how much to yield to the public, how much to pure ideological commitments. The absence of a viable democratic constitution and viable political expression from below leaves the highly centralized, absolutist government the task of gauging popular sentiment, the "popular will," etc., and consequently opens the way to serious error in making this allowance because of inaccurate measuring devices and the lack of institutionalized expression of public opinion, political heterodoxy, and the loyal opposition of the political outs. The capriciousness of intellectualistic constructs seems to be the price paid by theories which deny open-ended dialectics (whether of the Hegelian variety or not)—capriciousness which may prove far too expensive for whole countries to suffer in order to industrialize and spread culture and enlightenment to its masses.

ECONOMIC THEORIES

While he rejected what he called the "metaphysical" dialectic of Marxism, substituting for it his theory of historical jumps, Tkachev was sympathetic to Marxist historical materialism minus dialectic. The economic basis of society was, for Tkachev, extremely important; he was willing to accept the Marx-Engels formulation of the base-superstructure relationship between economics, politics, and culture. At the same time, Tkachev was not altogether successful in avoiding the paradox of holding onto a voluntaristic philosophy of historical progress and causation (in which he stressed the superstructure) together with a form of modified economic determinism (in which he stressed the base).

Man's ethical systems are mostly mere rationalizations for existing economic relations of a given society, Tkachev wrote. The same applies in general to political orders and law—they too are mostly rationalizations, outward forms, reflections of basic economic relations. Even science and art may function as a class science or a class art; all culture, in fact, may stem from or rationalize a given economic order. Tkachev wrote in an early article in *Delo:*

> All juridical and political phenomena represent in themselves nothing more than direct results of economic life. This juridical and political life is, so to speak, simply a mirror in which the economic life of a people is reflected.[38]

Tkachev's economic theory bore at this time, undoubtedly, the influence of Marx's *Zur Kritik der Politischen Oekonomie* (see n. 38, chap. V, p. 153).

Tkachev says that man, in apprehending this economic causation or determinism, should harness it for man's benefit; moreover, as we have seen, intervention by the state in the economic process—in fact, in society as a whole—can bring large-scale change, reform, regeneration of the old order.[39]

Economic relations between men in society, Tkachev wrote, tend to determine their ethics, art, science, and their political relations, but the particular bourgeois-capitalist economic determinism is not necessary. Its particular existence is not inevitable; Tkachev definitely does not accept any dialectical-materialistic scheme of historical determinism in the sense in which that scheme was interpreted later, for example, by George V. Plekhanov. Tkachev gives his own example—the breaking of dishes is caused by the law of gravity in a certain sense, but the dishes need not be broken because of the law of gravity. Like gravity, economic laws should be used positively, should be directed along lines different from the way these laws operate in the capitalist system. They can be harnessed in a new way only after profoundly changing the present bourgeois-capitalist political and social order—an admission on Tkachev's part that "economic *determinism*" is a somewhat exaggerated term to describe the way in which he considers economic law and the economic order to function. The manner in which Tkachev's voluntarism shunts aside nearly all kinds of scientific law in its path comes through in the following:

> Human reason, as the criterion of freedom, may bring about the flourishing of peace, love, and agreement among men, when the economic interests of these men—those principal springs, those prime-movers of all their thoughts and behavior—are arranged so as not to cause antagonism between men; when in their midst will be established full, indestructible solidarity. Accompanying the absence of this solidarity, egoistic reason, acting as the "highest criterion of human activity," will never be able to lead to the security of harmony, peace, love, and accord in human affairs and the unconditional reign of freedom.[40]

There are also several examples of Tkachev applying an economic-deterministic scheme to describe certain historical phenomena (e.g., the peasant wars in Germany), especially those events which superficially seem to be motivated by religion or some spiritual issue but which are truly motivated, Tkachev says, by economics.

Possibly through his reading of Adam Smith and J. S. Mill and from several other sources, Tkachev developed a point of view which seemed to be based on Marx and yet, as formulated by Tkachev, tended to be cast in utilitarian terms. Strictly speaking, he was not an avowed follower of Helvetius, Bentham, or Mill; in his criticisms of Mill, for example, he saw in utilitarian theories mere reflections and rationalizations of the capitalist economic base. And he attacked this capitalist influence in the strongest possible terms.[41] But when he was not preoccupied with the application of purely economic categories to the study of history or philosophy, Tkachev employed formulas which he appears to have gotten from Marx, but which he expressed in classical utilitarian terms. Moreover, instead of elaborating or improving on Marx, Tkachev seemed to be content to propagate what he called "the great *practical* importance" of economic materialism; such materialism, he emphasized, *"would concentrate the energy and activity* of those men who are sincerely devoted to social causes *on the truly essential points:* namely, the vital interests of the people. Economic materialism *would guarantee that they would gain the support of the most indispensable forces. . . .* It would be *a spur which would inspire direct action."*[42] One of the remarkable aspects of this statement about materialism is Tkachev's Machiavellian treatment of the *uses* to which ideology may be put—a somewhat cynical "exploiting of theory, not for the sake of whatever truth may be embodied in it as much as *for the political ends for which it can be used."*[43]

Another characteristic of Tkachev's economic theory is its emphasis upon egalitarianism, which constitutes an archaic element of the French Enlightenment;[44] Kozmin has speculated on Tkachev's possible acquaintance with the works of Buonarotti, which in turn reflect and record the theories of Babeuf.[45]

When it came to the economics of socialism, Tkachev did not display the same clarity as when he spoke of revolution or the revolutionary tactics necessary to bring about socialism. He only said that under the new order the "external law of supply and demand would cease to apply; a new measure would be substituted":

> It will be essential to find a new, more rational criterion for measuring the value of a unit of labor. But how will this be accomplished? How and with what can one measure the value of labor of each individual; at each separate moment? . . . The fact is that this problem can be solved more easily when the differences now existing between individuals will be reduced and when their equality, viewed from both the psychological and physical standpoint, becomes more absolute. The problem will be solved, the principle achieved, when everyone is unqualifiedly equal, when there are no differences between people which are based on intellect, morality, or physical appearance. Then, people will all have an exactly equal share in the returns of production and any special valuation of their work will become utterly superfluous. The reasons now given by reactionary economists for the existence of wages will vanish of themselves and with them the wages themselves.[46]

Equal sharing—possibly "to each according to his need"—would replace the classical capitalist system of value-determination through supply and demand, Tkachev said. Sometimes it appeared that Tkachev accepted the Marxian labor theory of value, as suggested in his criticism of the capitalist measure of value based on supply and demand:

> Under present economic conditions, the value of a given unit of labor is determined by merely external measures which have nothing to do with the intrinsic [*vnutrennemu*] value of the unit. The external measure is capricious and arbitrary—namely, supply and demand. Nothing is said in this connection about the fact that with this kind of evaluation wages are measured only in theory according to the real cost of labor whereas in actual fact wages are not measured this way and if they are, only to a very small degree.[47]

Determination of the wage bill, to a degree, is subject to workers' control. A general meeting of the members of a given producer's cooperative might determine what each would receive as a return on his labor.[48]

At the same time, in opting for a quasi- but not perfectly egalitarian society, Tkachev was cautious to qualify the equality in such a way as to *exclude* political or absolute legal equality (justice, Tkachev seemed to believe, must by its very nature be parceled out unequally, each receiving his due in a portion different from another)—excluding even perfect economic equality (unequal economic distribution must apply here also). Tkachev wrote:

> [Socialist equality] is not to be confused with political and legal or even economic equality. We are speaking of an organic, physiological equality brought about by the conditioning of education and the common living conditions.[49]

In another place, Tkachev spoke contemptuously of efforts to "level" society, "to create absolute equality and thereby paralyze and level [*uravnirovat'*] the struggle between human forces,"[50]—here, again, an anticipation of Stalinism. Obviously reverting to his basic theory of law and force, Tkachev seems to be attempting an amalgam between social Darwinism (competition between oppressive human forces leading to improvement) and socialism (bringing society closer to equality in both the material and spiritual sense). Whether such an amalgam is possible even in theory is open to doubt. It would seem, however, that Tkachev's theories led him to this dilemma, which he never appears to have resolved or even fully discussed.

An important element in Tkachev's approach to capitalism was his view that the antagonism imbedded in capitalist society (especially in the traditional capital vs. labor antagonism) was absolutely irreconcilable, given a capitalist social and economic order:

> The interest of the capitalist is diametrically opposed to that of the worker. Any sort of agreement between them is unthinkable. One will always aim at predominating over the other. At the present time, the interest of capital reigns supreme over that of the worker.[51]

In his concept of negative progress (see above, pp. 124–28), Tkachev rejects the "grave-digger" concept of Marx: that further economic progress under capitalist conditions necessarily speeds the process of the destruction of the capitalist order itself. On the contrary, said Tkachev, bourgeois progress *impedes* revolution. Meanwhile, until the socialist revolution and the postrevolutionary dictatorial state intervenes in the social and economic order, no reform measures, Proudhonist utopianism, etc., can bring any decisive change in the order. Peaceful, parliamentary solutions to problems which are impossible to solve by parliamentary or democratic means are merely ridiculous, Tkachev said. Speaking of reform under capitalism, Tkachev wrote:

> It is very, very sad, of course, that each step must be purchased at the cost of human blood, that each intelligent change in society must come crashing through under arms. . . . We think that the so-called road of peaceful reform and tranquil progress is one of the most impractical utopias ever thought up by man in order to soothe his conscience and to lull his intellect to sleep.[52]

Tkachev has nothing but contempt for liberal reformists of various stripes. Émile de Girardin (1806–1881), French journalist and liberal-conservative, was, according to Tkachev, a "bourgeois Utopian," whose philosophy was deceptive and reactionary.[53]

Not only was peaceful, parliamentary reform useless but also, wrote Tkachev, anticipating Lenin in his attack on the Economists, was the economic strike method of trade unions.[54] If, however, the strike could be transformed into a general political strike (a strike linked to political demands and containing revolutionary possibilities) and, by the breadth of its organized opposition to the capitalists and their political agents of the state, be transformed into a mighty revolutionary weapon, then the strike method would be useful.

TKACHEV'S USE OF ECONOMIC DETERMINISM

Tkachev's treatment of the problem of the unequal status of women in bourgeois society affords an example of how he employed his formulation of economic determinism. His principal writing on the question of women entitled "The Woman Question" was published in *Delo* in 1869. Besides the connection between capitalism and prostitution, hard conditions of labor, poverty, and illiteracy (not to mention commercialization of the family), Tkachev used his *Delo* article as a vehicle for explaining "the principle which has always remained true"—namely, the economic foundation and cause for various superstructural phenomena.

Speaking of this process in general, Tkachev wrote:

> I assert that all phenomena of a political, moral, or intellectual nature, in the last analysis, are the result of causal phenomena in the economic sphere and the "economic structure" of society, as expressed by Marx. The development and direction assumed by the economic bases of society are the condition for the development and direction assumed by political and social relations in general and make their mark on the intellectual process itself taking place in society—on its morals, on its social and political philosophies. Thus, in remaining true to this departure point[55] whenever I encounter a certain fact, some important event in the life of society, a theory of society, a moral princi-

ple or philosophy, I try above all to explain it in terms of the given economic relations, by various economic calculations and constructions. . . . This does not mean that I deny the historical importance of ideas or intellectual progress of all kinds. No, far from it. It is simply that I regard somewhat differently from the bards who argue for the limitless omnipotence of the human intellect the historical role played by ideas. An idea is always an embodiment, a reflection if you wish, of a certain economic interest; before the idea existed, there was a prior economic interest which gave rise to the idea. The accuracy of this concept may be tested against the history of the philosophy of the 18th century [which was the expression of prevailing economic interests].[56]

Turning directly to the topic of women and applying the useful economic outlook of Marx, he wrote:

I wish to view this question not from the position of abstract right nor from the standpoint of a physiologist or psychologist but from the standpoint of economics . . . eliminating all extraneous factors in determining how the historical development of the economy alone, without the intrusion of intellectual progress, has led the woman's problem to its contemporary situation in contemporary society. . . . The woman's question viewed as a function of the given economic conditions is the best means for representing the parallel development of the economic bases of society and the problem of women. The historical development of the economic foundations of society, as everyone knows, has taken place through three stages: the first being the passage beyond physical labor; the second, of fixed capital; the third, variable capital— the contemporary period. Using this formulation of the three periods, one may separate out all the phenomena of social and political life, since each of the periods has left its mark on these phenomena, giving them their character and direction. The question of women cannot be excluded from among these phenomena. This is what I wanted to say in my article. . . . I have come to the conclusion that the economic inequality of men and women is the inevitable, necessary result of those rooted economic bases which lie at the basis of a given economic *status quo*. On the other hand, these same bases, which have given rise to the inequality, are themselves threatened by their own consequences which will completely destroy this inequality. Women, entering the labor market along with men, will lower the level of the wages paid to both, increase poverty . . . , and make prostitution develop to an extreme. Thus, prostitution and poverty become the results [of inequality] and threaten society. . . . At the present time, all thinking people consider the women's demands for equality completely justifiable, a fact which helps increase the importance of the question. But I do not consider this relationship of the intelligentsia to the woman's question the reason why the woman's question has arisen but rather the result of economic development. But while this may explain how the question has moved to the forefront, I have not explained in my article how other circumstances, connected with economic conditions, bear upon the question of women (namely, the action of women members of the intelligentsia).[57]

We can see (in the last sentence of the above quotation) the voluntaristic note entering the discussion of economic determinism—the familiar difficulty stemming from what has been called the excessively mechanistic view of social determinism contained in Marxism.[58] In the last sentence above, Tkachev introduces the factor of the "thinking representatives," in this case, "women members of the intelligentsia," by which he means socialist-minded women. Within the bounds of the same article, "The Woman Question," Tkachev made an interesting attempt to reconcile the decisive actionism of "an intellectual minority" with the deterministic working of economic factors. In reading the following, one may judge for himself whether Tkachev's attempt has been successful:

In order to be victorious in practical life, an economic interest needs the following two things: material force and the organization of this force. Material force is, by and large, the majority of people who are naïve, unreflective, and incapable of strict, efficient organization. Therefore, for the victory of this or that social element, it must have on its side a part of the intellectual minority. This intellectual minority gives to the material force its needed organization and directs it to a conscious goal. From this it is obvious how important it is for social progress in general to have the victory of this or that idea [possibly "ideal"—A. L. W.], the spread among the intelligentsia of this or that philosophy or this or that moral point of view. From this it is also obvious what the role is played by ideas in the history of mankind. . . . How should we describe the relationship between all phenomena of social life—is it causal or is it one of coexistence? If it is mere coexistence, where may we find the cause of these phenomena? If it is causal, which of the social phenomena is causal and which of them effects of causes? Is it impossible that A could be the cause of B and at the same time B be the cause of A? Only one of the two may be one or the other—either A is the effect while B is the cause or A is the cause and B the effect—which is it? Is it possible that one cannot understand that the whole problem consists namely in this, whether A is the condition for B or the other way around? They cannot be both, and to say so is the height of nonsense for which even the urbane bourgeoisie have no excuse.[59]

Tkachev's discussion above of the role of ideas (or ideals) in order for material force to be directed toward a conscious goal does little in itself to clarify the relationship—one of tension in his theory—between economic determinism on the one hand and the ideas and wills of his enlightened intelligentsia on the other. It was perhaps his intention to say something like this, if we interpolate. Actual economic conditions make certain ideas practicable; one cannot seriously entertain the idea of making a wooden table without wood or the proper condition of labor. But just as important as the material at hand, if not more so, are the *goals* or the *form* under which future progress and social development are to take place. Crude economic determinism will tell one nothing about progress, Tkachev seems to say. Both the goals for progress and the *organizational means* by which a certain type of progress (true progress to Tkachev meant the advent of socialism) are the concern of the intelligentsia, just as all progress which has taken place in earlier history has been under the guidance of thinking representatives of a given class. Moreover, by his own thought and activity Tkachev indicated that he thought that dissemination of new socialist ideas for progress, organization of the means to bring it about, etc., were the indispensable prerequisites for achieving progress.

Thus, his superstructure is indeed active, both in the pre- and postrevolutionary periods.

UTILITARIANISM

Whether Tkachev's basic ethical principles or his modified economic determinism is nearer the center of his whole system must remain a moot question. Only an evaluation of Tkachev's inner thoughts and his motives could yield a definite answer— clearly an impossible feat. It can be seen, however, that the formulations structured by Tkachev around these two points— the ethical and the economic—are very closely linked together and may, in fact, be viewed as mutually determinant.

It should not be forgotten that Tkachev was above all a revolutionary first and a political philosopher second. This fact in itself results in his putting the greatest stress on the ethical foundations of an ideal new order.

Tkachev eagerly awaited the new age when rational men (all members of developed and regenerate society) would calculate their own best interests so intelligently, with so much imagination and foresight, that their self-interests would merge ultimately into the supremely rational interest to form one unwavering current of monolithic, altruistic solidarity. The truth of the utilitarian ethic, wrote Tkachev in his rationalistic manner, lies in the fact of its irrevocable, a priori truth (again, the archaic odor of the French Enlightenment and Age of Reason). Tkachev wrote:

> To show the *a priori* truth of this conception is not really very difficult. Individual interest, the tendency toward improving one's existence, enhancing one's pleasure, and his earthly possessions indisputably from the primary stimulus for individual good as well as for general good. And, also, the betterment of the welfare of man and the broadening of his means of

improvement are above all expressed in the guarantee of the accumulation of things and material goods.[60]

Hence, it naturally follows that, speaking generally, the historical tendency of man is to better his lot; Tkachev's optimism about continuing human progress throughout history must express itself above all in the economic interest of man which, moreover, provides the leaven and the genuine starting-point for an expression of this law as well as in politics. Thus we see that for Tkachev not only are simple economic interests the "principal springs and prime movers" of human behavior, but human egoism in matters of pleasure and avoidance of pain and the amassing of earthly material goods is a basic human attribute and primary stimulus for personal and social betterment.

Furthermore, Tkachev points to no decalogue or tablet, no specific calculus of pleasure by which one can read the timeless principles of good behavior.[61] Rather, he foresees a time when communal altruism combined with utilitarian, regenerate individualism will be able to exist side by side, when moral behavior will be rationally ordered by each separate, enlightened individual—somewhat like the behavior of the character Rakhmetov in Chernyshevsky's novel, *What Is To Be Done?* These rational "people of the future," as he termed them, also would somewhat resemble Nietzsche's supermen with this great difference: the whole society eventually would be composed of such harmoniously functioning and calculating individuals (the debt to Pisarev is particularly marked in this Tkachevist projection).

However, while placing this high value upon the individual, Tkachev, unlike the Nietzscheans or the Marxists, *ignored any threat to this individuality from the side of the state,* even in its most authoritarian posture immediately after the revolution (see above, pp. 101–102). Nor did Tkachev ever fully describe the ultimate withering away of the state: his respect for law and his realism with respect to the egoism of men, even regenerate men, were too great to permit him to envisage a future in which men would not stand in need of the instruction and sanctions forthcoming from law and the state. On the contrary, Tkachev welcomed the interference of the state as "the regulator of the social process," as we have seen, and could

not envision the state's resigning its function of positively educating the people toward utilitarian behavior and conserving
the utilitarian order. The state would have to indoctrinate the
citizens with utilitarianism and *protect* its dissemination after
the revolution for a protracted period of time which, Tkachev
stressed, meant a very long, unspecified amount of time. Just
when or how enlightened self-interest would be so widespread
so as to automatically merge into habitual, monolithic, and altruistic solidarity and social peace and harmony, Tkachev never
explained. Instead, Tkachev stressed the protracted period of
indoctrination and reeducation. Education for Tkachev was
an extremely important state function if the society were to
be reconstructed and defended from those who would restore
the old order. It is important here not to confuse Lavrovist
education (revolutionaries learning from the people) in the
*pre*revolutionary period with Tkachevist education *after* the
revolution and under the tutelage of the revolutionary state
dictatorship.

Education is the state's business; teachers should be em-
ployees of the state. Tkachev wrote:

> Only the state may remove the interference of
> the bourgeois into the education of the workers. Only
> the state alone can give to the 'societies of enlighten-
> ment' [cadres of state educators formed into associa-
> tions] the necessary legal support and material back-
> ing.[62]

This educational activity must set definite goals for itself in
order to teach the masses most effectively; its professorial ranks
must be filled with those "who are the most honorable and
therefore [!] most sympathetic to the interests of the workers."[63]

Tkachev meanwhile was most critical, even contemptuous,
of the Lavrovist-Populist view of education. Tkachev described
the Populist theories as follows:

> Out of the armory of civilization, out of its means
> of leading the masses forward, it [the Populist view-
> point] perverts education into a kind of eternal brake,
> into a weapon of stagnation and routine. Education
> can exert a beneficial influence on the people's develop-

ment only when it stands above the people's daily and historically determined needs; only when it pursues ideals which are more reasonable and broader than the people's; in a word, not by descending to the level of the people's interests [also possibly "demands"— A. L. W.] but by raising the people up to its level. If on the other hand education were to concern itself simply with the avoidance of conflict, with the wishes and goals of the undeveloped masses and were to decline to exert a forceful influence upon the young generation, then it must willy-nilly oppose every progressive movement and shape the youth merely according to the old pattern of their fathers. . . . Is it possible that our liberal ignoramuses do not understand that the voice of the people, their own voice, can have a decisive effect and importance only in the sphere of those simple affairs and problems directly concerning the disposition of their immediate, personal wellbeing? In the sphere of those problems concerning the education of their children, their voice has no importance.[64]

TKACHEV'S VIEWS ON PSYCHOLOGY AND AESTHETICS

Tkachev displayed a rather high degree of consistency when he touched areas relatively peripheral to his revolutionary core of social and political theory. Tkachev came close, in fact, to the Soviet theory of "socialist realism," a point of view which had been suggested to him by at least two immediate forebears, Dobrolyubov and Pisarev.

The most appropriate content of artistic works, Tkachev said, should be the actual empirical fact, even raw data, taken directly from real Russian social life. But the duty of the artist does not consist of merely reporting naturalistically what he sees about him or simply tallying up statistics. He has, a "synthetic" and "scientific" function:[65]

Science must wash all poetry into its broad stream. Only science, in fact, may save it from wild fantasy. Science alone can convey to it this sober realism without which poetry becomes sterile, useless, even pernicious amusement. There could never be too much science in it!

Science forces art, to the detriment of the latter's prejudices about "beauty" and "holiness," to remove the shrouds of idealism from those "most lofty" human feelings and to present them in the unsightly and thoroughly unpleasant form in which they appear in the eyes of scientific realism. . . . Politics, social economy, statistics, jurisprudence, the so-called "temple of art" from all sides are scattering the unfortunate poets and artists with their, the formers' conclusions, formulas, laws, abstracts, and codes.[66]

Viewed from the standpoint of the artist himself, artistic creation proceeds, according to Tkachev, as follows:

It is certain that at the present time . . . thanks to the development of our rational, abstracting faculties of our minds and, in fact, thanks also to the success attained by scientific psychology, this passive "association of ideas" [in the Humean sense] has weakened significantly. However, in the understanding of the half-educated masses a dose of a mystical attitude toward the writer is still prevalent. It tends to see artistic creation dominated by feeling-over-the-intellect. In the intellectual history of mankind, this was merely an early stage and constituted a period of mystical contemplation of nature and her phenomena, of immediate poetic expression, a period of high ecstasy and hallucination manifesting themselves in this or that art form. In a word, this was a period of the great activity of mere feeling and the complete absence of critical thinking and the truly cultured mind.[67]

The advent of modern science put an end to all this for Tkachev. He finds that scientific insight may be extended into the heretofore "fantastic realms." In certain respects, Tkachev's view of the development of human thinking suggests Auguste Comte's optimistic belief in laws of human development from the first stage of animism (savage, mass fantasy), to the second stage of religion, metaphysics and personal fantasy, to the last stage of positivism, which affords the only rational means of exhibiting the logical laws of the human mind which have hitherto been sought after by "unfit methods," the coming of "a new science: Social Physics."

In the following passage, taken from Tkachev's "The Significance of Art in the Intellectual History of Man,"[68] one finds traces of the latterday Soviet Communist theory of Socialist Realism:

> The thinker and the artist; scholar and poet; rationalism and creative power; in other words, science and poetry—two spheres into which the Western European mind is divided. Science and poetry share between them a whole *ager publicum*—and are becoming the sole possessors of our intellectual life. However, this double rule has rarely remained stable; sooner or later it has developed into a single rule. And judging by the present state of thought, it may with some probability be predicted that in the future poetry and the clergy, poets, and artists will be exiled from the civilized world just as they were exiled from Plato's Republic, although at that time with garlands of wool on their heads. Of course, this future does not bother contemporary artists, despite its grimness. . . . In our life there are many conditions favoring the flourishing of "art and poetry," and as long as these conditions persist their status is as firm as that of metaphysics or alchemy centuries ago. . . . Although art is still far from being completely ostracized, nevertheless without doubt our intellectual civilization, if it has not already begun to, in any case has nearly approached the period of the forerunners of such an ostracism.

Among the subjects suitable for artists' attention, Tkachev said, were: the ichthyosaurus, ammonite, fossils of the Pleistocene and Meistocene periods, "the rags and tatters of beggars." "It is a pity," he wrote, "that poets linger over their Apollos and Venuses. What is needed instead are poet-popularizers constantly controlling their fantasies with geological and paleontological texts."

To a degree, Tkachev had taken the heritage of Dobrolyubov's aesthetics and grafted it onto Comtean theories of the historical laws of human intellectual development and progress. In a sense Tkachev would agree with Comte's idea, an idea vaguely suggested earlier by Feuerbach, that man's intellectual development has led him to the place where science should be logically extended to the social and spiritual realm of man's activity. There is really nothing holy or mysterious about the human brain; sooner or later it can be subjected to scientific law just as other organs have been, Tkachev thought.

It is perhaps not surprising to find Tkachev listing Dostoyevsky as one of the authors least likely to qualify as a socialist and realist writer. *"Gospodin* Dostoyevsky," wrote Tkachev in "Sick People—*The Possessed,* a Novel by Fyodor Dostoyevsky in Three Parts," reprinted in *Delo,* Nos. 3, 4, 1873, "in all his belletristic writings confines himself exclusively to an analysis of the psychiatric anomalies of the human character and to describing the inner world of mentally ill people. It is therefore obvious that any kind of purposeful [*tendentsiozniye*] generalizations would be impossible in writing of this type. . . . Through his sick people, Dostoyevsky is himself relieved from having to pass any kind of judgment."[69] In words somewhat similar to those later spoken by Leo Tolstoy about Dostoyevsky (to Maxim Gorky), Tkachev complained that Dostoyevsky's "main stock in trade" consists in discussing "various idiots, maniacs, melancholics, epileptics." Dostoyevsky's purposefulness and idea, Tkachev further complained, is in constant struggle with his aesthetics, his first "I" with his second "I." What purposefulness [*tendentsioznost'*] there is in this author, Tkachev wrote, consists in saying that the dreams people have of the future are the possessions of sick people, "the 'possessed' who behave like evangelists, the products of a sick Russia." Linking Dostoyevsky to other romantic writers of the day, Tkachev indicts them all for ignoring positive, "living, free characters to whom petty-egoistic interests are alien, who are free of the usual disharmony and inability to show active and effective opposition to the oppressing influence of their 'environment.' . . . Their characters [those of Dostoyevsky and "other romanticists"] are by no means accidental creations. They are products of the petty-bourgeois mind. They are deeply imbued with the conditions of life of the petty-bourgeoisie, its family and social relationships, its theoretical ideas and moral outlook, with the whole range of its intellectual outlook."[70]

When it came to the depiction of Verkhovensky, the revolutionary in *The Possessed,* Tkachev regarded Dostoyevsky's characterization as "out-moded . . . the quintessence of egoism." Tkachev did not consider Verkhovensky to be a true revolutionary type as, say, the perfectly realistic and altruistic Rakhmetov of Chernyshevsky's *What Is To Be Done?* Verkhovensky is merely the vehicle for Dostoyevsky's usual preaching "of egoism as a great moral force giving birth to the luxurious wood of contemporary civilization."[71] Tkachev further accused Dostoyevsky of outright "falsification" [*fal'sifikatsiya*] of many of the so-called "sick people" of the younger generation of revolutionaries, falsification which is, moreover, deeply "harmful" to the cause.[72]

Tkachev did praise Dostoyevsky for his psychological insight, at least into mentally deranged types. But Tkachev had in mind, he thought, a much larger, therapeutic and analytical sphere of operation for both psychology and literature than the literature of the romanticists.

In his time Tkachev was familiar with the writings of such pioneers in experimental psychology as Wundt, Ribot, and Charcot. But Tkachev's own ideas dimly anticipated Pavlovism or behavioralism in their attempt to categorize and find a law-bound process in the mental development of mankind. Tkachev envisioned nothing less than the classification of every mental empirical datum. "The laws and secret mechanism of our mental life," he wrote, will be brought to light and studied in the near future and "the true cause and basic law of our psychic life" discovered:

> Of course, by "psychological knowledge" we do not mean knowledge which is raw, merely empirical, unclassified and uncategorized (which may well suit the tastes of certain pedagogues including Leo Tolstoy), but scientific, rational knowledge, which will have come as the result of long and thorough study in the science of psychology.[73]

And:

> Every science has the task of making scientific study of the phenomena observed by it; to study a phenomenon scientifically means to uncover its cause, to explain and define the laws which govern it. This is also the task of the psychologist. . . . Psychological

specialists will . . . reveal to us the secret mechanism of our mental life. . . . The method of psychology has not only changed [in some quarters] since the time of Aristotle, Pythagoras, Socrates, and Plato but has become weighted down with metaphysical philosophy.[74]

Medicine and physiology, Tkachev added, would be the means by which psychologists would be able to reveal the "secret mechanism" of the mind. The external world has been studied and its laws uncovered; next to be studied should be the internal world of the mind.[75]

When it came to literary criticism, Tkachev argued that objective criteria must be employed. Literary criticism, like creative art, is not to be an indefinite, "mystical," impressionistic thing as it had been up to his time, according to Tkachev. Tkachev presented two basic criteria which, he said, amount to a sociological viewpoint on the one hand and a psychological viewpoint, on the other. Of these two standards of judgment, he wrote:

In every literary work are contained two facts: the author's reproduction of the real social environment around him and the act itself of reproducing it—in other words, the sociological and the psychological viewpoints. From the standpoint of the sociological criterion may be distinguished, first, the social conditions which gave rise to the actual literary work; second, that social soil, those historical, economic, political-juridical factors which give social meaning to the raw, empirical phenomena and which are reproduced by the author and which influence the education of the persons' characters depicted in the work. From the standpoint of the psychological criterion, intellectual factors are investigated, also purely psychical factors participating in the creation of the actual work. Also the overall merit of these factors is judged in the light of the work produced with their help. Second, the psychological criterion analyzes characters presented by the author. Obviously, the most important critical elements are the intellectual ones, the intellectual forces of the author. Upon the strength of these forces will depend the critic's statement of his final preference. The critic must judge the intellectual attributes of the

author through his work; they point out to the critic
whether the author has demonstrated any capacity
for logical reasoning, a capacity for abstract thought
[from real life] or, on the contrary, for mere "creative fantasy. . . ." If there is abstract thought, then
the work will be truly purposeful in character. Then
the business of the critic will be to point out how the
social factors evoke this or that particular purposefulness and to elaborate its influence on the social
and psychic life of man. The predominating point of
view is the sociological, while the psychological plays
an important but subordinate role.[76]

Coming close to saying that his criticism might best be called
"Sociological" realism, Tkachev describes further what he
means by realistic criticism:

The method of realistic criticism is one of a
strictly scientific character, proceeding not from subjective feeling but from conclusions of a [sociologi-
cal] character, an analysis which always yields exact
examination. On the other hand, the method of aesthetic and idealistic criticism is in its very essence
purely subjective and incapable of discovering its own
errors.[77]

Tkachev cited his opponents' (subjectivists' and aestheticists')
view of art as the denial that the contemplation of the artist
is "a chain of logical conclusions," a worked-out analysis and
synthesis; they claim it to be only a number of random
revelations. In Comtean terms, again, such talk about revela-
tion merely shows, according to Tkachev, how man has not yet
completely liberated himself from "fetishism" and passed into
the realm of science.

Tkachev, perhaps anticipating Freud to an extent, describes the unconscious as follows:

Subjective psychology, by necessity, limits its
spheres of investigations to a small number of phenomena encompassed by our consciousness, by the merely
conspicuous processes of our psyche. But with these
processes all the content of man's psychic life is
scarcely exhausted. On the contrary, these conspicuous processes play only a very modest role, we may

say even a secondary role. Our brain, without the help of its conscious part, constantly perceives a mass of impressions which reach it by means of external as well as internal organs of our body. For example, between it (the brain) and the internal organs (organs of digestion, breathing, blood, circulation, sex, etc.) occurs an uninterrupted transfer of impressions out of which is formed, for the most part, the ground for our whole psychic life—that substratum we call temperament, our "moods," our "characters." Hence, it is obvious that the activity of the brain, when explained by these processes, plays the leading role in our spiritual life. . . . The objective method, taking the unconscious psyche for its departure point for the study of the conscious psyche, establishes . . . the whole of our internal world and delivers an entirely new mass of facts and phenomena into the realm of psychology —data without which it would be unthinkable to establish even an approximately true understanding of the laws and nature of our psychic life. . . . We are at present busily determining the precise nature of this unconscious process.[78]

These are the grounds for calling Tkachev a psychological reductionist who seeks an explanation for character, moods, temperament in man's physiology. In addition to his physiological approach, Tkachev emphatically attributed psychological effects to social causation:

Changes in external conditions become nervous changes; external forces change into intellectual and psychical forces. . . . Thus the key to the settling of one of the most difficult problems in contemporary scientific psychology has been found![79]

The political implications of a psychology which stresses external conditioning, along with internal factors, are perhaps obvious. For if changes in external (meaning largely social) conditions can effect changes in the mind, including its unconscious part, then a given political ruling group, charged with the task of remaking the society and "forcing consciousness" after the revolution, must logically assert itself in as many facets of the social environment of the citizens as possible —in biological science (indeed, all science), the economy, literature, fine arts, architecture, politics, etc., since all of these spheres involve determinant external conditions and are spring-boards or stimuli for social conditioning. In Stalin's promotion of Lysenkoism, to cite a single twentieth-century application of this outlook, biological science was to be viewed as a "party science," in that biologists were to teach and apply the principle of social conditioning (social Pavlovism) and the Lamarckian idea that conditioned reflexes and acquired characteristics may be passed on genetically to future generations (of humans as well as of plants and animals). As applied by Stalin,[80] this outlook had enormous political importance and could be regarded as making up a part of the very psycho-social foundations for building a socialist and fully communist society in the USSR. While discarding Lysenkoism, present-day leaders of the USSR have not entirely repudiated social Pavlovism. In any case, they appear to be continuing to apply it.

NOTES

1. Thoroughly within the Tkachevist (and perhaps also Leninist) tradition was the Stalinist program of collectivization of agriculture, the socialization of the Russian village, the recasting of village life along socialist and communist lines. Stalin characterized collectivization as, he said, a "reform *from above.*"

2. Tkachev, *Sochineniya*, III, pp. 88–89. Tkachev's letter was written in the form of an answer to an article by Engels for *Volksstaat* in 1874 entitled *"Émigré* Literature." In this article Engels strongly criticized Tkachev for the latter's attacks on Lavrov and the Lavrovist *Vpered!* Tkachev's letter, also written in 1874, appeared first in German as a pamphlet. It was published in Russian in the Kozmin-edited *Sochineniya* of 1933.

3. See *Reminiscences of Marx and Engels* (Moscow: Foreign Languages Publishing House, n.d.), an article in this volume by A. Voden entitled "Talks with Engels," pp. 325–34. Engels expressed his appreciation of Plekhanov to Voden, although he disagreed with Plekhanov's identification of Tikhomirov with the Narodnik terrorists and Populists. Later Voden writes: "Once, when he attributed to Tkachev thoughts which in substance were those of Bakunin, he lost no time in writing to me that after going to the source . . . he had come to the conclusion that he had taken one confused [*konfusionsrat*] person for another." We do not know if this mixup in Engels' mind pertained to the period of his correspondence with Tkachev or not. Engels replied to Tkachev's letter in an article in *Volksstaat* in 1875, which was again published in 1894 in a collection of articles by Engels that were translated into Russian and became well known to Russian Marxists of the nineties.

4. Kozmin writes on this point: "If we acquaint ourselves with what Tkachev was writing in the sixties, before his arrest in the Nechayev case, we will become convinced how opposed Tkachev was to any idealization of the Russian peasantry. . . . In 'Destroyed Illusions,' Tkachev labeled popular self-enlightenment an illusion . . . and spoke of the illusion about the alleged genius of the people. . . . In the opinion of the others [i.e., go-to-the-people Populists], the uncivilized crowd stood incomparably higher than the civilized crowd because of the former's immediate purity. In the uncivilized crowd was preserved everything glorious and great. But it needed instruction for the people to learn from it. In the uncivilized crowd, the civilized crowd must find its own rejuvenation. . . . Tkachev agreed with neither idea" (Kozmin, *P. N. Tkachev*, pp. 128–29).

5. *Ibid.*, p. 130.

6. It is quite striking to find Tkachev employing the term "village proletarians." But it must be recalled that Marx and Engels had earlier used the term, for example, in *The Address of the Central Authority to the Communist League*, April, 1850. The Basel Congress of the International (1869) addressed an appeal to the village proletariat to form "laborers' unions." See the discussion in David Mitrany, *Marx Against the Peasant. A Study in Social Dogmatism* (New York: Collier Books), pp. 66–67.

7. Tkachev, *Sochineniya*, I, 40–41. As we shall presently see, Tkachev makes a distinction between two types of peasants—the majority of proletarianized peasants (note Tkachev's free use of the word "proletarian," again anticipating Lenin) and the smaller number of petty peasant proprietors. The ruling class of bourgeois factory and land owners form an alliance, as it were, and hold down the poor peasant in the village. Tkachev uses the word *kulak* to describe the middle and better-off peasant.

8. Tkachev, *Sochineniya*, III, 91.

9. The full text of Engels' second attack on Tkachev (which Tkachev was never able to answer because of incapacity and finally death) may be found in Karl Marx and Friedrich Engels, *The Russian Menace to Europe—A Collection of Articles, Speeches, Letters, and News Dispatches, Selected and Edited*, Paul W. Blackstock and Bert F. Hoselitz, eds. (3d ed.; Glencoe: The Free Press, 1952); the citation is from pp. 232–33. Vera Zasulich made a somewhat fruitless attempt to obtain clarification from both Marx and Engels on their approach to the Russian question. All of this controversy, it should be noted, was well known to the Russian Marxists of the 1890's, including Plekhanov and Lenin.

10. *Ibid.*, pp. 234–35.

11. The original of this letter was found only in 1923 in the private papers of Paul Axelrod preserved in the archives of the German Social-Democratic Party in Berlin; a German translation of this letter was made by Boris Nicolaevsky in *Die Gesellschaft*, I, No. 4 (July 1924), 361–62. Hoselitz and Blackstock, *op. cit.*, pp. 278–79, note: "Zasulich and her friends could not make any use of this . . . in their discussions with . . . Russian Marxists. But less than a year later they got a statement from Marx on the same subject which was much more forthright and precise." To wit: "Russia forms the vanguard of the revolutionary movement of Europe" (*Ibid.*, p. 228). Marx continues with the Russian "spark" concept, that a Russian revolution would rebound back to Europe and be "a signal for a proletarian revolution in Europe." He adds that in this case the Russian commune could act as a starting point "for a communist course of development." All this is not very remote from Tkachev's view.

12. *Ibid.*, p. 217.

13. Both Marx and Engels could read Russian, although with what degree of facility is not clearly known. They did follow Russian socialist and revolutionary developments closely; Marx's admiration for Chernyshevsky and his originality is well known. A review of both Marx's and Engels' statements on Russia and the prospects of revolution in that country reveals a degree of contradiction. After a review of the literature, it is this author's opinion that the quotations given above seem best to sum up their approach to the problem of revolution in Russia. In a word, they were optimistic; they even entertained the notion that the spark ignited in Russia would set Europe afire. Their position undoubtedly influenced the more militant Russian Marxists.

14. F. I. Dan, *op. cit.*, pp. 95–97, makes essentially the same point. An interesting quotation of Lavrov's, reproduced by Dan (p. 82), illustrates his position: "Our social revolution must come out of the villages, not the cities."

15. Tkachev, *Sochineniya*, III, 243.

16. From Engels' letter to Joseph Bloch, 1890: "There is an interaction of all these elements [economic situation *and* various elements in the superstructure] in which, amidst all the endless host of accidents . . . the economic movement asserts itself as necessary. . . . We had to emphasize the main principle vis-à-vis our adversaries who denied it, and we had not always . . . the opportunity to give their due to the other elements involved in the interaction." And in his letter to Conrad Schmidt, 1890: ". . . what we call the *ideological outlook* reacts in its turn upon the economic base and may, within certain limits, modify it." To Franz Mehring, 1893: "Men make their history themselves, but not as yet with a collective will according to a collective plan."

17. Tkachev, *Sochineniya*, I, 36.

18. *Ibid.*, III, 473, in footnote by Kozmin.

19. Kozmin, *P. N. Tkachev*, pp. 67–69, from a *Delo* article of 1868.

20. *Ibid.*

21. Kozmin, *P. N. Tkachev*, p. 70, from "Sick People," *Delo*, IV (1873).

22. "Once setting for himself a definite end—namely, the achievement of such an order of things giving full recognition to and adoption of the principle *volus* [sic] *populi supreme lex esto*—Machiavelli," Tkachev wrote, "neglected no means which would lead directly or indirectly to this end. Machiavelli's understanding of truth and justice leads him to a simple calculation of what is useful or expedient; he denies natural law of the type taught by the Scholastics; he denies mystical morality; he freely admits of force in law and therefore all his actions are directed only toward making Italy above all a strong, united state. Thus, Machiavelli understood the essence of law and in this sense may be termed an authentic realist" (from an article in *Russkoye slovo*, 12 [1865], written by Tkachev and quoted by Kozmin, *P. N. Tkachev*, p. 89, where Kozmin notes that Machiavelli enjoyed great popularity among the youth of the 1860's). A poem addressed to Machiavelli written by I. I. Golts-Miller in the sixties was well known. One of the lines read: "The magnificent Machiavelli who struck such terror in the hearts of stupid people."

23. Engels was evidently doubtful about the success of a political leader, like Thomas Münzer (1489–1525), the German Anabaptist, whose ideas were "far in advance" of the prevailing social and economic environment. "What he can do," wrote Engels, "depends not upon his will but upon the degree of contradiction between the various classes, level of development of the means of production, etc. . . . In the interests of the movement, he is compelled to advance the interests of the alien class. . . . Whoever is put in this awkward position is irrevocably lost." Tkachev, on the other hand, was not so pessimistic and attributed Münzer's failure largely to a lack of *organizational skill*.

24. Tkachev, *Sochineniya*, III, 69–70. Tkachev was evidently one of the first socialist writers in Russia to employ the Russian word *kulak* to describe middle and well-to-do peasants. Tkachev's article, from which this warning of kulakization is quoted, is entitled "Tasks of Revolutionary Propaganda in Russia," was published in London in 1874, and was an attack on Lavrovism. Tkachev, in the manner employed by Lenin later, as has been mentioned already, often buttressed his argument about the bourgeoisation of Russia with impressive statistical data (cf. Lenin's *The Development of Capitalism in Russia*). Besides the kulaks themselves, added Tkachev, "stockbrokers and loansharks," once urban phenomena, were now in evidence in the village, which was rapidly assuming a bourgeois character.

25. From Tkachev's letter to Engels. The Western bourgeois state, Tkachev wrote to Engels, "stands with both feet in this capital," presenting a most difficult *obstacle to revolution in western Europe.* Not so in Russia, he maintained.

26. Tkachev, *Sochineniya*, III, 64–66. Tkachev was not altogether contemptuous, of course, of the "hurricane" quality of the "unconscious, disorderly . . . restiveness of the people" when it played a revolutionary, "destructive" role. Most of the time (in the usual nonrevolutionary situation), the people drift aimlessly when left to themselves, and become increasingly reactionary and bourgeois.

27. Tkachev, *Sochineniya*, III, 219, in which he describes the program and functions of *Nabat.*

28. *Ibid.*, III, 219–20.

29. *Ibid.*, III, 64.

30. Full quotation is above, pp. 54–56.

31. Tkachev, *Sochineniya*, III, 221.

32. *Ibid.*, III, 221.

33. *Ibid.*, III, 332, from Tkachev's "Anarchy of Thought."

34. *Ibid.*, III, 337.

35. See above, pp. 118–24, for Tkachev's application of the jump theory.

36. See above, pp. 92–97.

37. "Subjectivistic" in the sense that he attributed to himself and to his small group of Tkachevists a great degree of individual intellectual acumen and strength of will. Tkachev himself, of course, uses the word "subjectivistic" pejoratively.

38. From Tkachev's review of Yu. Zhukovsky's *Political and Social Theories of the 16th Century and Proudhon and Louis Blanc, Sochineniya*, I, 69–70. The article was written by Tkachev in 1866 and is one of the earliest incidents of a Russian social and political writer making direct attribution to Karl Marx; Tkachev's own footnote referred to Marx's *Zur Kritik der Politischen Oekonomie,* especially the preface to this work, published in June 1859—that is, five years before the establishment of the First International and eight years before the completion of the first volume of *Capital.* Despite its brevity and early appearance, it is considered to contain the formulation of the basic conceptions of historical materialism. Tkachev refers to Marx in his footnote as "the well-known German exile."

39. In this way Tkachev, an economic determinist of sorts, reveals the same type of contradiction sometimes detected in the writings of Marx and Engels. Engels, in particular, attempted to reconcile the concept of the base-determining-the-superstructure with the concept of the superstructure-reacting-upon-the-base—the key word being "reacting" upon the economy. See also Marx's *The Civil War in France,* particularly Engels' preface to it, where the Paris Commune coalition

of Blanquists and Proudhonists in 1871 are indicted for not having sufficiently utilized the powerful means of "the servant of society."

40. Tkachev, *Sochineniya*, II, 16–17.

41. See the frequently bombastic tone of Tkachev's review of the Zhukovsky book, *Ibid.*, I, 69, where Mill, although praised to an extent, is nonetheless stigmatized as a mere mouthpiece of the bourgeoisie.

42. Tkachev, *Ibid.*, I, 70. In other writings Tkachev is apt, as he was here, to measure the good or evil of a theory according to its *usefulness for the revolution* and to criticize opposing revolutionary theories if they "retarded" the revolutionary movement.

43. Stalin's well-known statement of the relationship between theory and practice is perhaps relevant here: "Theory can become the *greatest force* in the working class movement if it is *closely bound up with practical revolution:* for *theory alone can give the movement confidence, guidance, strength, and understanding . . . and clarify the process and direction of* class movements" [my italics—A. L. W.). Tkachev's manner of looking at the *function* of theory was rather prophetic of things to come—e.g., ideas to be found later in Sorel, Pareto, Lenin, Mussolini, Michels, Stalin, and so well explained and catalogued in Mannheim's *Ideology and Utopia*.

44. Venturi, *op. cit.*, p. 398.

45. B. P. Kozmin, *Ot devyatnadtsatovo fevralya k pervomy marta* (Moscow: Izdaniye Politkatorzhan, 1937), p. 138.

46. Tkachev, *Sochineniya*, I, 427.

47. *Ibid.*, I, 427. Here again there seems to be some support for Kozmin's contention against what other Soviet critics have said and still say today, that "Tkachev was the first person [in Russia] to understand the significance of Marxism and to adopt its theoretical principles, applying them broadly to various fields of science (Kozmin, *"Ocherki po istorii ratsionalizma,"* p. 120). At the same time, Kozmin was critical of those Russian historians who, he said, exaggerated the degree of Tkachev's acceptance of Marxism (see my discussion of 1920's dispute below, pp. 176–87). It is interesting to find that Tkachev used the Marxist term "wage slavery." "Intrinsic value" (for Tkachev) is value engendered by labor.

48. Tkachev, *Sochineniya*, I, 427. Engels in his preface to Marx's *A Critique of Political Economy* offers the general meeting of workers as a possible means of assisting in industrial management. At the same time, Engels, like Tkachev, had profound respect for authority, including the one-man variety as both of them often indicated—Engels, e.g., in his *Die Neue Zeit* article "On Authority"; Tkachev in numerous writings, in both the *Delo* and *Nabat* periods.

49. Tkachev is quoted in Venturi, *op. cit.*, p. 339.

50. Tkachev, *Sochineniya*, I, 19.

51. Quoted by Kozmin in *P. N. Tkachev*, p. 60, from an early article in *Delo*.

52. *Ibid.*, pp. 109–10.

53. Tkachev wrote a review of several of Girardin's works and utilized the occasion to declare many of his own ideas on the state, society, force and law, and so on. Girardin was critical of the provisional government in France in 1848 and supported the candidacy of the future emperor, Napoleon III, who had been, however, running for President of the Republic in the elections of 1848. Girardin became disillusioned with Napoleon, but when the liberal Émile Ollivier (1825–1913) joined Napoleon's cabinet in 1869 and led the ministry, Girardin gave his support to the "Liberal Empire" of Napoleon III. Girardin, a prolific writer, was the author of novels and plays in addition to numerous essays and books on politics.

54. Tkachev, *Sochineniya*, II, 7–9. This criticism of parliamentary "reformism," as Tkachev termed it, may also be found in his letter to *Vpered!* cited above.

55. It would not be far afield to suggest that Tkachev used this departure point (*iskhodnaya tochka*) not unlike an Archimedean point, a convenient means or starting-point, the assumption of which helps clarify conditions in society but which is true because it is *useful* in giving inspiration and direction to the revolutionary movement. See in this section the discussion of Tkachev's view of the usefulness of ideas and of modern science for which theoretical assumptions, non-Euclidean geometry—in short, *useful* mental constructs— give us a way "to act on earth and within terrestrial nature as though we dispose of it from outside, from the Archimedean point . . ." (Hannah Arendt, *The Human Condition* [Garden City: Doubleday and Company, 1958], pp. 238 and 368, where she quotes Whitehead on "organized thought" leading to "organized action").

56. Tkachev, *Sochineniya*, I, 445–46.

57. Arendt, p. 446.

58. Alfred G. Meyer has written (in *Marxism—the Unity of Theory and Practice* [Ann Arbor: University of Michigan Press, 1963], pp. 158–59, 73) : ". . . the Marxist tradition itself is strongly wedded to mechanistic thought. . . . The very terminology in which the functional theory of Marxism is couched betrays the deep roots with which it is planted in the soil of causal thought. . . . Another striking example of mechanistic thinking is the 'reflection' theory of knowledge, according to which ideas are the reflections of reality."

59. Tkachev, *Sochineniya*, I, 446. Here, interestingly, Tkachev is using the word "intellectual minority" in application to *any* era, to *any* type of society.

60. Quoted in Kozmin, *P. N. Tkachev*, p. 71, from an article that appeared in *Delo* in 1865.

61. Like most materialists, old and new, Tkachev was an atheist. And like some of his radical brethren Tkachev's anticlericalism and atheism left him with no divine support for the good life, either in the present or in a hereafter. Instead, he resorted to reason akin to Aristotle's "rational principle of man." The proof for his utilitarian ethic is stated as an a priori postulate analogous to a geometrical axiom.

62. Tkachev, "Ernst Becher's Labor Question in Its Contemporary Meaning and the Means to Its Solution," *Sochineniya*, V, 441–42. Kozmin notes that the article may have appeared in the regular *Delo* column, "New Books," *Delo*, No. 7 (1869).

63. *Ibid.*, V, 441. J. S. Mill, *Utilitarianism* (New York: E. P. Dutton, 1929), p. 31, wrote: "The whole force of education . . . should be directed as it once was in religion" toward turning out young utilitarians. But of course Mill rejected Jacobin means to effect reform.

64. From Tkachev's 1875 article in *Nabat*, "Teach the People or Be Taught by the People?" *Sochineniya*, III, 401–402. Tkachev's politics suggests a pyramid. At the bottom one finds a multitude of "simple affairs" concerning the petty daily existences of individuals. As one ascends up the pyramid, the problems become more important and universal and the authority of the state and state-run institutions correspondingly greater. Some of these most important problems *do*, of course, concern the individual's daily existence (e.g., the education of his children), but the transcendent importance of these problems demands their solution by the informed offices of the state and not by the uninformed offices of the masses.

65. Tkachev, "Poetry and Science," *Sochineniya*, VI, 492.

66. *Ibid.*, VI, 326.

67. *Ibid.*, VI, 330.

68. *Ibid.*, VI, 324–25.

69. *Ibid.*, III, 9.

70. *Ibid.*, III, 14.

71. *Ibid.*, III, 20.

72. *Ibid.*, III, 43.

73. "Pedagogy: the Legitimate Daughter of Psychology," *Ibid.*, VI, 447. This article was prompted by a book by the Russian psychologist, Mikhail S. Zelensky, whose views on psychology closely paralleled those of Tkachev.

74. *Ibid.*, VI, 452.

75. *Ibid.*, VI, 456–57.

76. "The Principles and Tasks of Contemporary Criticism," *Ibid.*, VI, 319–20.

77. *Ibid.*, VI, 322. Tkachev accused Pisarev of subjectivism.

78. *Ibid.*, VI, 457–58.

79. *Ibid.*, VI, 459.

80. Neo-Lamarckian Lysenkoism has been condemned officially in the post-Stalin USSR. But the institutions, by which most of this social conditioning was to take place, remain. Furthermore, in the post-Stalin period still more ingenious (if not farfetched) institutions have been planned with which to condition or recondition Soviet citizens so that they may become communist men (not unlike Tkachev's projection of people of the future). See author's article "The Boarding School," in *Survey* (July 1965), pp. 83–94. As explained in this article, the boarding schools, which are more than mere theoretical projections and already educate hundreds of thousands of Soviet youths and which are eventually intended to include most Soviet youth, are a purely communist institution designed for thoroughly "forcing consciousness" of the new society into young minds.

CHAPTER VI

Problems in Tkachevism

Several of Tkachev's concepts raise questions which are characteristic of his, as well as other Jacobin-oriented social philosophers. Other problems arise when comparisons are made between Tkachevism and Bolshevism (Leninism). These may be viewed within the following framework:

1. Problems of intellectual culture in the light of economic determinism and one-party dictatorship;
2. Tkachevism as seen from the point of view of ideology-*qua*-rationalization;
3. Tkachevism, Leninism, and Soviet historians.

ECONOMIC DETERMINISM AND THE INTELLECTUALS

Tkachev once wrote that Marx had "formulated [economic determinism] in a most exact and definite manner . . . although the idea was not new to our literature and was carried over like everything else of value in West European literature."[1] As has been discussed above in this study (Chapter IV, Economic Theories) Tkachev inclined toward modified economic determinism. One of the most famous pronouncements of this nature was:

> All juridical and political phenomena represent in themselves nothing more than direct results of economic life. This juridical and political life is, so to

speak, simply a mirror in which the economic life of a people is reflected.[2]

Some of Tkachev's writings and concepts in the 1860's and 1870's were so Marxist-sounding that some prerevolutionary and Soviet scholars went so far as to call Tkachev the first Russian Marxist, a status that has been extensively debated in the USSR.[3] Our present purpose here is not to argue this point or pass judgment on the degree of Tkachev's commitment to Marxism in general or economic determinism in particular. Taking his statements at face value, we will proceed to examine the consequences the theory has for Tkachev's total world outlook and for Jacobin-oriented politics.

Louis Fischer has recently observed:

> Today, in Russia, literacy is up, book sales are up, sputniks and missiles are up and apartment houses are up, but culture, which transcends all of these and consists primarily in the relationship of individuals to one another and of the state to man, is not up. If Khrushchev can be blotted out, where is the security and dignity of the ordinary people?[4]

Assuming that a degree of spiritual poverty (especially in Soviet belles-lettres) does exist in the USSR and that Fischer's two sentences *are* applicable to the USSR, to what degree may the Jacobinism in the Soviet ideological heritage help produce this state of affairs? What role is assigned to intellectuals, creative artists, the bearers of intellectual culture in systems of economic determinism? Marx and Engels and Tkachev could not avoid discussing to one degree or other the problems posed by these questions.

Marx and Engels and Tkachev, who treated a whole range of topics all the way from economics, politics, and psychology to family relations and the question of women, could scarcely leave aside the question of the role of culture in advancing the dialectical-materialistic process (for Marx and Engels, dialectical; for Tkachev, more voluntaristic with respect to historical causation).

Marx wrote, and Tkachev essentially agreed, "the class which represents in itself the ruling material force of society is at the same time the society's ruling spiritual [i.e., cultural— A. L. W.] force." Marx continues:

> The class which has at its disposal the means of material production disposes also, by the strength of this power, of the means of cultural production so that . . . in general all of those ideas which have not the means of spiritual production are subjugated and suppressed by that class.[5]

In another place, Marx and Engels wrote:

> Morality, religion, metaphysics, all the rest of ideology and their corresponding forms of consciousness thus no longer retain the semblance of independence; they have no history, no development. . . . Life is not determined by consciousness, but consciousness by life.[6]

Whenever Marx and Engels and Tkachev discussed the base and superstructure relationship in bourgeois society, they tended to lay primary emphasis on the economic base as the causative factor.[7] The spiritual culture, they said, is largely superstructural, a reflection (as in a mirror, Tkachev said), often a rationalization of the underlying productive relations and of the leading class commanding those relations.

From all this it seems strange to find that bourgeois consciousness may continue to lag over (according to Tkachev, for a protracted period) in the socialist phase when a new social and economic base is in the process of being laid—an idea which is more than implied in *The Critique of the Gotha Program,* for example. As the new economic base and corresponding social and political institutions are erected on this new proletarian-class base, one would expect that new reflections would soon begin to appear in the mirror of the socialist superstructure. Where Marx said that he was reluctant to "make recipes for future kitchens,"[8] Tkachev, and to a degree Lenin and other Bolsheviks, chose to emphasize the constructive functions of the socialist dictatorship-superstructure (especially after its destructive, antibourgeois phase had drawn to a close) in reeducating and regenerating Russian society.

But is there not an explicit contradiction here? If culture

is superstructural according to economic determinism, how can one of the images in the mirror—the political dictatorship—look back down on its socialist base and socialist society and dictate to that base and its intellectuals as, for example, in the USSR after half a century of socialist life and practice? If socialist productive forces are determinant with respect to nearly everything else in the society,[9] including its spiritual life, why is such interference from the side of the superstructure warranted or even possible, according to the theory?

Tkachev seemed to deal with this problem as arbitrarily as he did with his differences with the German First International and dialectical materialism, which he summarily dismissed, along with whatever Hegelianism was contained in it, as reactionary, an impediment to the forward-to-revolution line. Tkachev frankly infused *voluntarism* into his political philosophy where Marx and Engels were reluctant to take this step, although even they assigned an important role to leaders and organization in the period of preparing the proletarian revolution.[10] A revolution," wrote Engels, "is the most authoritative thing there is." Tkachev, Lenin, *et al.*, thoroughly agreed and added that *building socialist society* is uppermost among those authoritative things.

But, as we have observed, Marx refused to make recipes for future kitchens. Moreover, Marx and Engels devoted perhaps too little attention to problems of intellectual culture, its role in the history of ideas, in the conception and making of inventions, its function with respect to the base, and its role in the postrevolutionary period of building socialism. It is this inattention or obfuscation of the problem of culture and the role of intellectuals in society which has caused socialist culture either to be misunderstood (as to its function) or abused by ideologues in the fourteen one-party communist states carrying out socialist programs today.

Indeed, the political theories of Marx and Engels and Tkachev, Lenin, and others display a lack of clarity about the nature of the intellectual class or the role played by intellectuals before and after the revolution. Lewis Feuer, writing of the Marxist confusion about that " 'portion of the bourgeoisie [that] goes over to the proletariat, and in particular a portion of the bourgeois ideologists . . . ,' " asserts:

161

The motivations of revolutionary intellectuals would scarcely, however, fit into a pattern of determination [*by*] theoretical consciousness. . . . To have granted that revolutionary intellectuals were basically moved by ethical feelings, by principles of justice and equality, would have constituted a decisive departure from historical materialism.[11]

But Tkachev and others after him made just such a decisive departure when speaking of both the pre- and postrevolutionary periods. The socialist dictatorship of eminent representatives of the new ethos assumes the tremendous burden (tremendous for its arrogance as well) of administering and providing the ideological guidance of the whole reconstruction, reeducation, and regeneration of society—*the implanting of new ideas,* as Tkachev called it.[12]

How does this stress on the role of the socialist intellectuals with respect to the general public as well as to the party rank-and-file affect the problem of culture?

If Marx and Engels were hesitant to anticipate future recipes, Tkachev suggested and his successors actually moved ahead to a formulation of these recipes, ultimately arriving at party and bureaucratic control of the process of intellectual culture by means of official criticism, censorship, organization of artists' groups, even sometimes planning the output of all types of art, graphic and literary. The result often has been staleness and a "shoe-production point of view," as Ilya Ehrenburg and many others have complained.

It seems obvious that Tkachev's Marxist inclinations—his generally base-and-superstructure formulation—clashed with his voluntarism. Marx and Engels, on the other hand, perhaps succeeded in avoiding this dilemma by stopping the voluntaristic phase (if, indeed, that phase existed)[13] with the revolution, with the revolutionary overthrow of the old, bourgeois society. The "leap from necessity into freedom" would seem to imply organization, planning, authoritative leadership. But in speaking of the socialist period to follow, Marx and Engels appeared to remain true to their economic determinism and dialectical materialism; they evidently expected a new socialist culture to rise almost naturally out of the regenerated soil of socialist productive relations and the socialist *gemeinwesen.*

Writing and reflecting about Russia, the backward "giant that came late," Tkachev, anticipating Lenin and his successors, would not, or could not, resign himself to such a metaphysical or "pedantic" (Tkachev said) conceit about economic causation or the dialectical process of history. We recall Tkachev's words: "A revolutionary minority is no longer willing to wait but must take upon itself the forcing of consciousness upon the people." Or, "The minority [of intellectuals] will impart a considered and rational form to the struggle, leading it towards predetermined goals, directing this coarse material [the masses] towards ideal principles." Thus, despite Tkachev's mirror metaphor of his description of the economic base as "the principal springs . . . prime-movers of thoughts and behavior," superstructure in his view is extremely active before, during, and after the revolution. Tkachev applied the voluntaristic outlook particularly to the period after the revolution.

Still, Tkachev (and others who have attempted a similar theoretical feat) have provoked a dilemma, one that began to perplex Lenin near the end of his life.[14] The voluntaristic trend in Tkachevist as well as Leninist thought has tended to confuse what should not be confused—namely, the truism that without a freely developing culture creative and unimpeded intellectual imagination and inventiveness with minimal interference from political authorities at the top, ill effects are likely to result. The springs of intellectual imagination and invention may dry up or become routine; a black market in paintings, essays, and novels may develop. More important for the rulers themselves, the legitimacy of the regime may assume an artificial quality and its descendent plans lack the wholehearted, energetic, and unmanufactured support of the citizens. The lack of grassroots heart and the spontaneous expression of popular feeling (whether of disgruntlement or loyalty) tend to detract from the regime's base of popular support and the creditability of its programs and pronouncements. This may lead eventually to an overall weakening of the effect of the regime's planning and execution of its national purposes.[15] The Soviet press provides abundant examples of artificially whipped-up enthusiasm, in part the product and effect of a descending mode of political power.[16] Loyalty of the ruled to the rulers may break down altogether, as in Communist Hungary in 1956 or Communist China since 1966. Descending-power regimes assiduously set about organizing outlets or safety valves for the release of popular dissatisfaction ("let a hundred flowers bloom," said Mao Tse-tung in his effort in 1956–1957 to cope with the "contradictions problem" in Communist China).

It is doubtlessly true that excessive voluntarism and one-party dictation and authoritarianism, when carried over from the revolutionary phase into the postrevolutionary phase of constructing socialism and communism, may produce a number of bad side effects in the nation's culture which tend to *interfere with the very building of socialism and communism,* as well as with the process of human "creative evolution," quoting Professor Merriam (in footnote 16). Among the phenomena or bad effects of this voluntarism and authoritarianism are:

1. Creating sensitivity or suspicion in the citizenry about the legitimacy of the oligarchical regime—the result of weakly-developed popular support at the grassroots, support which is stronger when it is freely expressed and not forced or "rigged";
2. Drying up—or the threat of it—of the sources of various creative springs—evidenced in the USSR, particularly in literature and music; less so in cinematography (where the very genres tend to encourage experimentation) and in natural science (which is considered in the post-Stalin era to be relatively apolitical);
3. Working havoc with the official ideology whose theory of economic determinism, when applied to the last stage of building communism, would seem to make one-party dictation an anachronism, a fact which changing of the term "dictatorship of the proletariat" to "all-people's state" or "all-people's party [CPSU]" does not cancel.

The party ideologues in the USSR, as Zbigniew K. Brzezinski has pointed out, are continually in frenetic pursuit of all means to buttress the official ideology of the regime, since the ideology is so deeply involved in the very legitimization of the regime:

. . . the role of ideology involves the almost frenetic efforts of the regime to indoctrinate the masses. It is not an exaggeration to say that indoctrination has replaced terror as the most distinctive feature of the relationship of the regime to society, and perhaps even of the system itself as compared to others. With the destruction . . . of organized intermediary groups between the regime and the people, with the basic outlines of the new society erected, the emphasis on class struggle has given way to a massively organized effort to instill in the Soviet people the values of the ruling party. The closer one studies the Soviet political system, the more one becomes impressed by the totality of the effort and the energy and resources committed to it. There is just no comparable example elsewhere to this total effort (in the words of *Pravda*, September 14, 1960) "to rear the new man." While the Party often meets with major difficulties because of boredom, hostility toward uniformity, absence of free contacts with the West, and disbelief and/or just formal acquiescence, it is able to exploit a very major advantage—that it is in a position to link the process of ideological indoctrination with technical modernization of society, which has become the universally accepted good in our age. It is not an accident that, in all recent discussions of propaganda, the Party has been stressing the need to link the two, and because of its monopoly of power the Party can make modernization seem like the consequence of its ideologically inspired action. The organizational compulsion of the Party for ideology-action thus becomes the source and the means of modernization, thereby strengthening the Party's social legitimization.[17]

We would add to Brzezinski's incisive remarks that the frenetic quality of the regime's ideology-action is whetted by the dilemma we have discussed in the third point above—that the economic determinism vs. "political determinism" (voluntarism) problem existing in the half-century-old "socialist" Russia would seem eventually to help "erode" (to use another of Brzezinski's terms) the official ideology and its endeavors to legitimize one-party rule and the machinations of the oligarchs—e.g., the *coup* in Moscow of October 13–14, 1964, by which Khrushchev was thrown out of office and the Brezhnev-Kosygin regime installed.

It should be pointed out that not all Russian Marxists (not all Bolsheviks either) have permitted revolutionary voluntarism or postrevolutionary intellectualism and Jacobinism to undercut their basic Marxist theory of economic determinism or dialectical materialism. This is eliminated by their hesitancy about predicting future kitchens as we noted in the case of Marx. For example, Plekhanov, "the father of Russian Marxism," once wrote:

> There is no power on earth which would be able to say to art: "You must head in this or that direction," just as there is no power on earth which might prescribe this or that direction to science or philosophical thought.[18]

Of course, Plekhanov's rather rigid adherence to Marxist historical materialism and economic determinism tended to save him from the *degree* of voluntarism found in his Bolshevik opponents. But occasionally, even among the Bolsheviks, one could find the same hesitancy about cultural dictation. For example, Trotsky:

> Our Marxist perception of the objective social dependence and social utilitarianism of art, when translated into political terms, in no way anticipates aims to command art by means of decrees or dictation. It is not true that for us only that which expresses the worker is new and revolutionary—nonsense! It would be ridiculous to demand of poets that they describe a factory smokestack or rebellion against capital. It is obvious that the new art cannot help but be organically situated in its attention in the midst of the proletarian culture. The plough of the new art can in no way be limited to any restricted plot of earth—on the contrary, it must cultivate the whole field up and down.[19]
> For it [dialectical materialism], art . . . is always socially dependent, historically utilitarian from the point of view of the objective historical process. Art searches, by means of its necessary rhythm of words, into dark, human moods, merges thought with feeling or opposes them to one another, enriches the spiritual experience of the individual and the collectivity, refines feeling, makes it flexible, sympathetic, resounding, broadens the capacity for thought along

no single road of experience, and nourishes individuality, the social group, and the nation.[20]

Art must mark out its own path. The methods of Marxism are not methods of art. The Party leads the proletariat, but not the historical process.[21]

These Marxist pronouncements tended to be forgotten (and perhaps still are in the USSR) when the meaning of Stalin's conception of artists, writers, and philosophers as "engineers of the human soul" began to sink into Soviet society and become a part of the functioning of the one-party oligarchy.

TKACHEV AND IDEOLOGY-*QUA*-RATIONALIZATION

Nowhere did Tkachev display his avowed Machiavellianism more clearly than when he discussed the practicality and usefulness of certain ideologies, considered apart from whatever truth they may contain. We recall that he spoke in this way of Marx's materialist outlook when he said that it had "great *practical* importance." The ideology, he said, would "concentrate the energy and activity of those men who are sincerely devoted to social causes on the truly essential points: namely, the vital interests of the people." Economic materialism would guarantee that they would gain the support of the most indispensable forces. It would be a spur which would inspire direct action.[22]

Hans Morgenthau, perhaps inspired by the work of Mannheim and others, tends to view ideology as mere rationalization of the brute facts of acquiring and retaining political power. Applying this kind of analysis to Tkachevism and modern Jacobinism, we may see *an apparent relationship between ideological formulations and actual social, intellectual, or national-cultural factors existing at the time or in the era in which the ideological formulations were made.* When examining this relationship, one might keep in the back of his mind Bertrand de Jouvenel's statement about ideology: "The logic of a revolutionary epoch is to be found not in the ideas but in the facts. . . . The central fact is the erection of a New Power."

To illustrate the way in which Tkachevist-Leninist ideology was congruent with social, economic, and intellectual conditions extant in Russia at the time of its formulation, I have quoted below a number of excerpts from the writings of major theorists, grouped according to ideas and conditions that were current in late-nineteenth-century Russia. Is this congruence merely evidence that Tkachev, Lenin, and the others were men of their time, who drew their modes of thought and expression from the common fund of information and ideas that was available to all their contemporaries, and whose ideals were founded on empirical bases? Or does it show that they were sophists and opportunists who cynically took advantage of existing conditions and intellectual fashion to propagate their ideas and, ultimately, to seize power in Russia? For example, science and scientific method enjoyed great repute at the end of the nineteenth century. Many thought that absolute scientific truths about human society could be found that were analogous to the recently discovered truths about geology, biology, and physics. Did these thinkers share that belief, or did they realize that for an ideology to be *convincing* to intellectuals and quasi-intellectuals it would have to employ scientific jargon and even, perhaps, be called a science, as were the ideologies of Tkachev and Lenin? There is no simple answer to the question: Certainly each of these men, at one time or another, adopted an admittedly Machiavellian approach to the problem of dealing with the masses. Just as certainly each of them sought to remodel society on an ideal plan, in reaction against a social order that had grown intolerable. Nevertheless, the extent of their altruism is worth pondering, and the reader is invited to consider it in relation to the following quotations. Note also the similarities between the views of Tkachev and Lenin.

SUITABILITY OF IDEOLOGY TO THE FACTUAL OR "LOGICAL" SITUATION OR PREMISE

Russian Situation

Existence of a small, rationalistic intelligentsia for whom the nineteenth-century Age of Science and its irrefutable postulates seemed to suggest the applicability of science to the actions of men in society and to politics which, for some, became a kind of social physics.

Ideological Rationalization

Communism proceeds not from principles, but from facts. . . . What still survives of all former philosophy is the *science* of thought and its laws—formal logic and dialectics. Everything else is merged into a positive *science* of nature and history.—MARX[23]

Marxism is the *science* of the laws governing the development of nature and society, the science of revolution of the oppressed and exploited masses, the *science* of the victory of socialism in all countries, and the *science* of building a Communist society.—STALIN[24]

The essence of any *science*, be it astronomy, biology, or history, is similar—it always concerns itself with the laws governing the given phenomena. . . . We must be able to bring social empirical facts under the control of *science* and thereby bring order[25] and harmony out of the chaos of social empirical data.—TKACHEV[26]

Science Demands Scientists

Talented scientific minds are needed to perceive scientific truth, organize the raw data, formulate systems of thought and programs of action. They understand "necessity" and are prepared to help it realize itself. They may or may not be actual members of the class which necessity uses to effectuate its purposes. What is important is that they be enlighteners, bearers, popularizers of the new science. It is not expected that they can constitute more than a tiny minority of the population.

Ideological Rationalization
of the Demand for Scientists

The dictatorship of *individual persons* has very often been in history the expresser, bearer, and guide of the dictatorship of revolutionary classes—of this the experience of history speaks undeniably.—LENIN[27]

Modern socialist consciousness can arise only on the basis of *profound scientific knowledge*. . . . The vehicles of this science are not the proletariat, but the *bourgeois intelligentsia*.—LENIN[28]

The *intellectuals* in our party make up a much larger percentage than in West European parties.—LENIN[29]

The objective [economic process] is *perceived* first of all by the *leaders of the Communist Party,* who derive from these economic processes political conclusions and indicate the measures that are necessary to ensure the victory of the New over the Old.—STALIN[30]

Thinking representatives of the given class [are those who have] the necessary knowledge and experience—the necessary political instinct for rapid and correct solution of intricate political problems.— LENIN[31]

The *minority* [*of intellectuals*] will impart a considered and rational form to the struggle, leading it towards predetermined goals, directing this coarse material [the masses] towards ideal principles. . . . The uncivilized crowd is too crude and ignorant to discern the causes of its hard pressed condition and itself find the road to its amelioration.—TKACHEV[32]

Russian Situation

Revolution in a backward country like Russia with a large mass of illiterate peasants, a weakly developed proletariat and bourgeoisie, and hence few bourgeois liberties, in a country where the few urban administrative centers dominate the whole country—revolution in such a country should be organized and concentrated in these few key centers of control. A tiny minority bred in these urban centers exists and is prepared to lead the revolution and impose its program upon the vast majority lying both within and especially without the urban centers.

Ideological Rationalization of Rule by a Minority Over the Majority

The importance of the proletariat is *far larger than the actual number of persons who compose it.* This is why the proletariat, *although it may compose a minority of the population,* is capable of triumph over the bourgeoisie. . . .

It is particularly characteristic of workers' political parties that they can embrace only a *minority of their class.* . . . Thus, we are obliged to admit that *only this conscious minority* may lead the masses and carry them along behind it. . . .

The capital cities or large trading and industrial centers . . . to a significant degree decide the political fate of a nation. Gentlemen "Socialists" regard state power as some sort of sacred thing, an idol, or as some resultant vector of interacting forces expressed by voting, an absolute of "authentic democracy."— LENIN[33]

An attack at the *center of power* . . . could lead to positive and lasting results.—TKACHEV[34]

The peasants . . . [try to save] themselves from extinction . . . as fractions of the middle class. They are, therefore, not revolutionary, but conservative. Nay, more—they *are reactionary*, for they try to roll back the wheel of history.—MARX[35]

They have described and still describe the childish tale about the proletariat . . . "convincing" a majority of the toilers and winning them lastingly to their side via elections. . . . Only after beating the bourgeoisie over the head and seizing the power in the state can the sympathy and support of the petty-bourgeois strata [that is, *the peasant majority*— A. L. W.] be won. . . . Partisans of the Second International say in their propaganda . . . that the proletariat must first achieve a formal expression of the will of the majority of the population . . . and then after that transfer the power to the proletariat. This *misconception* overlooks the fact that bourgeois parties rule mostly because they are able to deceive the masses of the population, due to the oppression of capital . . .—LENIN[36]

The *proletariat* indeed comes forward here in Russia as the *representative of the whole nation,* of everything vital and honest in *all* classes.—LENIN[37]

If you leave the people to themselves, they will build nothing new. . . . The peasant loves traditional forms of his life and does not want to lay a finger on them. . . . One can imagine how quickly and successfully we could carry out our socialist principles if the program depended on one-sided local wishes and *capricious arbitrariness of the routine-ridden majority!*—TKACHEV[38]

When we speak of the will of a nation, do we by any chance mean the opinions of that nation? Not at all. . . . We are for the proletarian class dictatorship.

Thus it is clear from this what we mean when we refer
to the will of the nation. . . . *Claims based on universal suffrage mean nothing and prove nothing to
us.*—OSINSKY[39]

The *real* majority of the people . . . is *not to be
understood in a formal [referendum] sense.*—
TROTSKY[40]

[The Party is] a minority of a minority.—
LENIN[41]

Foe of New Socialist Dictatorship Is Liberalism

An absolutist system finds its most formidable (and logical) foe to be liberalism—the system in which political power
changes hands periodically and in which political opposition
is permitted expression through rival political parties, the
press, public opinion, pressure groups, and so on. Liberalism
implies toleration of a variety of social and political philosophies, no one of whch is permitted to establish an irremovable
monopoly on truth.

Ideological Condemnation of Liberalism

Universal tabulation of votes . . . only proves
always to be a mere *fiction, a fantastic right,* and
from this right flow benefits to those whose interests
have nothing to do with those of the workers.—
TKACHEV[42]

Petty-bourgeois democrats [are people] who call
themselves "socialists" but are really *henchmen of the
bourgeoisie.* . . . The bourgeois, German Social-
Democratic Party, the strongest party in the Second
International, was the most active party in Germany
in preparing an attack on the Soviet Union.—LENIN[43]

. . . the transference of all power to the Constituent Assembly [representing a variety of political
forces—A. L. W.] is the same thing as agreement
with the *malignant bourgeoisie.* . . . The Russian
Bolshevik Soviets hold the best interests of the toilers
enormously higher than the interests of a treasonable
agreement with the *bourgeois parties.*—LENIN[44]

Liberalism began to lose its progressive character
with the coming onto the scene of the proletariat.
. . . In the epoch of the general crisis of capitalism,

the development of *liberalism* has led to the elimination of differences between liberals and the conservatives.—LENIN[45]

To decide once every few years which member of the ruling class is to oppress and suppress the people in parliament—there you have the real essence of *bourgeois parliamentarism.*—LENIN[46]

The struggle for life or death against capital, to demand of the proletariat that it piously observe the *demands of political democracy* would be the same thing as demanding of a man who is defending his life and existence against *highway robbers* that he observe the artificial and conditional rules of French wrestling, which have been established by his enemy. —LENIN[47]

They [moderate socialist and liberal opponents] have not understood that a vote within the framework, the institutions, within the habits of *bourgeois parliamentarism* is part of the *bourgeois state apparatus,* which must be smashed and broken up from top to bottom in order to realize the dictatorship of the proletariat, for the transition *from bourgeois democracy to proletarian democracy.* . . . They have not understood that all serious questions of politics are decided *not at all by votes, but by civil war.*—LENIN[48]

. . . only force can give meaning to right.— TKACHEV[49]

[*Bourgeois democracy*] puts the *particular* interest above the *general* interest, the *partial* above the *whole, egoism* above *altruism.*—TKACHEV[50]

The revolutionary minority, having freed the people, . . . directs the destruction of the enemies of the revolution. In this manner, the minority can deprive the *enemies* of all means of resistance and counterattack. Then it can proceed to the introduction of new, progressively communist elements into . . . the national life.—TKACHEV[51]

Civil liberty and freedom for capital—this is a *contradiction* which cannot be resolved [under capitalism].—TKACHEV[52]

The *bourgeois political freedom* of Western Europe is profitable only for those who have the possibility and the leisure to enjoy this freedom. . . . The interest of the capitalist is diametrically opposed to the interest of the worker. *Any sort of agreement between them is unthinkable. One will always aim at predominance over the other.* At the present time the interest of capital reigns over that of the worker.—TKACHEV[53]

It is very, very sad, of course, that each step must be purchased at the cost of human blood, that each intelligent change in society must come crashing through under arms. . . . We think that the so-called road of *peaceful reform* and *tranquil progress* is one of the most *impractical Utopias* ever thought up by man in order to soothe his conscience and to lull his intellect to sleep.—TKACHEV[54]

The history of the workers movement now shows that in all countries . . . communists will go through a struggle (which has already begun) above all and chiefly against the movement's own form of Menshevism.—LENIN[55]

What conclusions may be drawn from these comparisons?

First, it suggests that suitability (in the Russian case, at least) of *ideas to situation* may be something more than mere accident or coincidence, as the rather impressive suitability of the ideas of Tkachev, Lenin, *et al.*, to Russian conditions appears to have been. Much of this suitability, of course, depends squarely on how one expresses or views the concrete situation or the environment. We are assuming here that the concrete situation, conditions, and premises are herein described more or less as the political observers and actors quoted on the left would have viewed or actually did view them. We are also saying something more: that in retrospect there was considerable basis for their assessing the concrete situation the way they did since they wished to succeed—and did—in actualizing the political power and ideological goals contained in their programs. For example, scientism did have considerable appeal for Russian intellectuals at the turn of the century; it therefore seems natural that political appeals might be stated *scientistically,* as in fact they most emphatically were by the Bolsheviks.

Second, it would be premature to conclude that the ideologists deliberately quoted or cooked up the ideas, not because they actually believed in them, but merely to find suitable or expedient rationalizations. And yet a number of political scientists have more than implied that ideology consists of little more than just that: Machiavellian "window-dressing" (even "ritual," according to Erich Fromm) in order to gain, legitimize, or hold political power in the state. Would it not be more objective to say that the ideas may be at best an unconscious reaction to the concrete situation, at worst self-conscious products of fanatical minds bent on imposing those ideas on the public at all cost, supported in the use of coercion by a clever estimate of the weaknesses and susceptibilities of their victim?

A rather sophisticated view of ideology is that it serves the purpose of rationalizing the callous deeds of unrestrained political power. Political actors, according to that analysis, rightly employ ideology as a camouflage or a pontifical ethic to salve consciences, justify necessary evils, and win support among the innocent. Man is, in that view, reduced to a neurotic creature so content with his illusions that he need not trouble to improve reality.

The world of humane letters has produced a number of spokesmen for a different attitude toward the function of ideology. To them it is natural and good that man speculate upon the better and even the best, that he strive to act in a manner likely to realize his ideals, and that he place over himself leaders to effect these aims. Given these assumptions, ideology becomes a definition of the ideal way of life and a plan of action for realizing that ideal.

If ever there existed a state and an elite that, by the depth and breadth of its political power, had the possibility of imposing successfully (or unsuccessfully) its own ideal pattern upon the world, it is the Soviet Government and Communist Party. They have *proved* that ideology can be, indeed, the most "virile of actualities." The power-for-power's-sake school leaves unanswered the whys and wherefores of the present Soviet institutions, way of life, and tactical schemes. Why, for example, did the Bolshevik leadership choose collective farms in the USSR and again in its satellites instead of free cooperatives or state subsidies to agriculture in order to guarantee more grain for export and for the cities? Why was the swallowing up of key economic, political, and cultural posts by a single-minded, disciplined political party considered preferable to the distribution of these posts among a variety of more or less autonomously competing groups within a framework of patriotic loyalty and fair play? Why was the self-perpetuation and co-option of leaders deemed preferable to elections, periodic house cleanings of the leaders, and greater participation of the ruled in selecting and checking their rulers? Answers to these questions are not likely to be found by reference solely to power for its own sake. There are, after all, many ways of acquiring, holding, and using power. And there are as many corresponding ideologies and programs.

TKACHEVISM, LENINISM, AND SOVIET HISTORIANS

The victory in Russia of the most radical wing of Russian Marxism and the establishment of the one-party dictatorship, which was soon to exercise control over all media of communication in the country, shortly after 1917 led to a somewhat one-sided emphasis in the study of the history on Marxism and other types of socialism existent in prerevolutionary Russia. Historians (some excepted, of course), acting as full-fledged propagandists of the new regime, began to trace an alleged basic line of development of socialism in Russia leading inevitably up to the Bolshevik victory in November 1917. One may observe the tendency of Soviet historiography from the revolution to the imposition of Stalin's one-man rule and narrowing of the party line on historiography (in part a *kulturkampf*, in part Stalin's method of intimidating and silencing certain individual intellectuals and groups of intellectuals) to single out the *most radical* figures in the revolutionary past of the nineteenth century. But there was rarely agreement between the historians on how to gauge the significance of this or that revolutionary doctrine in terms of future developments and the eventual triumph of Bolshevism. Many of the debates and differences continue in severely truncated form to the present.[56]

What influence on Bolshevism was credited to Tkachev by the Leninist historians of the early postrevolutionary period before Stalin's imposition of the Lenin Cult?

Any treatment of Tkachev confronts the Soviet historian with a number of obvious hazards. First, do some of the obvious resemblances of Tkachev's outlook to that of Lenin warrant calling Tkachev "the first Bolshevik," as some have actually called him?[57] If so, does such a description fit the concept of historical materialism, which asserts a rather strict dependence of ideas upon historical development and establishes the irreversibility of the upward-spiraling historical process? And what of the stature and originality of Lenin and the Bolshevik party, if it turned out that Lenin and his followers were in some sense imitators of some proto-Bolshevik forerunner?

Second, if the past and certain revolutionary figures of the past were "Bolshevized" by Soviet historians, these same Soviet historians would find themselves in agreement with any number of exile publicists living in the West who were violent critics of the Soviet regime and making free use of the term "Blanquist" or even *buntarist* (*putschist*) to describe Lenin, the wily conspirator.[58]

Although a number of figures took part in the 1920's debate on the degree of Bolshevism in Tkachevism, the principal ones were Professor M. N. Pokrovsky, B. P. Kozmin, B. I. Gorev, S. I. Mitskevich, and N. N. Baturin. To a degree, it was Pokrovsky, perhaps the most reputed among the five authors listed, who initiated the debate. For example, in his authoritative *Essays on the Russian Revolutionary Movement in the Nineteenth and Twentieth Centuries* (*Ocherki russkovo revolyutsionnovo dvizheniya XIX–XX vv*), published in Moscow in 1924 (which had followed some articles and lectures by Pokrovsky in which his views had become widely known), Pokrovsky indicated how Bolshevizing the prerevolutionary past could be accomplished in the case, for example, of Zaichnevsky's proclamation, *Young Russia*. Pokrovsky called this proclamation "the first Bolshevik document in our history."[59] However, since Pokrovsky's historical investigations took him over such a broad reach of Russian history, it is more useful here to select two of the above historians to illustrate the debate over Tkachev, Tkachevism, and Bolshevism. These two are Mitskevich and Baturin.[60] But first, let us examine Gorev.

In many respects, it seems that, besides Pokrovsky's lectures, B. I. Gorev's book on Auguste Blanqui (see n. 62) was a milestone marking the beginning of serious investigation of the Blanquist element in Russian prerevolutionary thought, particularly as that tendency appeared congenial to Bolshevism. Gorev, who became a Bolshevik in 1905 after having been a prominent member of the League of Struggle for the Liberation of the Working Class, later went over to Menshevism but rejoined the Bolsheviks in 1920; this "renegadism" somewhat detracted from the authority of his assertions with respect to Tkachev and Lenin's debts to Tkachev and Tkachevism.[61] Gorev's book, *Auguste Blanqui*,[62] made the point that elements of Blanquism in Marxism boiled down to three basic organizational and tactical elements: the conspiratorial party; the minority's seizure of power; and the dictatorship of the revolutionary vanguard after the seizure of power. Gorev attempted to prove that all these Blanquist elements in Marxism constituted an important part of Bolshevism as well.

Two articles soon followed the appearance of Gorev's book. One supported the Gorev view of the kinship between Leninism and Tkachevism and the affinity of both to Marxism, while a second follow-up article strongly attacked Gorev and contained a veiled threat (motivated in part by Gorev's recently discarded Menshevism).

The first pro-Tkachev-Lenin-kinship article was written by S. I. Mitskevich,[63] an old Bolshevik Party member and doctor of medicine who in the immediate postrevolutionary period (beginning in 1918) headed the Moscow Department of Education; it was entitled "The Russian Jacobins," published in *Proletarskaya revolyutsiya* (*Proletarian Revolution*) in 1923. In this article and in one other written two years later in answer to Baturin, Mitskevich singled out a number of ideas which he said had "entered into the basic fund of Bolshevik ideology." He qualified his position to an extent by adding that since Tkachev spoke of a "revolutionary party" rather than the proletarian class-qua-class, there is no question of "an identity with Bolshevism . . . but rather one of analogy; otherwise, Tkachev would be a Bolshevik, or, vice versa, the Bolsheviks would be Tkachevists."[64] Perhaps his most significant statement, and one that apparently provoked Baturin's hostile rebuke, was:

> Nevertheless, it is an irrefutable fact that *the Russian Revolution proceeded to a significant degree according to the ideas of Tkachev,* with the seizure of power made at a time determined in advance by a revolutionary party which was organized on the principle of strict centralization and discipline. And this party,

having seized power, is working in many respects as Tkachev advised.[65]

Mitskevich added that he found in Tkachev's thoughts elements which are of proletarian socialism. . . . [Zaichnevsky] and Tkachev, more than any of the others, succeeded in overcoming bourgeois ideology, which was so familiar to the Russian revolutionaries of the 1860's and 1870's.[66]

N. N. Baturin made his appearance in print after Mitskevich's first article. He was undoubtedly encouraged in his attack on Mitskevich by the bitter onslaught which had earlier appeared under the mysterious by-line of "Sineira" (an allusion to Tacitus' phrase, "sine ira et studio" [without anger or passion]) who had attacked Gorev in 1923 and written his rebuttals in *Proletarskaya revolyutsiya* in 1924 and again in 1925.[67]

The essence of Baturin's attack (we shall ignore the motivation and customary in-fighting among Soviet academicians, sometimes for official Party favor) was that Mitskevich had been "blind" to the petty-bourgeois essence of Tkachevism.[68] Tkachev had no understanding of classes, class struggle, or their role in history, as presented by Marx and Engels. Moreover, Mitskevich's comparisons of Tkachevism to Leninism were superficial; whatever similarities there may have been were purely accidental. Baturin took Mitskevich to task for not emphasizing Tkachev's peculiar jump theory of historical development, which, he said, had nothing to do with the Marxist (or Leninist) philosophy of history as dialectical. Moreover, it was strongly suggested by Baturin that Mitskevich had erred because of the fact that he himself was not a pure and orthodox Marxist-Leninist.

Mitskevich struck back in the "Answer to Baturin." He wrote:

Let Comrade Baturin not tell me that they [the Russian Jacobins] were not genuine proletarian socialists. I know that, but I also know that it is necessary to think dialectically and not to limit oneself to saying yes, yes and no, no. The Russian Jacobins were the forerunners of Russian revolutionary Marxism, but they were not yet revolutionary Marxists.[69]

Mitskevich then repeated the Lenin quotation from *One Step Forward, Two Steps Backward.*

Mitskevich also made some extremely interesting observations about Russia as a *special case,* noting how well *both* Tkachevism and Leninism were suited to this Russian situation.[70]

In his "On the Problem of the Roots of Bolshevism—An Answer to Comrade Baturin," in *Katorga i ssylka,* No. 3 (16), 1925, Mitskevich asserts:

> The principal cause of the analogy [between Tkachevism and Bolshevism] lies deep within the peculiarities of Russian history and Russian social life.[71]

Mitskevich then lists these peculiarities which led Tkachev and the Bolsheviks to use similar tactics and devise, in some respects, similar programs.[72]

1. Russia exceeded the West European countries in the "intensity" of its class contradiction and class struggle;
2. The dictatorship of the Tsarist ruling circles ("Tsarist absolutism") caused much popular dissatisfaction and frequent uprisings and *Pugachevshchina;*
3. The conditions of poverty under which the intelligentsia lived;
4. Absence of any possible legal expression for political opposition or the grievances of the working class;
5. The "retarded" development of capitalism in Russia;
6. The active interference of the state in what little industry there was "[creating] an illusion of the artificiality and the lack of any roots [of capitalism in the society]"; therefore, the overall weak development of Russian capitalism facilitating its overthrow.

In commenting on the above examples of Russian peculiarities, Mitskevich notes how both Tkachevism and Bolshevism treated each of the special Russian conditions. But his discussion is extremely terse, indirect, even coy—perhaps to a degree reflecting his desire (by the mid-twenties and Stalin's accretion of power) to avoid a too acrimonious debate which would only invite the concern of the highest officials of the Party, especially in the aftermath of Lenin's death. Mitskevich implies that these six Russian peculiarities *were just as true of the Russia of Tkachev's time as they were of Lenin's some thirty-*

five years later. The essence of his discussion of Russian peculiarities, as it pertains to the kinship problem, consists of the following.

Tkachev (and Lenin) were right in their estimate of the *weakness* of Russian capitalism and of the Tsarist state (or at least, Tsarism's periods of waxing and waning power, depending on its foreign and domestic engagements and problems). Also, the Tsarist state (unlike those of the bourgeois West) and capitalism lacked roots in the depths of Russian society—thus, the artificiality of the state (meaning by "state" the Tsarist *government*,[73] Mitskevich maintained) and of capitalism and the expediency of toppling this regime at its heart and center in the capital (for Lenin, the Provisional government of Kerensky, a bourgeois regime, was just as weak and vulnerable as the Tsarist state, even the weakest link in the bourgeois chain) ; that the retarded development of capitalism in Russia was an advantage to the proletarian cause, an *advantage* that could not last long if the revolutionaries delayed their *coup* (a point made by Lenin late in 1917) ;[74] and that the Tsarist state had set a pattern of sorts which by its nationalization of various industries, would facilitate the etatization of all of Russian industry and, in fact, the whole economy by the "worker's *half* state," as Lenin called it in *State and Revolution* in an early anticipation of the contemporary Lassalleist concept of the "all people's state" (cf. CPSU Program adopted at the Twenty-second Party Congress in 1961), which is also a kind of half state theory.

Mitskevich also had some interesting (and at times rather original) things to say about the origins of Russian socialism; his remarks here are, to a degree, related to the whole question of Russia as a special case.

According to Mitskevich's viewpoint, some of which may be traced to Tkachevism and to statements made by Lenin, Russian socialism arose from:

1. The influence of the European socialist movement;
2. Development of large Russian industry;
3. Absence of any deep-rooted or extensive petty-bourgeois peasant land ownership (Stolypin's reform had not time to work any major changes in Russian peasant life, al-

though it might have had it been allowed to continue);
4. Lack of experience to be gained from a rapidly-developing working class;
5. Close ties between the Russian working class and the peasantry "which nourished the idea that their aims were indistinguishable in the Russian revolutionary movement"[75] (that is, from Tkachev's and Lenin's point of view, certainly not Plekhanov's or the Socialist-Revolutionaries'!).[76]

In expanding on these points, Mitskevich maintained that Russian capitalism did not really begin to sink roots in Russian society until the 1890's when peasant ties with the urban workers were not broken, as they were in West European countries. He then states:

> The condition for our victory consisted in the formation of our party which had taken over the old Russian revolutionary traditions. . . . This assured the victory of the working class.[77]

Mitskevich then taunts Baturin, pointing out that Marx himself had favorably regarded the Russian revolutionary movement and called it the vanguard of the whole revolutionary movement of Europe (in Marx's Preface to *The Communist Manifesto*), the spark and signal which would herald the revolution in the West and in which both revolutions would complement each other. Mitskevich adds that Marx could hardly have said these things about the Russian socialists if he had thought that they were lackeys of the bourgeoisie or liberals, as Baturin seems to suggest they were.[78]

Speaking of Marx, Mitskevich further notes in the course of his argument with Baturin that he took a profound interest in the *Program* of the People's Will (*Narodovol'tsi*) group; Mitskevich speculates that Marx may have even helped edit it.[79] "We read in this *Program*," says Mitskevich, that:

> The people, while rising up, must choose their Provisional Government from among the workers or people known for their loyalty to the people's cause. . . . *After* the uprising has been victorious throughout the whole country, when land, factories, and mills have passed into the hands of the people, *when in the*

> *state there will be no other militia than the people's*
> *own . . . then the people will send its own repre-*
> *sentatives to a Constituent Assembly.*[80]

Mitskevich asserts that a historian may form actual links with members of the People's Will *who later were to become Marxists and still later Bolsheviks,* especially those who had worked in the midst of the *urban* laborers.[81]

The debate was abruptly ended even before Stalin's famous letter to *Proletarskaya revolyutsiya* in 1931, entitled "On Certain Questions of the History of Bolshevism."[82]

This letter marked the climax of a period which had already begun soon after Lenin's death when the Stalin machine's control over the country's media began to move ahead. The Stalin letter, summing up and attempting to justify what had already been carried out as the Party's "General Line" on historiography several years before, stated that "rotten liberalism" afflicts certain kinds of Bolsheviks, that "certain *'litterateurs'* and 'historians' have attempted to drag Trotskyite trash masked as contraband into our literature [which] must be met with a determined attack by Bolsheviks. . . . It is impossible to permit literary discussion with Trotskyite smugglers." Although Trotskyites were singled out, this term was, and had been earlier, merely a euphemism employed by Stalin to stigmatize as "contraband" or "bourgeois objectivity" any true objectivity or free opinion about the Russian revolutionary past. Any questioning of the cult of the absolute originality of Lenin was forbidden and is still forbidden in the USSR today. One after the other, various journals began to apologize for so-called past errors, among them *Katorga i ssylka* for its tolerance of the Tkachev-Lenin kinship controversy. From this time on, objectivity began to disappear steadily from Soviet history books and journals, not to mention from literature in other fields of study as well.

M. N. Pokrovsky, one of the first to note a kinship between the ideas of Tkachev and Lenin, and his school of history, as well as specialists on Russian Jacobinism and Blanquism, were all silenced. Some of the victims of Stalin's later trials, held in 1936–1938, many of them Old Bolsheviks, were in fact accused in part of having distorted the past, true Party history, and old Party disputes. The result was a general leveling of historiography to the mean of the Party's General Line, as Stalin and his group defined it. Boris P. Kozmin himself, who survived the purges, reprisals, dismissals, and banishments, began to modify his approach to the Russian revolutionary past.

As we have indicated, Kozmin took on the job of editing Tkachev's works (the *Sochineniya*), which began to appear with Volume I in 1932. However, although the *Sochineniya* was to have comprised seven volumes, the seventh never appeared and the edition ended with Volume VI in 1937. That last volume contained no preface by the editor, though such prefaces were customarily included in volumes of this type in the Soviet Union. Although Kozmin lived until 1958, no explanation was ever given for his abandonment of the *Sochineniya*.

As far as other historians and their commentaries on Tkachev were concerned, throughout the Stalin period and today Soviet historians simply revert to the viewpoints of Mitskevich's detractors, Messrs. "Sineira"[83] and Baturin. Baturin had written by 1930:

> *To compare Marxism and Blanquism is wrong. Marxism is a great crossroads on the road of humanity, while Blanquism is only one of many country roads. . . . The ideas of Tkachev were not the ideas of the October Revolution but of the Great French Revolution, and none of the truly revolutionary elements in the ideas of the Russian Jacobins went beyond the ideas of the French Revolution. The revolutionary ideas of Zaichnevsky and Tkachev are not the roots of Bolshevism at all, but the last blossoms of the Great French Revolution on unreceptive Russian soil.*
>
> We find absolutely no elements of proletarian socialism in the social programs of Zaichnevsky and Tkachev. Instead, we find in them all the marks of petty-bourgeois social utopias. Between these reactionary utopias and Bolshevism you cannot place an equal sign or deduce any kind of analogy whatsoever [italics are mine—A. L. W.].[84]

By the time Baturin and others had finished with Tkachev and the Russian Jacobin tradition, there was very little left to say at all of a positive nature about Tkachev other than that he was "an outstanding revolutionary-democrat," which is the current line in Soviet journals, encyclopedias, and textbooks.[85]

The 120th anniversary of the birth of Peter Nikitich Tkachev (June 29, 1964) was passed over in silence by Soviet historical journals. Likewise, in 1966, the 80th anniversary of Tkachev's death (January 4, 1966) was ignored in soviet publications. Meanwhile, anniversaries of other less controversial and interesting revolutionary figures were duly recognized— e.g., the 150th anniversary of N. P. Ogarev's birth was widely commemorated in 1963.

Even Tkachev's name rarely appears in print now in the USSR. And when it does, it is most assuredly *not* accompanied by any such apposition as "the forerunner of Lenin" or "the first Bolshevik," descriptions of Tkachev that, as we have seen, have been given at various times by Western and Soviet historians.

Today in the USSR Tkachev continues to be treated as a "Blanquist . . . *zagovorshchik* . . . *putschist,*" at best a misguided Narodnik—but surely not as a proto-Bolshevik.

His concepts are regarded as if they were nineteenth-century anticipations of Maoism or Red Guard extremism. Sometimes Tkachevism is attacked without mention of its inventor. For example, in his long *podval* in *Pravda* (September 30, 1966) entitled "Evolutionary and Revolutionary Forms of Social Development," Professor M. Rozental condemned the Tkachevist concept of "historical leaps" (*istoricheskiye skachki*), at least as applied on mainland China in the form of the "Great Leap Forward." Indeed, as Rozental remarks, Lenin did speak of leaps (*skachki*), for "without a leap, without a revolutionary transformation of the old forms of life, no new social order could be brought about." But, Rozental continues, "Marxism-Leninism and anarcho-conspiratorial Blanquism have nothing in common."

Neither Stalin nor the thirty-year campaign of silence about Tkachev can erase what has already been written and recorded by memoirists, friends of Lenin, Russian historians, and by Tkachev himself—even though some of this material may be difficult to examine through normal channels in the Soviet Union.

The Lenin Library in Moscow, as the author found on inspecting the card catalogue in June 1966, lists only one work, not by, but about Tkachev (a pamphlet written by B. P. Kozmin). Even Lenin's personal library contained more than this about Tkachev. The same catalogue lists dozens of titles by or about countless other revolutionaries of the second half of the nineteenth century. But the six volumes of Tkachev's works, published in the USSR between 1932 and 1937, are not listed among the 22 million titles in the Lenin Library, nor are dozens of *Soviet* works about Tkachev (they are available, however, in several libraries in the U. S.). Moreover, the latest edition of the *Malaya Sovetskaya Entsiklopedia* (the third edition), the most complete large-scale Soviet encyclopedia, gives this *Narodnik,* as it calls him, a short two-paragraph article in Volume IX (press date 1960) and omits the apposition "revolutionary-democrat" which had often accompanied Tkachev's name in earlier editions of both the *Great* and *Small Soviet Encyclopedias.* Many other examples could be given (e.g., recent articles on revolutionary movements published in Soviet historical, philosophical, or literary journals) of the silent—or, when he is mentioned in passing, distorted—treatment of Tkachev.

And the policy may have had some success, as conversations with young university educated members of the Soviet postwar generation have indicated. The author found, when he asked several of them about Tkachev in the summer of 1966, that such persons responded blankly with "Who?" This was not the answer when the conversation turned to Chernyshevsky, Bakunin, Nechayev, Lavrov, or Mikhailovsky.

In their treatment of Tkachev, Party historians of both the Stalin and post-Stalin periods prudently continue to overlook even such unimpeachable sources as Lenin's close collaborator, Bonch-Bruyevich, when, as we have seen above, they clearly refute official history.

A volume just published in the USSR, *Ocherki istorii istoricheskoi nauki v SSSR* (*Notes on the Historical Development of Historiography in the USSR*), Volume IV, 1966, discusses this problem, among others, but in a very condensed form. The authors, all of the USSR Academy of Sciences, assert that "a struggle for the correct Marxist conception of revolutionary Populism was not resolved successfully in the beginning." The book then all too briefly reviews the controversy between S. I. Mitskevich and B. P. Kozmin on the one hand and N. N. Baturin and the Party-liners on the other.

As the authors state, the issue over Tkachev concerned the degree of both Marxism and proto-Bolshevism contained in his writings. The 1966 Soviet work asserts that Pokrovsky erred in regarding Tkachev as "the first Russian Marxist," as did Mitskevich and Kozmin in designating Tkachev "as a forerunner of the Bolsheviks" or in thinking that the concept of Soviet power and the dictatorship of the proletariat was developed from Zaichnevsky's *Young Russia* and from Tkachev.[86] Baturin's position, according to the authors, "was supported by a majority of researchers" and was a conception which was "more thoughtful and consistent, representing a Marxist-Leninist point of view."

Ocherki makes an interesting admission in regard to the Stalinist attack on the historians (particularly on Pokrovsky) and their treatment of revolutionary Populism as an ideology with Marxist overtones: "Under the influence of the cult of Stalin's person, obvious exaggerations arose in the treatment of Populism. The thesis slowly came into force that Populism was 'the most evil opponent of Marxism.'"

CONCLUDING OBSERVATIONS

Tkachev was keenly aware of the efficacy of political power. He seemed to feel that as society grew more industrial, or that as the state began to acquire mightier weapons, power would become even more crucial and efficacious with respect to society and to all aspects of human life. Tkachev reflects that tendency of thought, in part attributable to Rousseau, which calls for the intrusion of the public into the private, not for the sake of the public alone, but in the name of the general welfare of both the public and private domains.[87] What might be called the psycho-social function of the state makes a striking contrast to the old view, so dominant in the nineteenth century, of atomistic individuals living in a society in which, for Adam Smith and Herbert Spencer, they mechanically act upon one another externally and with a harmonious result. Tkachev rejected this on several grounds; the way he rejected it resembles certain contemporary fascist and communist theories.

Tkachev strongly denied that individuals may be considered to any degree truly self-subsisting, especially in unregenerate bourgeois or semibourgeois society. Far from it; they are hopelessly *dependent* and are caught up in an unrelieved circle of routine (*rutina*) out of which no exit *known to the masses themselves* is possible. Only an intellectual proletariat (as Pisarev once described the radical intelligentsia) can lead the masses out of their vicious circle. The individual-centered psychology of Dostoyevsky appears to Tkachev to be "sick"; Hegel's phenomenology of the spirit is "pedantic rubbish"; Lavrov's democratism and individual-centered sociology (the same could be said of other prerevolutionary theorists) is viewed by Tkachev as "reactionary," "subjectivistic," and "counterrevolutionary," mere offsprings or rationalizations of Western bourgeois utilitarianism, atomistic individualism, and so on. A pejorative frequently used by Tkachev was "pessimistic." He found a good deal of pessimism in the writings of Dostoyevsky. "Optimism" to Tkachev meant to have faith in the power of human reason and of individually rational men (and for Tkachev there are very few of them), in their capacity to work great changes in society. Tkachev in general accepted Comte's doctrine of the ascending evolution of the human intellect and like Comte was contemptuous of what he considered "subjectivistic" and "metaphysical" philosophy, particularly as found in German philosophy and socialism.

Thus, only a strong will tied to a rational intellect (possessing a socialist outlook and total commitment to revolution) and organized with other wills and special intellects as a revolutionary elite with subordination of parts to the ruling center (representing the whole) are capable of bringing about man's progress despite, Tkachev (and Lenin) leads us to think, the opinions of the mass man, whom he calls the "routine man." Social Darwinism, if it implies an inexorably improving condition of man, a mechanistic conception in which improvement takes place automatically without a clearly expressed efficient cause bringing the improvement, is rejected by Tkachev; for a similar reason, we recall, Tkachev rejected the determinism of the Marxian dialectic. There is little place in either, Tkachev implies, for the *intellect-will action of an elite.* Here is the traditional voluntarism vs. determinism contrariety, and Tkachev favors the first. Optimism is not already engendered in the social process; it must be inserted and infused coercively into it by the elite-become-educators in the constructive phase of the revolution.

The modern aspect of this Tkachevian position consists in Tkachev's emphasis on what might be called the penetration of the individual mind through avenues of *public* control and influence. In repudiating the walled-off individual and the unassailable inner-sanctum quality of an "atomic" individual, Tkachev places the emphasis on the interdependence aspect of human society (spiritual and material) and seeks to exploit this interdependence through institutional reform designed to remake man under the "New Principle," i.e., altruism and communism. He almost seems to accept alienation of most individuals (but clearly and obviously *not* of his voluntaristic, autonomously willing and thinking elite) as a fact of life. To Tkachev, the masses seem destined to "find themselves in others," a fact which is utilized by the socialist dictatorship to create what will be in fact a new type of dependence (or, better, interdependence), a new type of collectivized personality which the masses must imitate. If they *are* left to their *own* designs and pleasures, the *old and encrusted routine* will continue because the principle of individualistic egoism aims only at its own satisfaction, not at any higher, loftier principle.

In the manner in which he regards propaganda or even political theories as either beneficial or harmful, as either useful or useless to the Cause, Tkachev anticipates some updated versions of Machiavellianism and exploitation of mass alienation. In other words, given the mass man's unconscious enslavement and inability to attain self-awareness and "consciousness" (knowledge), his shadowy life of self-gratification and ego-centered economic motives, almost any means should and must be employed by the revolutionary minority to make the revolution, over the heads of the masses, if necessary, employing the most extravagant agitational slogans, promises of future satiation, and so on. Tkachev seems to be appealing to what Karl Jaspers has called "a blind political will." He seems to be calling the dissatisfied masses, even the modestly educated among them, to escape from freedom:

> The alternative method of renouncing a true political life is to surrender to a blind political will. One who does this is discontented with his life and complains of environing circumstances, *regarding them, instead of himself,* as the cause of the happenings of his life. . . . Such vociferous would-be participation is the most widespread manifestation of a *reputed* political knowledge and will. Persons of this kidney stumble along through the times able to make trouble and stir up strife, but utterly incapable of discovering the true path.[88]

Tkachev seems to understand that this kind of stumbling, troublemaking, political man was or would be a prevalent type in modern society and that he could be exploited for the Cause. Let these disgruntled and faceless fanatics curse their circumstances (blaming the bourgeois system of production and distribution) and stir up trouble; the elite can make good use of such vociferous disgruntlement. But as for devising the programs for changing the circumstances or the human products of the circumstances and accomplishing the revolution—that was the exclusive right of the elite rulers, not of the distorted and flawed human products of the old social and economic system, the routine-ridden and shortsighted masses.

Self-awareness and true freedom seemed, for Tkachev, to belong only to his elite intellectuals-become-revolutionaries. Presumably, such consciousness might slowly be acquired later by the many, although Tkachev made no such prediction. However, the installation of a dictatorship tends to keep the monopoly of political knowledge in the hands of a small elite. By means of its broad controls over society, the collective dictatorship does little or nothing to promote a general liberation from a new routine and from outer-directedness; in fact, it is in its interests to *promote* alienation and outer-directedness under a new flag. Few, if any, safeguards against abuse of state power can exist in a system of personal or committee dictatorship. One gathers from reading Tkachev that to allow safeguards is to weaken the state, an eventuality that Tkachev's philosophy, like Lenin's, will not permit if the goals the dictatorship has set for itself are to be realized.

Tkachev seems oblivious to the danger of man becoming a mere cog of the political and administrative machinery.[89] It has been confessed in the Communist world that the Stalin period actually witnessed a new type of socialist alienation. Professor Gyorgy Lukacs has remarked:

> [Communist writers] must learn how the best writers [in the West] are fighting against alienation. In the end, we shall find political allies among them. It is the task of literature to paint a picture of the enormous alienation that was the product of the Stalinist era and to help in overcoming it.[90]

Professor Eduard Goldstuecker, a Czechoslovak authority on Franz Kafka who was imprisoned for ten years under the Stalin regime, wrote in communist Czechoslovakia in 1964:

> Technical civilization, alone and of itself, produces anti-humanism and dehumanizing pressure on each individual. Modern civilization draws the individual from the collective, even when it creates enormous new collectives, and makes the individual feel lonely. In a society where religion has ceased to be the cement and connecting link creating ethical inhibitions, it must be replaced by something else. And this something is, in the first rank of importance, art.[91]

Though Tkachev was not conscious of the problems that were to arise in an industrialized society organized along one-party socialist lines and with political leaders who alleged themselves to be endowed with superhuman philosopher-king qualities, present-day scholars within socialist countries are. They seem to yearn for a rebirth of spontaneity, which they deem essential to art and human existence, and for the spiritualization of man's life through art, replacing religion and politics in this function. At the same time, this newly-demanded freedom for art in communist countries contradicts the descending, indoctrinational role of the socialist state and the role assigned by it to the writers to act as "engineers of human souls." One-party states, moreover, have seemed reluctant to yield to any revitalized spontaneity after the revolution, possibly for the same reason that Tkachev feared and opposed spontaneity before the revolution: it is difficult to direct and may lead to disharmony, multiplicity of political programs, parties, philosophies, organizations, and "a hundred flowers." Under conditions of self-perpetuating one-man or one-party rule, communist ideology would thus become simply one more political philosophy, one of several alternative roads to human happiness. This could lead in turn to the disenthronement of Tkachevism-Leninism, Stalinism, or any other political orthodoxy as the one true faith and state philosophy. And the removal of this important ideological prop, which is used to legitimize the rule of the communist oligarchs, could lead to the removal of the oligarchs themselves.

NOTES

1. Tkachev quoted in Kozmin, *P. N. Tkachev*, p. 54.

2. Tkachev, *Sochineniya*, I, 69–70.

3. See pp. 65–66n, 187.

4. Louis Fischer, "Lenin's Legacy," *Columbia University Forum*, VII, No. 4 (Fall 1964), 9.

5. Quoted in *The Role of the Foremost Ideas in Social Development*, a pamphlet lecture by F. V. Konstantinov (Moscow: Vsesoyuznoye Obshchestvo dlya Rasprostraneniya Politicheskikh i Nauchnikh Znanii i Izdatel'stvo *Pravda*, 1947), pp. 17–18.

6. Karl Marx and Frederick Engels, *The German Ideology* (New York: International Publishers, 1939), p. 14.

7. In making this statement, the author is well aware of the exhaustive disputes, some of which went on in Marx and Engels' own time, as to the degree of determinism in their "economic determinism." Engels, for example, as we have pointed out elsewhere above, referred to an "interaction" between base and superstructure in which the superstructure may "react back upon the base." See pp. 151n, 192n.

8. Quoted from Marx, *A Contribution to a Critique of Political Economy*, in Vernon Venable, *Human Nature: the Marxian View* (New York: Alfred A. Knopf, 1946), p. 177.

9. Several critics of Marxism have pointed out that Marx's deterministic scheme breaks down in still another respect: If inventions cause the appearance of new productive forces which in turn lead to new productive relations, how can inventions be conceived invented at all if spiritual culture is not free to develop independently? This is

the very nature of the spirit in which Marx and Engels tend to deny intellectual culture when they say, for example, that "it has no history" or is a mere reflection of the base (which inventions radically alter!).

10. Compare *Communist Manifesto*. Perhaps the most familiar authoritarian statement by either Marx or Engels is the latter's article, "On Authority," published in *Die Neue Zeit*, XXXIII, Band I (1913–1914), 37–39, translated to English in *Marx and Engels—Basic Writings on Politics and Philosophy*, ed. Lewis S. Feuer (Garden City: Doubleday, 1959), pp. 481–85.

11. Lewis S. Feuer, "Marx and the Intellectuals," *Survey*, No. 49 (October 1963), p. 102. The "portion of the bourgeoisie" quotation is from *The Communist Manifesto* and is quoted by Feuer.

12. Hannah Arendt has observed: ". . . striking similarities between the organizational devices of the *movement* and . . . totalitarian *state* are hardly surprising," *op. cit.*, p. 412.

13. Some Marxist critics point to the spontaneity quotation from *The Communist Manifesto* as an example of an anti-authoritarian and even democratic strain in Marxism: to wit, that the revolution is accomplished by the "overwhelming majority of proletarians" *through their own efforts.*

14. Compare Fischer, *op. cit.*, *Forum*, p. 8. Fischer observed: "I find that Lenin was at his most brilliant [toward the end of his life]." Fischer believes that Lenin at last began to become conscious of the dilemma, but knew of no solution to it.

15. "[Public] cooperation does not signify the absence of order, hierarchy, discipline, leadership—all of which may flourish in its domain—but signifies relatively light emphasis on brute force and relatively heavy emphasis on the attractive forces of the community—the use of less force and more flowers, of the *miranda* of politics rather than its *horrenda*. . . . The greatest of all revolutions in the whole history of mankind is the acceptance of creative evolution as the proper role of man, for this will eventually transform the spirit and the institutions of education, of industry, and of government, opening a broad way to the realization of the highest and finest values of human life, in a form of organization where leaders no longer scream and curse and threaten and where men no longer shuffle, cringe, and fear but stand erect in dignity and liberty and speak with calm voices of what clear eyes may see." From the concluding pages of Charles E. Merriam, *Systematic Politics* (Chicago: University of Chicago Press, 1946), p. 345.

16. A post-Khrushchev statement of the ideology-action function of the Party oligarch is the following, from *Pravda*, January 12, 1965, "Organization—a Leninist Principle," by V. Stepanov: "The people properly view the Party as the sovereign of their thoughts. . . . Party organizations have the honorable and important duty of forming public

consciousness and public opinion, on which people's behavior often depends."

17. Zbigniew K. Brzezinski, *Ideology and Power in Soviet Politics* (New York: Frederick A. Praeger, 1962), pp. 79–80.

18. From Plekhanov's notebook reproduced in *Literaturnoye Nasslediye G. V. Plekhanova* (Moscow: Gosudarstvennoye Sotsial'no-Ekonomicheskoye Izdatel'stvo, 1936), p. 201. In *Plekhanov—Father of Russian Marxism*, Samuel H. Baron has, for some reason, ignored this aspect of Plekhanov's outlook.

19. Leon Trotsky, *Literatura i revolyutsiya*, Soil Publishers of the Central Board of Political Education (Moscow, Krasnaya Nov', 1923), p. 125.

20. *Ibid.,* p. 123.

21. *Ibid.,* p. 131.

22. Tkachev, *Sochineniya,* I, 70. See discussion above, pp. 130–131.

23. Karl Marx, *Selected Works* (Moscow: Institut Marksa-Engelsa, 1933), I, 15 (italics in the quotations are mine—A. L. W.).

24. From Stalin's *History of the CPSU(b)—Short Course* (New York: International Publishers, 1939), p. 355.

25. A "Russian Thomas Huxley," an opponent of a too-wide application of science, was a rare phenomenon in Russia. For an excellent book, dealing with the sometimes too-wide application of science by social scientists of the nineteenth (and twentieth) centuries, see F. A. Hayek, *The Counter-Revolution of Science. Studies on the Abuse of Reason* (Glencoe: The Free Press, 1955).

26. Tkachev (*Sochineniya,* I, 35, 67) went so far as to say: "Human thinking has its own laws . . . i.e., it would never say that two plus two equals five, no matter how great its freedom." Dostoyevsky's "underground man" denied this! At the same time, Tkachev warned that the use of the word "science" might be abused by certain party-minded individuals: "We must not confuse empirical fact with scientific fact using the word 'science' to describe one's *own* political economy, history, jurisprudence and psychology."

27. Lenin, *Sochineniya* (4th ed.), XXVII, 240–41.

28. Lenin, *What Is To Be Done?, Ibid.,* V, 32–33, 40.

29. Lenin, quoted by Lewis Feuer, *op. cit.,* p. 104.

30. Stalin in *Voprosy filosofii,* VIII, No. 5 (1952), 60 (up to now the quotation has never appeared in English, to my knowledge). The remainder of the quote sounds like Plato's cave allegory in *The Republic.*

31. V. I. Lenin, *Detskaya bolezn' "levizny v kommunizme"* (Moscow: Orgiz, 1945), pp. 6–7, 21–22.

32. Tkachev, *Sochineniya,* III, 491–92.

33. Lenin, *Sochineniya* (4th ed.), XXX, 50, made a series of observations stressing the importance of the "vanguard of the vanguard" located and based in the cities, representing the proletariat and even the whole society, despite the proletariat's being a small percentage of the total population.

34. Tkachev, *Sochineniya*, I, 48, footnote.

35. *The Communist Manifesto* (Chicago: Kerr and Co., 1940), pp. 26–27.

36. Lenin, *Sochineniya* (4th ed.), XXX, 245–50.

37. Lenin, *Sochineniya* (4th ed.), XXI, 254.

38. Tkachev, *Sochineniya*, III, 256.

39. The Bolshevik leader Valerian V. Osinsky, at the Eleventh Party Congress.

40. From Trotsky's *History of the Russian Revolution* (New York: Simon and Schuster, 1937), III, 177.

41. Lenin in "The Tasks of the Third International," July 14, 1919, and at the Second Congress of the Communist International, July 23, 1920. The "true will" of the majority as expressed by a very small minority is not only a concept of Russian Communists but was occasionally utilized by the German National Socialists: "The True Will of the people cannot be revealed through parliamentary votes and plebiscites. . . . The will of the people, in its pure and uncorrupted form, can only be expressed through the leader. Thus, a distinction must be made between the supposed will of the people in a parliamentary democracy, which merely reflects the conflict of various social interests, and the true will of the people in the Leader-State, in which the collective will of the real political collective is manifested. . . . Such a collective will is not a fiction, but a political reality." (From Ernst Rudolf Huber, *Verfassungrecht des grossdeutschen Reiches* [Hamburg, 1939], pp. 194–98.) Hajo Holborn observed in "Origins and Political Character of Nazi Ideology," *Political Science Quarterly* (December 1964), that Hitler in *Mein Kampf* "used almost Marxist terminology in deriding the stupidity of the bourgeoisie and the old upper classes for being hampered by humanitarian scruples and for their inability to conceive of better programs than the restoration of the German frontiers of 1914." Holborn did not note the several appeals by Hitler to the readers of *Mein Kampf* to learn organizational and propaganda technique from the Bolsheviks of Russia. The same could have been said by Hitler of several of the concepts of Tkachevism and Leninism.

42. Tkachev, quoted by Kozmin, *P. N. Tkachev*, p. 105.

43. Lenin, quoted by Stalin, *Problems of Leninism* (New York: International Publishers, 1934), p. 420.

44. Lenin, *Sochineniya* (4th ed.), XXII, 186–87.

45. "Liberalism," *Malaya Sovetskaya Entsiklopediya,* V (1959), 539–40.

46. Lenin, "The State and Revolution," *Sochineniya* (4th ed.), XXI, 400.

47. *Kommunisticheskii Internatsional* (3d ed.; Moscow: No. 1, May 1, 1919), p. 14 (quoted in Alfred G. Meyer, *Leninism* [New York: Frederick A. Praeger, 1957], p. 69).

48. Lenin quoted in *ibid.*, pp. 69–70.

49. Tkachev, quoted by Kozmin, *P. N. Tkachev,* p. 105.

50. Tkachev, *Sochineniya,* III, 66.

51. *Ibid.,* III, 266.

52. *Ibid.,* II, 48–49.

53. Tkachev, quoted by Kozmin, *P. N. Tkachev,* p. 60.

54. Tkachev, quoted by Kozmin, *Ibid.,* pp. 109–10. Marx himself did not entirely rule out the possibility of intolerance after the revolution: ". . . the bloody birth pangs of the new society . . ." (Marx and Engels, *Werke* [Berlin: Dietz, 1959], V, 457).

55. Lenin, "Leftwing Communism—An Infantile Disease," *Sochineniya* (4th ed.), XXXI, 71.

56. Among current subjects and topics of historical debate are: Dostoyevsky and the degree to which his literature is realistic against the degree to which it is reactionary; the definition of the term *Narodnik*—whether *Narodnichestvo* is to be regarded as an early analogous form of Menshevism or whether parts of it may be called "revolutionary and democratic" while still suffering certain deficiencies; countless other debates concerned with major or minor phases of the literary or revolutionary activity of Ogarev, Pisarev, Dobrolyubov, *et al.* As we shall see, nearly perfect silence surrounds the subject of Tkachev, the few scattered comments being exceptional.

57. S. I. Mitskevich, "Russkiye Yakobintsy," *Proletarskaya Revolyutsiya,* XVIII–XIX, Nos. 6–7 (1923), 12.

58. One such émigré in the 1920's, S. P. Melgunov, wrote: "Notorious Leninism . . . is nothing more than Old Russian Nechayevism, a particular Russian brand of Blanquism, modernized by Marxist terminology and deepened to incredible dimensions. . . . Its true ideological forefather is . . . Tkachev" (*N. V. Chaikovskii v gody grazhdanskol voiny* [Paris, 1929], p. 10). Yarmolinsky, Karpovich, Dan, Slonim, Golddenveizer, Nicolaevsky, to name a few, may be added to this list of *émigrés.*

59. In an early writing by Pokrovsky, an article entitled "Lenin in the History of the Russian Revolution" (Lenin v istorii russkoi revolyutsii), *Molodaya gvardiya,* No. 203 (1923), 244.

60. In addition to the articles by Mitskevich and Baturin cited below, this author has examined B. I. Gorev, *Ogyust Blanki* (Moscow:

Gosudarstvennoye Izdatel'stvo, 1921), which provoked the following articles: "Are there Elements of Blanquism in Bolshevism?" (Yest' li v Marksizme elementy Blankizma?), *Pechat' i revolyutoiya*, Book V (1923), 112–15, by the pseudonymous "Siniera"; B. Gorev's "Does Ideological Resemblance of Marxism to Blanquism Offend Marxism?" (Obidno li dlya Marksizma ideinoe rodstvo s Blankizmom?), *ibid.*, Book V (1923), 115–19; books or articles by Yarmolinsky, Karpovich, Dan, Nicolaevsky, *et al.*, cited in the Bibliography or elsewhere in this study. Gorev, a former Menshevik, was incidentally the author of a Soviet encyclopedia on Tkachev (*Entsiklopedicheski Slovar'* [7th ed.; Moscow: Russkovo Bibliograficheskovo Instituta Granat, 1927], XLI, Part VIII, cols. 217–19). The pseudonym "Sineira" was used by an unknown adherent of the Party's orthodox view toward Tkachev in opposition to the position taken by Pokrovsky (to an extent), Mitskevich, and Gorev, which is explained in the following pages of this study.

61. V. Varlamov, "Bakunin and the Russian Jacobins and Blanquists as Evaluated by Soviet Historiography," *Research Program on the USSR* (New York: East European Fund, Inc., 1955), including an important list of books and articles on this subject compiled by B. I. Nicolaevsky.

62. I have used another edition of Gorev's work on Blanqui, a volume containing various essays by Gorev (including the one on Blanqui) entitled, *Ot Tomaca Mora do Lenina—1516–1917—Populyarniye ocherki po istorii sotsializma v biografiakh i kharakteristikakh*, (4th ed.; Moscow-Petrograd: Izdatel'stvo L. D. Frenkelya, 1923), pp. 28–34. Among the other essays by Gorev in this volume are extremely interesting treatments of Lassalle, Proudhon, Bakunin, and Lenin himself, in which thought-provoking comparisons as well as contrasts are made between the political thought of Lenin and that of the others, going all the way back to Thomas More. To my knowledge, the book has never been cited in English, nor is it listed in the Varlamov-Nicolaevsky bibliography cited above.

63. I have found the following biographical information on Mitskevich, Sergei Ivanovich, 1869–1944 (mostly from the *Small Soviet Encyclopedia*—he is not mentioned in *Great Soviet Encyclopedia* of the 1930's): graduate of Moscow University, 1893, doctor of medicine; a Marxist by 1892; in the People's Will movement, 1893–1894; exiled to Yakutsk in 1897 and returned to Moscow in 1903; in 1905–1906 participated in Bolshevik revolutionary work in Moscow, then in Nizhni-Novgorod; in 1914, was located in Saratov, contributing to the Bolshevik press; head of the Moscow Department of Education in 1918; helped organize the Museum of Revolution in Moscow, 1924–1934, and eventually became its director. His name is omitted from the *Great Soviet Encyclopedia* (1950's ed.), but has turned up in the post-Stalin *Small Soviet Encyclopedia*.

64. In Mitskevich's "Answer to Baturin," *Katorga i ssylka* No. 3 (16), (1925), p. 93.

65. *Proletarskaya revolyutsiya*, Nos. 6–7 (18–19), (1923), p. 16.

66. Mitskevich, *op. cit.*, *Katorga i ssylka* (1925), p. 95. Gorev had already reminded his readers (in his book on Blanqui) that it was Lenin himself who had once written in *One Step Forward, Two Steps Backward:* "A Jacobin, indissolubly linked with the organization of the proletariat, conscious of his class interests, is a revolutionary Social-Democrat" (V. I. Lenin, *Shag vpered, dva shaga nazad* [Moscow: Gospolitizdat, 1961], pp. 171–72). Lenin often called Bolsheviks "contemporary Jacobins" and Mensheviks "contemporary Girondists" (p. 171). Included in Lenin's personal library, by the way, was Kozmin's *P. N. Tkachev.*

67. N. N. Baturin, "On the Heritage of the 'Russian Jacobins' " ("O nasledstve 'russkikh yakobinssev' "), *Proletarskaya revolyutsiya*, No. 7 (30), (1924), pp. 82–89; same author, "More on the Flowers of Russian Jacobinism" ("Yeshcho o tsvetakh russkovo yakobintsva"), *Proletarskaya revolyutsiya*, No. 8 (43), (1925). Baturin's two articles were later published posthumously in the Stalin period in his *Sochineniya* (Moscow-Leningrad: Gosudarstvennoye Izdatel'stvo, 1930), pp. 373–80 and 392–405. (This information was provided by Boris I. Nicolaevsky.) Baturin, Nikolai Nikolayevich (Zamyatin) (1877–1927), is described in the *Small Soviet Encyclopedia* (3d ed.), I (1958), 835, as a professional revolutionary, propagandist, and historian; graduate of Petersburg University; entered RSDLP in 1901 as a Bolshevik; helped Bonch-Bruyevich organize the library and archive of the Central Committee of the RSDLP (b); after the Revolution, on the editorial staff of *Pravda* and lecturer in history at Sverdlovsk University.

68. Baturin. "On the Heritage of 'Russian Jacobins,' " *Proletarskaya revolyutsiya*, No. 7 (30), (1924), p. 83.

69. Mitskevich, "An Answer to Comrade Baturin" ("Otvet k tovarishchu Baturinu"), *Katorga i ssylka*, No. 3 (16), (1925), p. 93.

70. The Varlamov study does not discuss this part of Mitskevich's presentation of the case for kinship between Tkachevism and Leninism. But to this author it is *most* interesting! Dan touches on the problem (in *Proiskhozhdeniye bol'shevizma*) but only episodically and without reference to the debate of the 1920's.

71. Mitskevich, *op. cit.*, pp. 95–96.

72. *Ibid.*, p. 96.

73. One of Baturin's arguments against the Bolshevism contained in Tkachevism was that Tkachev's neglect of class struggle and the bourgeois-class base of the Tsarist *state* was a non-Marxist phenomenon in his thought. Both Gorev and Mitskevich rebutted this argument by pointing out that Tkachev's use of the word "state," when applied to Tsarism, should be interpreted to mean the "Tsarist *government*," Tsarist officialdom, the Court, etc.; Tkachev, it will be recalled, had

maintained that the Tsarist state (*gosudarstvo*) "hangs in the air . . . possesses no roots." Gorev and Mitskevich affirm this and add that *Lenin believed this too.* Kozmin too supported this Gorev Mitskevich view, in a footnote of Tkachev's in *Sochineniya* (see n. 86 below).

74. One of his most famous statements, issued in the form of a letter to the Bolshevik Central Committee on the evening of November 6th: "We must not wait! We could lose everything! [We have] an advantage if we seize power now." Other examples of such Leninist advice against delaying may be found in Lenin's utterances and letters of late 1917 to the Bolshevik Central Committee.

75. Mitskevich explains that what he has in mind here is the fact that Russian peasants very often were part-time peasants and part-time proletarians, moving to and from the villages and cities, depending on the season and opportunities for work. Both Tkachev and Lenin noted this phenomenon, too.

76. Mitskevich, *op. cit.*, p. 96.

77. *Ibid.*, p. 97.

78. *Ibid.*, pp. 98–99.

79. *Ibid.*, p. 98.

80. *Ibid.*, p. 99.

81. *Ibid.*, p. 101.

82. The pertinent quotations from Stalin's letter may be found in Varlamov, *op. cit.*, pp. 26–27.

83. For meaning of pseudonym, see p. 179.

84. *Ibid.*, p. 28.

85. Compare *Small Soviet Encyclopedia*, under "Tkachev" (3rd ed.), IX (1960): "Tkachev did not understand the class content of the state and maintained that the Russian state had no roots and was supposedly 'suspended in the air' " (col. 353—a short, unsigned article of about 100 words).

86. M. V. Nechkina, *et al.*, *Ocherki istorii istoricheskoi nauki v SSSR* (Moscow: Akademiya Nauk, Izdatel'stvo "Nauka," 1966), IV, 360.

87. G. D. H. Cole wrote of Rousseau's concept of the state: "The state exists and claims our obedience because it is a natural extension of our personality" (Introduction, J.-J. Rousseau, *Social Contract* [New York: E. P. Dutton, 1950], p. xlvii); Rousseau himself wrote: "The better the constitution of a state is, the more do public affairs encroach on private in the minds of the citizens" (Book III, chap. XV). At the same time, Rousseau's writings suggest germs of the alienation concept found in Marx's *Philosophic Manuscript* (and before Marx unwittingly suggested a new form of world alienation; Arendt sees it arising in the communism of the *gemeinwesen*), prompted by Hegel's *Phenomenology of the Mind.* In the discourse on

inequality, Rousseau protests that the "social man lives constantly outside himself . . . so that he seems to receive the consciousness of his own existence merely from the judgment of others concerning him"; and, "It now became the interest of men to appear what they really were not." But the new personality to be received by man in a regenerate society, according to Rousseau, tends to be a public personality ("the public is the truest judge of morals").

88. Jaspers, *op. cit.*, p. 9.

89. A charge hurled at Stalin by a protesting post-Stalin poet in *Pravda* on October 21, 1962.

90. Quoted in *The New York Times*, Jan. 16, 1965, p. 1, under the headline, "New Red Debate: Man's Alienation—Theory Questions Marx View Blaming Only Capitalism."

91. *Ibid.*

APPENDIX

Tkachev's Writings

Besides the published writings of Tkachev, both in Russia and abroad, a number of other works did not get into print at the time they were written. They were confiscated by the Third Section, the Tsarist security police. The Soviet editor principally responsible for locating Tkachev's writings, Boris P. Kozmin (1883–1958), made most of these confiscated manuscripts available to the reader by reproducing them in *Izbranniye Sochineniya* published in the 1930's (see Bibliography, below). Volume 4 of the *Sochineniya*, pp. 449–454, contains a comprehensive list of Tkachev's writings, published and unpublished. Below are the more representative articles and pamphlets of Tkachev, as given in the *Sochineniya*, some of which are cited in this book and some of which are believed to have been read by Lenin. They are listed chronologically. Asterisks indicate the writings with a strong proto-Bolshevist tendency.

"Mirovoi sud" ("World Court"), *Vremya* (*Time*), 1862, No. 11.

"Raboche-vospitalel'niye zavedeniya dlya nesovershennoletnikh prestupnikov" ("Reform Schools for Underage Criminals"), *Yuridicheskii Yestnik* (*Juridical Messenger*), 1864, No. 1.

"Amerikanskiye tyur'my" ("American Prisons"), *Delo* (*The Cause*), 1867, No. 3.

"Proizvoditel'niye sily rossii," ("Russian Productive Forces"), *Delo*, 1867, Nos. 2, 3, 4.

"Noviye knigi (L'yuis i Dzh. S. Mill'. A. Kont i polozhitel'naya filosofiya)," ("New Books [Louis and J. S. Mill. Auguste Comte and Positivism]"), *Delo*, 1867, No. 9.

"Nemetskiye idealisti i filisteri" ("German Idealists and Philistines"), *Delo*, 1867, Nos. 10, 11, and 12.

"Noviye knigi (I. Bentam. 'Izbranniye sochineniya')" ("New Books [J. Bentham. 'Collected Works']"), *Delo*, 1867, No. 12.

* "Gosudarstvo i yevo predely v svyazi s sovremennymi voprosami administratsii, zakonodatel'stva i politsii" ("The State and Its Prerogatives in the Spheres of Administration, Legislation, and the Police"), *Delo*, 1867, No. 2.

"Noviye knigi (A. Smit. 'Issledovaniya o prirode i prichinakh bogatstva narodov')," ("New Books [A. Smith. 'An Inquiry into the Nature and Causes of the Wealth of Nations']"), *Delo*, 1868, No. 2.

"Noviye knigi (V. Tsimmerman. 'Istoriya krest'yanskoi voiny v Germanii')," ("New Books [V. Zimmermann. 'The History of the Peasant War in Germany']"), *Delo*, 1868, No. 4.

"Lyudi budushchevo i geroi meshchanstva" ("People of the Future and Heroes of the Petty Bourgeoisie"), *Delo*, 1868, Nos. 4–5.

"Noviye knigi (I. Pryzhov. 'Istoriya kabakov v rossii v svyazi s istoriyei russkovo naroda')," ("New Books [I. Pryzhov. 'The History of Taverns in Russia and Their Connection with the History of the Russian People']"), *Delo*, 1868, Nos. 9–10.

* "Podrastayushchiye sily" ("Rising Forces"), *Delo*, 1868, Nos. 9–10.

* "Razbitiye illyuzii" ("Destroyed Illusions"), *Delo*, 1868, Nos. 11–12.

"Zhenskii vopros" ("The Woman Question"), MS. written in 1869.

"Predisloviye i primechaniya k knige Ernesta Bekhera, 'Rabochii vopros v yevo sovremennom znachenii i sredstva k yevo razresheniyu' " ("Preface and Notes to Ernest Becher's book, 'The Worker's Question at the Present Time and Means to Its Solution' "), MS. written in 1869.

"Bardi frantsuzskoi burzhuazii" ("Bards of the French Bourgeoisie"), *Delo*, 1869, No. 3.

* "Nedodumanniye dumy" ("Unthinkable Thoughts"), *Delo*, 1872, No. 1.

"Nedokonchenniye lyudi" ("Incomplete People"), *Delo*, 1872, Nos. 2–3.

* "Statisticheskiye primechaniya k teorii progressa" ("Statistical Notes for a Theory of Progress"), *Delo*, 1872, No. 3.

"Spasenniye i spasayushchiyesya" ("The Saved and the Saviors"), *Delo*, 1872, No. 10.

"Statisticheskiye ocherki rossii" ("Statistical Notes on Russia"), *Delo*, 1873, Nos. 1, 4, 5, 7 and 10.

"Pozhary v rossii" ("Fires in Russia"), *Delo*, 1873, No. 2.

* "Tendentsioznii roman" ("The Tendentious Novel"), *Delo*, 1873, Nos. 2, 6, and 7.

"Pis'mo iz Velikikh Luk" ("Letter from Velikie-Luki"), *Vpered! (Forward!)*, Vol. 2, 1873.

"Tashkentskiye rytsari" ("The Knights of Tashkent"), *Delo*, 1874, No. 11.

* "Zadachi revolyutsionnoi propagandy v rossii. Pis'mo k redaktoru zhurnala *Vpered!* ("The Tasks of Revolutionary Propaganda in Russia. Letter to the Editor of the Journal *Forward!*"), (without designation of place of publication), 1874.

* "Otkrytoye pis'mo g. Fr. Engelsu" ("Open Letter to Mr. Engels"), Zurich, 1874 (in German).

"Belletristy-empiriki i belletristy-metafiziki" ("Belletristic Empiricists and Belletristic Metaphysicians"), *Delo*, 1875, Nos. 3, 5, and 7.

* "Narod uchit' ili naroda uchit'sya" ("Be Taught by the People or Teach the People?"), *Delo*, 1875, No. 4.

* "*Nabat*. Programma zhurnala." ("*Nabat*. Program of the Journal"), Geneva, 1875.

* "Itogi" ("Conclusions"), *Nabat*, 1875, No. 1.

* "Nashi illyuzii" ("Our Illusions"), *Nabat*, 1876, Nos. 2–3.

* "Revolyutsiya i gosudarstvo" ("Revolution and State"), *Nabat*, 1876, Nos. 2–3.

* "Anarkhiya mysli" ("Anarchy of Thought"), *Nabat*, 1875, No. 1.

* "Narod i revolyutsiya" ("The People and Revolution"), *Nabat*, 1876, Nos. 5–6.

* Revolyutsionery-reaktstionery" ("Revolutionary-reactionaries"), *Nabat*, 1876, No. 5.

* "Anarkhicheskoye gosudarstvo" ("The Anarchical State"), *Nabat*, 1876, Nos. 5–6.

"Literaturnoye popurri" ("Literary Potpourri"), *Nabat*, 1876, Nos. 4, 5, 6 and 8.

* "Vozmozhna li sotsial'naya revolyutsiya v rossii v nastoyashcheye vremya" ("Is a Social Revolution Possible in Russia at the Present Time?"), *Nabat*, 1876, No. 6.

* "Organizatsiya sotsial'no-revolyutsionnoi partii" ("The Organization of a Social-Revolutionary Party"), *Nabat*, 1876, Nos. 7–8.

* "Minuta nastala" ("The Minute Has Arrived"), *Nabat*, 1876, No. 7.

"Pedagogika—rodnaya dochka psikhologii" ("Pedagogy—the Legitimate Daughter of Psychology"), *Delo*, 1876, No. 11.

* "Nakanune i na drugoi den' revolyutsii" ("On the Eve and the Next Day of the Revolution"), *Nabat*, 1876, Nos. 11–12, and 1877.

"O pol'ze filosofii" ("On the Use of Philosophy"), *Delo*, 1877, No. 5.

* "Zhertvy dezorganizatsii revolyutsionnykh sil" ("Victims of the Disorganization of Revolutionary Forces"), *Nabat*, 1878.

* "Revolyutsiya i printsip natsional'nosti" ("Revolution and the National Principle"), *Nabat*, 1878.

* "Salonnoye khudozhestvo" ("Art of the Salons"), *Delo*, 1878, Nos. 2 and 4.

* "Novy fazis revolyutsionnovo dvizheniya" ("New Phase in the Revolutionary Movement"), *Nabat*, 1878, Nos. 5–6.

* "Printsipy i zadachi real'noi kritiki" ("The Principles and Tasks of Real Criticism").

"Muzhik v salonakh sovremennoi belletristki" ("The *Muzhik* in the Salons of Contemporary Belles-Lettres"), *Delo*, 1879, Nos. 3, 6, 8, and 9.

* "Shto zhe teper' delat' " ("What Is To Be Done Now?"), *Nabat*, 1879, Nos. 3–5.

"Utilitarnii printsip nravstvennoi filosofii" ("The Utilitarian Principle in Moral Philosophy"), *Delo*, 1880, Nos. 1, 7, and 8.

"Gniliye korni" ("Decayed Roots"), *Delo*, 1880, Nos. 2–3.

"Predisloviye k romanu N. G. Chernyshevskovo 'Shto delat'?" (Preface to N. G. Chernyshevsky's novel *What Is To Be Done?*), *Ni Dieu, ni maitre*, 1880, No. 2.

* "Oratory-buntovshchiki pered russkoi revolyutsiyei. Na temu: neobkhodimo pristupit nemedlenno k tainoi organizatsii, bez kotoroi nemyslima politicheskaya bor'ba" ("Orator-rebels Before the Russian Revolution. On the Theme: the Necessity of Proceeding Immediately with Secret Organization Without Which the Political Struggle Is Unthinkable"), Geneva, no date.

BIBLIOGRAPHY

Books

Arendt, Hannah. *On Revolution.* New York: Viking Press, 1965.
———. *The Human Condition.* Garden City: Doubleday and Company, 1958.
———. *The Origins of Totalitarianism.* New York: The World Publishing Co., 1963.
Aristotle. *The Basic Works of Aristotle.* Edited and with an Introduction by Richard McKeon. New York: Random House, 1941.
Arkhiv Zemlyi i volyi i narodnoi volyi. Compiled by V. R. Laikin and N. L. Pivovarskii. Moscow: Izdatel'stvo Vsesoyuznovo Obshchestva Politkatorzhan i Ssilno-Poselentsev, 1932.
Axelrod, P. B. *Perezhitoye i peredumannoye.* Berlin: Izdatel'stvo Z. I. Grzhebina, 1923.
Baron, Samuel H. *Plekhanov—the Father of Russian Marxism.* Stanford: Stanford University Press, 1963.
Belyayev, Ivan D. *Krestyaniye na rusi.* Moscow: Izdaniye Knigoprodavtsa A. D. Stupina, 1903.
Berdaev, Nicholas. *The Origins of Russian Communism.* New York: Charles Scribner's and Sons, 1937.
Bervi, V. V. (N. Flerovsky). *Polozheniye rabochevo klassa v rossii.* Moscow: Gosudarstvennoye Sotsial'no-Ekonomicheskoye Izdatel'stvo, 1938.
Blackstock, P. W., and Hoselitz, B. F. (eds.). *The Russian Menace to Europe (by Karl Marx and Frederick Engels).* A Collection of Articles, Speeches, Letters, and News Dispatches. Glencoe: Free Press, 1952.
Bogucharskii, Vasili Y. *Istoriya politicheskoi bor'by v 70–kh-80–kh gg. XIX veka.* Moscow: Izdaniye Russkoi Mysli, 1912.
Boiko, Yuri. *Rosiske narodnitstvo yak dzherelo leninizmu-stalinizmu.* Munich, 1959.
Bonch-Bruyevich, Vladimir Dmitriyevich. *Izbranniye sochineniya v trekh tomakh.* Moscow: Izdatel'stvo Akademii Nauk SSSR, 1961.
Broad, C. D. *Scientific Thought.* Paterson: Littlefield, Adams, and Co., 1959.
Brzezinski, Zbigniew K. *Ideology and Power in Soviet Politics.* New York: Frederick A. Praeger, 1962.
Burtsev, Vladimir L. *Za sto let—1800–1896.* Collection of Social and Political Writings. London: Russian Free Press Fund, 1897.

Burtt, E. A. *The Metaphysical Foundations of Modern Science*. Garden City: Doubleday and Company, 1932.

Bystryansky, V., and Mishin, M. (eds.). *Dictatorship of the Proletariat*. Collection of articles on the subject by Marx, Engels, Lenin, and Stalin. New York: International Publishers, 1936.

Carr, E. H. *Studies in Revolution*. New York: Grosset and Dunlap, 1964.

Chang, Sherman H. M. *The Marxian Theory of the State*. Philadelphia: Spencer, Inc., 1931.

Chernyshevsky, Nicolai G. *Polnoye sobraniye sochineniya*. Vol. 1. Compiled by B. P. Kozmin. Moscow: Gosudarstvennoye Izdatel'stvo, 1939.

———. *What Is To Be Done?*, 4th ed. New York: International Book Store, n. d.

Curtiss, John S. (ed.). *Essays in Russian and Soviet History*. New York: Columbia University Press, 1963.

Dan, F. I. *Proiskhozhdeniye bol'shevizma. K istorii demokraticheskikh i sotsialisticheskikh idei v rossii posle osvobozhdeniya krestyan*. New York: Izdatel'stvo Novaya Demokratiya, 1946.

Dobrolyubov, N. A. *Polnoye sobraniye sochinenii*. Moscow: Gosudarstvennoye Izdatel'stvo, 1934–1939.

Duverger, Maurice. *Political Parties. Their Organization and Activity in the Modern State*. New York: John Wiley's Sons, 1961.

Eagan, J. M. *Maximilian Robespierre*. New York: Columbia University Press, 1938.

Eastman, Max. *Artists in Uniform: A Study in Bureaucratism*. New York: Alfred A. Knopf, 1934.

Eddington, Sir Arthur. *The Nature of the Physical World*. Ann Arbor: Ann Arbor Paperbacks, n. d.

Engels, Frederick. *Socialism: Utopian and Scientific*. New York: International Publishers, 1935.

Feuer, Lewis (ed.). *Marx and Engels—Basic Writings on Politics and Philosophy*. Garden City: Doubleday and Company, 1959.

Figner, Vera. *Studencheskiye gody*. Moscow: Golos Truda, 1924.

Fischer, Louis. *The Life of Lenin*. New York: Harper and Row, 1964.

Flerovsky, Michael. *Russia—A History and Interpretation*. 2 vols. 1953. New York: The Macmillan Company.

Footman, David. *Red Prelude: The Life of the Russian Terrorist Zhelyabov*. New Haven: Yale University Press, 1945.

Frank, Philip. *Modern Science and Its Philosophy*. New York: Collier Books, 1961.

Galaktionov, A., Nikandrov, P. *Istoriya russkoi filosofii*. Moscow: Izdatel'stvo sotsial'no-ekonomicheskoi literatury, 1961.

Gamow, George. *One, Two, Three . . . Infinity—Facts and Speculations of Science*. New York: Viking Press, 1964.

Gorev, B. I. *Na ideologicheskom fronte*. Moscow-Petrograd: Gosizdat, 1923.

Gorky, Maxim. *Days with Lenin*. New York: International Publishers, 1932.
Grazia, Alfred de. *Politics and Government—The Elements of Politi cal Science*, Vol. 1. New York: Collier Books, 1962.
Haimson, Leopold H. *The Russian Marxists and the Origins of Bolshevism*. Boston: Beacon Press, 1955.
Hayek, F. A. *The Counterrevolution of Science—Studies in the Abuse of Reason*. Glencoe: Free Press, 1964.
Hertzen, Alexander I. *Memoirs*. New York: Alfred A. Knopf, 1922.
Hook, Sidney. *From Hegel to Marx: Studies in the Intellectual Development of Karl Marx*. Ann Arbor: University of Michigan Press, 1962.
Huxley, Thomas Henry. *Selections from the Writings of T. H. Huxley*. New York: Appleton-Century-Crofts, 1948.
Ivanov-Razumnik, R. V. *Istoriya russkoi obshchestvennoi mysli*, 2d ed. Petersburg: M. M. Stasyulevich Tipografiya, 1908.
Kautsky, Karl. *The Dictatorship of the Proletariat*. Ann Arbor: University of Michigan Press, 1964.
Kliuchevsky, Vasili O. *Proiskhozhdeniye krepostnovo prava v rossii*. From a Collection of Articles. Petrograd: Komissariat Narodnovo Prosveshcheniya, 1918.
———. *Kurs russkoi istorii*. Moscow: Gosudarstvennoye Sotsial'no-ekonomicheskoye Izdatel'stvo, 1937.
Kornilov, A. A. *Modern Russian History*. New York: Alfred A. Knopf, 1926.
Koyre, Alexandre. *From the Closed World to the Infinite Universe*. New York: Harper and Brothers, 1957.
Kozmin, Boris P. *Nechayev i nechayevtsi*. Moscow: Gosudarstvennoye Sotsial'no-ekonomicheskoye Izdatel'stvo, 1931.
———. *Ot deviat'nadtsatovo fevralya k pervomu marta*. Moscow: Izdaniye Politkatorzhan, 1937.
———. *P. G. Zaichnevsky i "Molodaya Rossiya."* Moscow: Gosizdat, 1932.
———. *P. N. Tkachev i revolyutsionnoye dvizheniye 1860–kh* Moscow: Novy Mir, 1922.
———. *Russkaya sektsiya pervovo internatsionala*. Moscow: Izdatel'-stvo Akademii Nauk SSSR, 1957.
Kuklin, G. A. *Itogi revolyutsionnovo dvizheniya v rossii*. Geneva: Biblioteka Russkovo Proletariya, 1903.
Lampert, E. *Sons Against Fathers: Studies in Russian Radicalism and Revolution*. (New York: Oxford University Press, 1965).
Lemke, M. V. *Politicheskiye protsessy v rossii 1860–kh gg.*, 2d ed., Moscow: Institut Marksa-Engelsa, 1923.
Lenin, V. I. *Detskaya bolezn' "levizny" v kommunizme*. Moscow: Orgiz, 1945.
———. *Dve taktiki sotsial-demokratii v demokraticheskoi revoliutsii*. Moscow: Gospolizdat, 1959.
———. *Shag vpered, dva shaga nazad*. Moscow: Gospolizdat, 1961.

————. *Sochineniya*, ed. L. B. Kamenev, 2d ed. Moscow-Leningrad: Gosudarstvennoye Izdatel'stvo, 1926.

————. *Sochineniya*, 4th ed. Moscow: Gosudarstvennoye Izdatel'stvo Politicheskoi Literatury, 1950.

————. *State and Revolution.* New York: International Publishers, 1932.

————. *The Proletarian Revolution and the Renegade Kautsky.* New York: International Publishers, 1934.

————. *Toward the Seizure of Power.* New York: International Publishers, 1932.

————. *What Is To Be Done?* New York: International Publishers, 1929.

Levin, Sh. M. *Obshchestvennoye dvizheniye v rossii v 60-70-e gg. XIX v.* Moscow: Izdatel'stvo Sotsial'no-ekonomicheskoi Literatury, 1958.

London, Kurt. *The Seven Soviet Arts.* London: Faber and Faber, Ltd., 1937.

Lossky, N. O. *History of Russian Philosophy.* New York: International Universities Press, 1951.

Mannheim, Karl. *Ideology and Utopia.* New York: Harcourt, Brace, and World, 1936.

Marcuse, Herbert. *Soviet Marxism—A Critical Analysis.* New York: Vintage Books, 1961.

Martin, Kingsley. *French Liberal Thought in the 18th Century.* London: Turnstile Press, 1929.

Marx, Karl. *Capital.* 3 vols. Chicago: Kerr and Company, 1906.

————. *Critique of the Gotha Programme.* New York: International Publishers, 1938.

————. *Selections on Art and Literature.* New York: International Publishers, 1947.

———— and Friedrich Engels. *Karl Marx and Frederick Engels, Correspondence: 1846–1895.* Translated by Dona Torr. New York: International Publishers, 1934.

————. *Manifesto of the Communist Party.* Moscow: Foreign Languages Publishing House, 1957.

————. *Selected Works.* 2 vols. Moscow: Foreign Languages Publishing House, 1962.

————. *Sochineniya.* 2nd ed. 30 vols. Moscow: Gosudarstvennoye Izdatel'stvo, 1928–1933.

————. *Werke.* 34 vols. Berlin: Dietz, 1959.

Masaryk, Thomas G. *The Spirit of Russia.* New York: Macmillan and Company, 1919.

Mavor, J. *An Economic History of Russia,* Vol. 2. New York: E. P. Dutton and Company, 1924.

Maximoff, G. P. *The Political Philosophy of Bakunin, Selected Writings of Bakunin.* New York: The Macmillan Company, 1953.

Mazour, Anatole G. *The First Russian Revolution: 1825.* Berkeley: University of California Press, 1937.

Melgunov, S. P. *N. V. Chaikovskii v gody grazhdanskoi voiny.* Paris, 1929.

Merriam, Charles. *Systematic Politics.* Chicago: University of Chicago Press, 1936.

Meyer, Alfred G. *Leninism.* New York: Frederick A. Praeger, 1957.

———. *Marxism—The Unity of Theory and Practice.* Ann Arbor: University of Michigan Press, 1963.

Michels, Robert. *Political Parties—A Sociological Study of the Oligarchical Tendencies of Modern Democracy.* New York: Dover, 1959.

Miluikov, Paul. *Russia and Its Crisis.* Chicago: University of Chicago Press, 1905.

Mill, John Stuart. *Auguste Comte and Positivism.* Ann Arbor: University of Michigan Press, 1961.

———. *Utilitarianism.* New York: E. P. Dutton Company, 1929.

Mosca, Gaetano. *The Ruling Class.* Edited and revised by Arthur Livingston. New York: McGraw-Hill Book Company, 1939.

Nechkina, M. V., *et al. Ocherki istorii istoricheskoi nauki v SSSR.* Moscow: "Akademiya Nauk, Izdatel'stvo Nauka," Vol. IV, 1966.

Nomad, Max. *Apostles of Revolution.* New York: Crowell-Collier Books, 1961.

Narodovol'tsiya—Sbornik III. Compiled by A. V. Sakimova-Dikoskaya, M. F. Frolenko, *et al.* Moskva: Izdatel'stvo Vsesoyuznovo Obshchestva Politkatorzhan i Ssilno-poselentsev, 1931.

Pares, Bernard. *A History of Russia.* New York: Knopf, 1947.

Payne, Robert. *The Fortress.* New York: Simon and Schuster, 1967.

Piontkovskii, A. A. *Ucheniye Gegelya o prave i gosudarstve.* Moskva: Gosudarstvennoye Izdatel'stvo Yuridicheskoi Literatury, 1963.

Pisarev, Dmitri I. *Izbranniye filosoficheskiye i obshchestvenno-politicheskiye stat'i.* Compiled by V. S. Kruzhkov. Moskva: Gosudarstvennoy Izdatel'stvo Politicheskoi Literatury, 1944.

Plamenatz, John. *German Marxism and Russian Communism.* London: Longmans, 1954.

Plato. *Dialogues.* Translated by Jowett. New York: Tudor Publishing Company, 1947.

Plekhanov, G. V. *Literaturnoye naslediye,* ed. P. F. Yudin, I. Udal'tsev, and R. M. Plekhanov, *Sbornik III.* Moskva: Gosudarstvennoye Sotsial'no-ekonomicheskoye Izdatel'stvo, n. d.

———. *Nashi raznoglasiya.* Petersburg: Novy Mir, 1906.

———. *Sochineniya,* 3d ed., D. Ryazanov (ed.). Moskva: Institut Marksa-Engelsa, 1922.

Pokrovsky, Mikhail N. *Ocherki russkovo revolyutsionnovo dvizheniya, XIX–XX vv.* Moskva: Krasnaya Nov', Glavpolit prosvet, 1924.

Polevoy, Y. Z. *Zarozhdeniye Marksizma v Rossii.* Moskva: Izdatel'stvo Akademii Nauk SSSR, 1959.

Possony, Stefan T. *Lenin. The Compulsive Revolutionary.* Chicago: Henry Regnery Company, 1964.

Prawdin, Michael. *The Unmentionable Nechaev. A Key to Bolshevism.* New York: Roy Publishers, Inc., 1961.

Preobrazhensky, A. G. *Etymological Dictionary of the Russian Language.* New York: Columbia University Press, 1951.
Pushkarev, S. G. *Rossiya v XIX veke* (1801–1914). New York: Izdatel'-stvo imeni Chekhova, 1956.
Rappoport, Angelo S. *Pioneers of the Russian Revolution.* London: S. Paul and Company, 1918.
Reshetar, John S. *Concise History of the Communist Party of the Soviet Union.* New York: Praeger, 1960.
Robinson, Geroid T. *Rural Russia Under the Old Regime.* New York: Longmans, 1932.
Rousseau, J. J. *The Social Contract and Discourses.* Introduction by G. D. H. Cole. New York: E. P. Dutton, and Co., 1950.
Russell, Bertrand *The ABC of Relativity.* New York: Mentor, 1958.
Scharndorff, Werner. *Die Geschichte der KPDSU.* Munchen: Gunter Olzog Verlag, 1961.
Sel'skii, E. *Po puti k svobode.* Moskva: F. Y. Burche, 1907.
Shapiro, Leonard. *The Communist Party of the Soviet Union.* New York: Random House, 1960.
Shub, David. *Lenin.* Garden City: Doubleday, 1948.
Smith, T. V. *Democracy versus Dictatorship.* Manasha: National Council for the Social Studies, 1942.
Spitzer, Alan B. *The Revolutionary Theories of Louis Auguste Blanqui.* New York: Columbia University Press, 1957.
Stalin, J. V. *Problems of Leninism.* New York: International Publishers, 1934.
Sullivan, J. W. N. *The Limitations of Science.* New York: Mentor, 1933.
Talmon. J. L. *The Origins of Totalitarian Democracy.* New York: Praeger, 1960.
Tkachev, Peter Nikitich. *Anarkhiya mysli. Sobraniye kriticheskikh ocherkov P. N. Tkacheva.* London: Izdaniye Zhurnala Nabat, 1879.
———. *Izbranniye literaturno-kriticheskiye stat'i.* Moskva: Zemlya i Fabrika, 1928.
———. *Izbranniye sochineniya,* ed. Boris P. Kozmin. 6 vols. Moskva: Gosudarstvennoye Sotsial'no-ekonomicheskoye Izdatel'stvo, 1932–1937.
Tonnies, Ferdinand. *Fundamental Concepts of Sociology.* New York: American Sociological Series, 1940.
Towster, Julian. *Political Power in the USSR.* New York: Oxford Press, 1948.
Treviranus, C. R. *Revolutions in Russia: Their Lessons for the Western World.* New York: Harper and Brothers, 1944.
Trotsky, Leon. *Literatura i revolyutsiya.* Moskva: Krasnaya Nov', Tsentral'nii Otdel Politicheskovo Obrazovaniya, 1923.
———. *Permanentnaya revolyutsiya.* Berlin: Izdatel'stvo Granat, 1930.
———. *Terrorism and Communism.* A Reply to Karl Kautsky. Ann Arbor: University of Michigan Press, 1961.
———. *The History of the Russian Revolution.* 3 vols. New York: Simon and Schuster, 1937.

Tucker, Robert. *Philosophy and Myth in Karl Marx.* London: Cambridge University Press, 1951.

Ulam, Adam B. *The Bolsheviks: The Intellectual and Political History of the Triumph of Communism in Russia.* New York: Macmillan Company, 1965.

Utechin, S. V. *Russian Political Thought. A Concise History.* New York: Praeger, 1963.

Valentinov (Vol'skii), N. V. *Vstrechi s Leninym.* New York: Izdatel'-stvo Imeni Chekhova, 1953.

Varlamov, V. *Bakunin and the Russian Jacobins and Blanquists as Evaluated by Soviet Historiography.* New York: Research Program on the USSR, East European Fund, Inc., 1955.

Vasetskii, G. S., and Kosichev, A. D.; Mamedov, Sh. F.; Shestakov, M. G. (ed.). *Ocherki po istorii filosofii v Rossii (vtoraya polovina XIX i nachalo XX veka).* Moskva: Izdatel'stvo Moskovskovo Universiteta, 1960.

Venable, Vernon. *Human Nature: Marxian View.* New York: Knopf, 1946.

Venturi, Ranco. *Roots of Revolution. A History of the Populist and Socialist Movements in Nineteenth Century Russia.* New York: Knopf, 1960.

Vernadsky, George. *A History of Russia.* Philadelphia: Blackiston, 1944.

Whitehead, A. N. *Science and the Modern World.* New York: Mentor, 1960.

Wilson, Edmund. *To the Finland Station.* New York: Harcourt, Brace and Company, 1940.

Windelband, Wilhelm. *A History of Philosophy.* 2 vols. New York: Harper, 1958.

Yarmolinsky, Avrahm. *Road to Revolution. A Century of Russian Radicalism.* London: Lassell and Co., Ltd., 1967.

Zasulich, V. I. *Sbornik stat'ei,* Vol. I. "Zhan-Zhak" Russo. Berlin: O. N. Rutenberg, n. d.

Zetkin, Klara. *Reminiscences of Lenin:* London: Modern Books Ltd., 1929.

Zilliacus, Konni. *The Russian Revolutionary Movement.* London: Bradbury, Agnew, and Company, 1905.

Articles

Barghoorn, Frederick. "The Russian Radicals of the 1860's and the Problems of the Industrial Proletariat," *The Slavonic Review* (March, 1943), pp. 57–69.

Baturin, N. N. "O nasledstve 'Russkikh Yakobintsev," *Proletarskaya Revolyutsiya,* No. 7 (30) (1924), pp. 82–89.

———. "Yeshcho o tsvetakh Russkovo Yakobinstva," *Proletarskaya Revolyutsiya,* No. 8 (43) (1925), pp. 97–100.

"Zaichnevsky," Bol'shaya Sovetskaya Entsiklopediya* (1st ed.), III.

Bonch-Bruyevich, V. D. "Vospominaniye Lenina," *Krasnaya Letopis,* No. 3 (48), (1932), pp. 113–15.

Cheshire, H. T. "The Radicals of the Sixties and Their Leaders," *The Slavonic Review* (June, 1922), pp. 110–20.

Curtiss, John S., and Inkeles, Alex. "Marxism in the U.S.S.R. Recent Revival," *Political Science Quarterly* (September, 1946).

Fedoseyev, P. N. " 'Manifest Kommunisticheskoi Partii' Marksa i Engelsa v materialisticheskoye ponimaniye istorii," *Vsesoyuznoe Obshchestvo po Rasprostraneniyu Politicheskikh i Nauchnikh Znanii Akademiya Nauk, Izdatel'stvo Pravda,* (Moskva: 1948).

Feuer, Lewis. "Marx and the Intellectuals," *Survey,* No. 49 (October, 1963), pp. 101–25.

Fischer, Louis. "Lenin's Legacy," *Columbia University Forum* (Fall, 1964), pp. 6–10.

Gorev, B. I. "Obidno li dlya marksizma ideinoye rodstvo s Blankizmom," *Pechat' i Revolyutsiya,* V (1923), 115–20.

Karpovich, Mikhail. "A Forerunner of Lenin: P. N. Tkachev," *The Review of Politics* (July, 1944).

Kozmin, B. P. "Tkachev i Lavrov," *Voinstvuyushchii Materialist,* I (1924).

Lemke, M. V. "K biografii P. N. Tkacheva (po neizdannym istochnikam)," *Byloye,* VIII (1907).

Magidoff, Robert. "Readers and Writers in Moscow," *New York Times Book Review* (February 29, 1948).

"Molodaya Rossiya," *Malaya Sovetskaya Entsiklopediya* (2d ed.), III.

"Petr Nikitch Tkachev," *Malaya Sovetskaya Entsiklopediya* (3d ed.), IX.

Miluikov, Paul. "The Influence of English Political Thought In Russia," *Slavonic Review* (December, 1926).

Mitskevich, S. I. "Otvet tovarishchu Baturinu," *Katorga i Ssylka,* No. 3 (16) (1925), pp. 92–101.

———. "Russkiye yakobintsi," *Proletarskaya Revolyutsiya,* Nos. 7, 8 (1923), pp. 119–21.

Nicolaevsky, Boris, I. "Materialy i dokumenty. Tkachev i Lavrov," *Na Chuzhoi Storone,* No. 10 (1925).

———. "Pamyati poslednevo Yakobintsa," *Katorga i Ssylka,* No. 11 (1926).

Pokrovsky, M. N. "Lenin v istorii russkoi revolyutsii," *Molodaya Gvardiya,* Nos. 2, 3 (1923), pp. 241–45.

"Sineira." "Yesli v marksizme elementy blankizma?" *Pechat' i Revolyutsiya,* Vk(1923), 112–15.

Stepanov, V. "Organizatsiya—leninskii printsip," *Pravda* (January 12, 1965).

Vishniak, Mark. "Ideiniye korni bol'shevizma," *Novy Zhurnal,* XXVII (1949).

Weeks, Albert L. "The Politics of the Soviet Boarding School," *Survey* (London): July, 1965.

———. "The First Bolshevik," *Problems of Communism,* October-November, 1967.

Index

Alexander I, 33n

Alexander II, 3, 41; emancipation of peasants, 16–17, 25, 29, 33n, 49, 67n

Alexander III: assassination of, 3; and Lenin's brother, 3

Alienation: Tkachev on, 190–91; Lukacs on, 191

Anarchism: of Bakunin, 31, 95; Tkachev on, 55, 95; future society and, 101

Archimedean point, 155n

Aristotle, 146

Artel', 12, 20, 118

ARTS:
science rescues, 141–43; "socialist realism," 141–43; "subjectivism" of opposed by Tkachev, 144–45, 153n; "sociological realism," 147; Marx and, 160; workers' state and, 162–63; Trotsky and, 166; Plekhanov and, 166

Atheism, Tkachev and, 156n

Atomistic individualism, 187–89

Augustine, 105n

Axelrod, P., 3; Plekhanov's letter to (admitting his Jacobinism), 39n; on Tkachev's Nabat, 53–56; on Tkachev's idea of progress, 54–55; on Tkachevism-Bolshevism kinship, 55–56; Perezhitoye i peredumannoye cited, 69n, et passim

Babeuvian communism. See Communism

Bakunin, M., 13; Jacobin phase of, 31; rejection of Jacobinism, 37n, 109n, 119; his Obschina against Tkachevtsi, 54

Ballod, P., 45

Base and superstructure. See DETERMINISM

Baturin, N. (Zamyatin): in 1920's controversy about Tkachev, 179–84, 187; biographical sketch of, 198n

Bazarov, 21, 26

Belinsky, V., 18

Berdayev, N., compares Russian revolutionism to "religion," 34n

Blagosvetlov, G., 43–44

Blanqui, A., 78, 104nn; assessment of Tkachev's debt to, 104nn, 178

Blanquism. See JACOBINISM

Boarding schools. See Education

BOLSHEVISM: resemblance to Tkachevism, viii–ix, 6, 8n, 168–85, et passim; Soviet discussion of Tkachevism-Bolshevism kinship, 6, 168–85, et passim; in Zaichnevsky's Young Russia (1862), 28–29; on "bearers of revolutionary consciousness," 55–56. See also JACOBINSON; LENIN

Bonch-Bruyevich, B.: on Lenin as follower of Tkachev, vii, 4–5, 186, et passim; organizes library in Geneva, 4–5; biographical sketch of, 7n

Boborykin, P., on Tkachev's personality, 65n

Brezhnev, L., 165

Brzezinski, Z., quoted on ideology, 164–65

Buonarotti, L., 131

Capitalism, Tkachev on, 128–38, et passim

Catechism, Tkachev's and Lenin's compared, 107n. See also Nechayev; TKACHEV.

Catherine II, 9

"Center(s) of power," Tkachev on seizure of power in, 78, 86

Note on the Author

Albert L. Weeks has been working in the Russian field continuously since 1946 when he began his graduate work in Russian History at the University of Chicago. He received his M.A. at Chicago in 1949 and went to New York to continue his graduate work, entering the Russian Institute at Columbia University in the same year. He received a grant from The Carnegie Corporation to complete his Ph.D. He received the Certificate of Study of the Russian Institute in 1960 and his Ph.D., in Political Theory, at Columbia in 1965.

Besides his formal education in Russian affairs, Dr. Weeks has used his knowledge of the Soviet Union in several capacities: He worked in the U.S. Department of State and Free Europe, Inc. for a total of six years. He visited the Soviet Union in the summer of 1966 where he conducted research. Since 1962 Dr. Weeks has acted as a radio and T.V. commentator on the world's Communist press, the first program of its kind on the air. The weekly program is currently carried over WNBC-Radio. Dr. Weeks has also served as editoral advisor for The Current Digest of the Soviet Press, published by the American Council of Learned Societies at Columbia University. He has contributed to The American Slavic Review, The Annals of the American Academy of Political and Social Science, The New Republic, The New Leader, The Reporter, Problems of Communism, Survey, and other publications.